The Administrative 'Revolution' in Whitehall

A Study of the Politics of Administrative Change in British Central Government since the 1950s

G.K. FRY

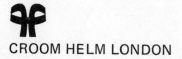

CROOM HELM LONDON

© 1981 G.K. Fry
Croom Helm Ltd, 2-10 St John's Road, London SW11

TO MY CHILDREN

Printed and Bound in the United States of America

CONTENTS

Contents

Preface

PREFACE

The Administrative 'Revolution' in Whitehall is the study of
administrative change in British central government since the
1950s which I promised in my book, The Growth of Government
(Frank Cass, 1979). This promise was easy to make because the
University of Leeds had already granted me sabbatical leave in
1976-77 to undertake the research for this present book. I had
the original idea for this book in the late 1960s. Indeed, the
broad thesis of The Administrative 'Revolution' in Whitehall
was anticipated in the remarks made on institutional reform in
my book, Statesmen in Disguise (Macmillan, 1969).
     The sub-title of this present book indicates its style
and content. It is about the politics of administrative
change. It is an interpretative essay of assessment. It
assumes knowledge of the basic facts and events. The Administrative 'Revolution' was largely over by 1976, but facts and
events down to the Conservative Election victory of May 1979
are taken into account. The author is aware that the interpretation given is based on political views which are
unfashionable in British intellectual life, and particularly
in academic life; but he believes that the interpretation is
one based on evidence.
     I have been fortunate in the amount of help which I have
received from friends and colleagues at the University of
Leeds, particularly Owen Hartley, James Macdonald and Alan
Deacon; and also from former colleagues Carey Jones and my
wife, Heather Fry. Lord Boyle, the Vice Chancellor, has been
very generous with his time and help too. I acknowledge the
help also of Kirsty Larner of the University of Glasgow.
However, when I say that none of these scholars can bear any
responsibility for what appears in this book I am not being
merely formal. Their views are not my views. I am
responsible for the contents of this book.
     The staff of the Brotherton Library at Leeds, and
particularly the Inter-Library Loan Service were very helpful
in locating the literature for this book. I am especially
grateful to Jenny Cooksey, Yvonne Fennell, Tim Hargreave and
Ruth Taylor. To the extent that the literature was from

government sources, I am grateful to the Controller of Her Majesty's Stationery Office for general permission to quote from its published material.

The Select Bibliography means what it says. It contains a selection of the books and articles and government papers that I have found most useful in writing this book.

As regards the References, in the case of books and articles listed in the Select Bibliography, only the name(s) of the author(s) and the date of publication are given. Government publications listed there are referred to with brevity too. When consistent with clarity, all the references in a paragraph of the text have been grouped together.

I take this opportunity of thanking Janet Brown and Sheila Hartley for reading the proofs.

Having dedicated my last book to my wife, I dedicate this one to my children.

G K FRY

Chapter 1

THE ADMINISTRATIVE 'REVOLUTION'

An Administrative 'Revolution' has taken place in British
central government since the 1950s.   Tinkering with the
machinery of government and its manning has been a characteristic of British political life during the period. Few parts
of central government, from the Treasury downwards, have
escaped being either reformed, rationalized, or reorganized.
New departments and other governmental bodies have been
created. Only some of them survived. The mechanisms for
trying to control public expenditure were overhauled. The
office of Parliamentary Commissioner for Administration was
introduced. The Civil Service was reformed. So was the
Foreign Service. At the end of all this activity, there was a
massive pile of paper - White Papers, Green Papers, the
Reports of Royal Commissions and other investigatory bodies
and their evidence, Acts of Parliament. Yet, what had this
orgy of reform, rationalization and reorganization actually
achieved ? What was the reality behind this facade of reform?
The scale of central government and the expenditure needed to
sustain it was of record peacetime levels. Contrary to the
claims of the reformers, neither this scale of activity nor
the reshaping of government machinery has led to an economic
and social order capable of arresting the country's long
relative decline. That plainly required more than an
Administrative 'Revolution'.
        This book is about the Administrative 'Revolution'. It
deals with the major reforms, rationalizations and reorganizations that have taken place in British central government
since the 1950s. This book attempts to take a synoptic and
analytical view of these changes and to examine institutional
developments in the context of changes in policy. It is a
study of the politics of administrative change. Unlike the
dominant sentiment of the time, this book is intended to be
impartial on the question of whether or not reform is 'a good
thing'. The evidence assembled suggests that some of the
changes were worth the effort. Several were not. Others
were never really made. For, the assumption behind the
Administrative 'Revolution' that the machinery of government
was sufficiently malleable to be made to fit the chosen role

for the State proved to be erroneous. That being so, the fundamental question had to be asked: what role could the State satisfactorily play ? In the end, the pressure of events forced that question to the fore, and opened up the prospect of more fundamental changes.

Chapter 2

THE ORIGINS OF THE ADMINISTRATIVE 'REVOLUTION'

Why did the Administrative 'Revolution' take place ? What
made change — and the appearance of it — so essential from the
end of the 1950s onwards, when at that decade's beginning all
was complacency ?

First, from the aftermath of Suez onwards, Britain's
international role came under greater scrutiny than before.
Among the consequences of the end of Empire, and of the
realization that Britain was no longer a Great Power, were a
succession of changes in governmental organization for defence
and external relations.

Secondly, and also from the mid-1950s, it became increasingly obvious that there was no sign of an arrest in the long
term decline of the British economy relative to that of its
major international competitors. The search for an 'economic
miracle' took the form of a greater role for the State, as if
government could secure 'national efficiency'. One result was
a development of governmental machinery for economic policy
making and planning, and for micro-economic intervention.

Thirdly, it came to be widely believed that the machinery
of British government itself needed substantial change. The
tone of much of that machinery had been set when the role of
the State was limited. Could such a machinery serve the
Positive State well ? Moreover, such was the scale of the
commitments that the Positive State entailed that — in the
context of the country's economic difficulties — there was a
continuing inducement to make governmental institutions, new
or old, more efficient. A series of investigations into
government machinery resulted, and a spate of reorganizations
and rationalizations followed them. At the end of it all, it
was debatable whether the activity was worthwhile. What was
indisputable was that government had grown still more.

I   NOT SUCH A GREAT POWER: THE QUEST FOR A ROLE

That Britain saw herself and was seen as a Great Power for so
long after 1945 was not surprising. She had been a Great
Power for a long time before 1945. She had been the dominant
world power in the nineteenth century. She had been on the

3

victorious side in the First World War, after which her Empire had reached its fullest extent. She had been one of the leading founder members of the League of Nations, as she was to be of the United Nations. She derived immense prestige from the fact that she had been the only country to have fought the Second World War from start to finish on the anti-Axis side. Indeed, as long as Winston Churchill, her war leader was present on the political stage - which he was until 1955 - Britain's reduced status in the world was hidden, particularly from herself. For, despite the formal result, Britain had been one of the losers of the Second World War.

This was obscured because Churchill did not only make history. He wrote it. The six volumes of his history of the Second World War became the popular version of Britain's and his role in it. The author was scrupulously fair to his hero, not least in his valiant fight for more rearmament and against the British foreign policy of Appeasement before the war itself. Churchill's response to the unenviable position that Britain found herself in by the end of the 1930s was essentially romantic. Cometh the hour of destiny - 1940 - cometh the man - himself. All was to be sacrificed to the overriding - and in itself excellent - aim of expunging the obnoxious Nazi Germany and her allies from the face of the Earth. Churchill's crusade was immensely popular with his fellow countrymen, whose response was magnificent. Their reward and their leader's was to share in the glory of victory in 1945. The Americans and the Russians took the spoils. Churchill's Iron Curtain warnings came late in the day. Before the war, the Appeasers had sensed that the price of undermining Nazi Germany's dominant position in Europe would be to install in her place another totalitarian regime - the Soviet Union. Such was Britain's weakness, however, that had she stood aside from a Nazi-Soviet conflict, she would have had to hope for the result to be an exhausted draw. Even a fully rearmed Britain could not have hoped to defeat the winner. For the Appeasers had been right in their belief that Britain simply did not have the resources to wage war at that level without bankrupting herself. She had not been able to finish on the winning side in the First World War without American intervention. This was bound to be so with a second total war. The Americans proved to be willing again to act as a financier for the British war effort. As Neville Chamberlain anticipated, however, it took an attack on her territory to directly involve America in the fighting. Even after the Japanese attack on Pearl Harbour, it remains doubtful that President Roosevelt could have declared war on Japan's ally, Nazi Germany, had not Hitler, crazily, declared war on the USA first. Churchill and Britain had gambled everything on the USA, and the gamble had come off, if only just. 'Victory at all costs' was what Churchill had proclaimed to be Britain's war aim in 1940. Others calculated the costs. Even with the peace, the differences in British and American interests - both in Europe and as regards the Empire - were such that an alliance with the Americans was bound to have a heavy price. In 1945, the junior partner in the 'special relationship' was bankrupt; and - in Churchill's phrase at the time of Munich - this was 'only the beginning of the reckoning'. If this was victory, it was one with many of the characteristics of a defeat, and it was little the better for not being seen as such.

Britain continued to act as a Great Power. Following Churchill's lead, her politicians saw Britain as the over-lapping area in three international circles: the Common-wealth, the Atlantic Community (by which politicians meant the USA), and Europe. This gave Britain a world role and one in which she did not have to choose between the various circles. Indeed, to closely integrate with, say, Europe was seen as threatening Britain's position in the other circles. Only integration with Europe was really on offer.[1]

That the opportunity of a close association with Europe was not established when Britain could have shaped a Western European Community to her liking was later to be a cause for costly regrets. The openings scorned by Ernest Bevin and Sir Anthony Eden in their respective tenures of the Foreign Secretaryship down to 1955 seem obvious in retrospect. Yet, immediately after the second total war in continental Europe in their lifetimes, Bevin and Eden can be forgiven for viewing European involvement beyond defence commitments with suspicion. Germany and Italy had just been Britain's enemies. Italy had a powerful Communist minority, even more substantial than that of France. Germany's 'economic miracle' and as yet successful venture in liberal democracy still lay in the future. France was politically unstable until the Fifth French Republic established itself from 1958 onwards, and she was not without her instabilities even after that. In Bevin's case, he was a member of the Attlee Labour Government, which having emphasized the role of the State in British society had little wish to diminish that role by ceding powers to any supra-national European authority. As for Eden, even in Opposition between 1945 and 1951, he showed none of the interest in West European unity that other Conservatives such as Churchill and Harold Macmillan displayed. Eden was very much his own Foreign Secretary in Churchill's peacetime administration after 1951. His antipathy towards European unity seems to have been one decisive factor in Britain not espousing that cause in the first half of the 1950s when she still seemed to have the prestige to lead it and on her terms.[2] More important was that Eden was not alone in believing that Britain did not need to choose Europe. Moreover, there continued to be little evidence that there was any domestic political mileage or much political sentiment in favour of closer association with Europe.

The Commonwealth and Empire still did attract political and popular support, if in varying degrees and in varying

5

ways. This was unsurprising, given that the Old Commonwealth countries – New Zealand, Australia, Canada, and South Africa – had been settlement colonies and had fought side by side with Britain in two world wars. Links of settlement were also strong with colonies such as Kenya and Rhodesia, where there was also white settlement. In addition, there was in some parts of British society a sense of imperial mission in relation to the many other underdeveloped countries over which Britain still presided as a colonial power. Nevertheless, this sense of mission had been strongest in relation to India, and as early as 1947 the Indian sub-continent had to be given its independence from British rule. Indian self government had been anticipated as a long term possibility. Humiliation at the hands of the Japanese in the Second World War – especially the symbolic defeat at Singapore in 1942 – had made Indian independence an immediate inevitability. It was a massive step towards the end of Empire. Thus, the imperialist lament in Look Back in Anger: 'I think the last day the sun shone was when that dirty little train steamed out of that crowded, suffocating Indian station ... I knew in my heart it was all over then. Everything.' It was, indeed, all over. The supposedly radical John Osborne who wrote the lines knew it, and seemed to resent it. Others chose to hide from the reality, and not only in the Conservative Party, which had tried to be the Party of Empire. For, deep down in many an upper and middle class Labour breast beat the heart of the District Officer, who to his friends was the epitome of constructive colonialism with a helping hand to the needy, and to his enemies was a self indulgent paternalist. It was fitting that Labour was in office when the multi-racial Commonwealth was founded with the decision on independence of India, Pakistan and Ceylon to freely associate themselves with the British Crown. This opened up the prospect of the Gold Coast, Nigeria, Malaya and all the other colonies doing the same when their turn came. That Burma had declined to associate herself from the outset was a fact that was glossed over. The problem of what place there would be for South Africa in a multi-racial Commonwealth when she herself practised racialist policies was left for the future. So was the problem of what happened if substantial numbers of New Commonwealth citizens exercised their right to emigrate and to settle in the so-called mother country. Such prospective problems seemed a small price for a role as Head of the Commonwealth that appeared to be a surrogate for Empire. Yet, in Britain's reduced economic circumstances, one question, still thought almost indecent to ask, pressed for an answer: from the British point of view, did the Commonwealth and Empire mean a profit or a loss ? Only in the Middle East – the Empire of oil – could the unequivocal reply of profit be made.3 It was in the Middle East that Britain was to find out just how little power she had left to sustain her pretensions.

That Britain was able to keep her Great power pretensions

as long as she did was because the Americans allowed her to keep them. It was a long standing British belief that she had a 'special relationship' with the USA, and one that was as important to the Americans as it was to herself. This belief was encouraged by the wartime alliance, and - within limits - flourished as long as memories of that alliance were vivid on the American side, and the USA thought she needed Britain for a particular role. The limits were set by the Americans. It was like a one-sided love affair in which one partner - Britain - was devoted, and the other found it convenient to have her around. The failings of the loved one were either discounted or ignored. The American urgings - which varied in intensity - that Britain should find another home in some kind of United States of Europe were ignored. That, immediately after the war, the Americans acted as if the dissolution of the British Empire was the first object of their foreign policy was discounted. So was contemporary American behaviour which treated the British economy as a serious rival, and one to be crushed. The terms of the American Loan were resented but largely because Britain had expected a loving gift. All was forgiven when the USA finally chose to confront the Soviet Union from 1947 onwards, the Cold War began in earnest, and Marshall Aid flowed. Bevin had soon recognized that Left (Labour Britain) could not talk to Left (Communist Russia) when the other half of the conversation was being conducted by Stalin. Bevin then did all he could to draw American men and money into Western Europe. For Bevin, the high point of his Foreign Secretaryship was signing for Britain the document which set up the North Atlantic Treaty Organization in 1949. Britain herself made a contribution in maintaining conscription, and in developing her own atomic weapons. At the time of the Korean War, she sent troops to aid the Americans and rearmed massively. Britain had some room for initiatives of her own. Britain recognized Communist China in 1950. Eden played an important part in finding a solution to the Trieste problem in 1953, and in securing Austrian independence two years later. Eden also played a leading role at the Geneva Conference over Indo-China in 1954, helping to secure a settlement which the Americans seem to have found pleasing.4 As long as Britain kept to what the Americans defined as her place, they allowed her to play out her Great Power fantasy. The Americans came to be so considerate in their treatment of Britain, that such as Eden could not detect the reality.

The Suez crisis of 1956 spelt out Britain's real position in the world for all who wished to see. The crisis began when the Egyptian dictator, Nasser, nationalized the mainly British owned Universal Suez Maritime Company in July 1956. It ended in political disaster for Britain. She was led into that disaster by Eden, by this time Prime Minister. What was obscured by the predictable moralizing of the Gaitskellite Labour Opposition to the eventual British military intervention were the very real practical objections to such intervention. Even if Britain had thought herself able to make the immediate military response necessary to be effective, she would still have had to face the problem of how to hold down the surrounding area sufficiently firmly to allow the Suez Canal to function smoothly. Two years before, Egyptian hostility had persuaded Eden, when Foreign Secretary, to evacuate British troops from the Suez Canal Zone. That hostility was scarcely likely to be diminished by a British invasion of Egypt. There was the very real possibility of the Canal being blocked, thus directly affecting the supplies of Middle Eastern oil that Britain deemed vital to her. This is what Eden meant in giving the melodramatic message for Secretary of State Dulles: 'the Egyptian has his thumb on our windpipe. Tell Mr Dulles I cannot allow that'. It was for Dulles to do the allowing. American acquiescence, let alone support, was always unlikely in an election year in which President Eisenhower was running as the Prince of Peace. A military intervention could not be a success in the face of American disapproval, such was her economic leverage on Britain, who would be dependent on her for oil too should the Canal be blocked. In the wings, in retirement, the combative Churchill recognized the reality: 'I should have exerted all my strength and persuasion to win the Americans round to our point of view, but if I had failed in this, I would never have gone forward alone'. Negotiation was the only practicable policy. Nasser himself, having correctly anticipated that it would take three to four months for Britain to organize a military intervention expected 'a sort of settlement' in the meantime. With the Suez Canal operating well, a settlement was the only sane solution. By October, Fawzi, the Egyptian Foreign Minister, had drawn up a scheme which Selwyn Lloyd – Eden's Foreign Secretary – later admitted would have given Britain what she wanted in terms of guarantees that the Canal would be operated in the interests of all who used it. In December, Eden conceded that Fawzi's scheme contained the broad lines of an agreement. By then, it was too late. Eden had set his heart on an armed intervention in Egypt, and, with the aid of the French and the Israelis, this took place in November. Nasser expected 'world opinion' to save him. American concern for 'world opinion' did save him. Such was the economic pressure applied to Britain that, having started to take back the Suez Canal by force, the invaders were them-selves forced into a cease-fire by the Americans twenty-four hours short of taking the now blocked and useless waterway. Commented Churchill: 'I am not sure I should have dared to start; but I am sure I should not have dared to stop'. A humiliating withdrawal followed. Eden had acted to topple Nasser – whom he ludicrously compared with Hitler – and to assert Britain's position in the Middle East.5 His perverse achievement was to considerably strengthen the prestige of the Egyptian dictator, and to demonstrate Britain's weakness not merely in and to the Middle East but to the whole world. At the same time, and in massive contrast, a real Great Power, the Soviet Union was able to ruthlessly suppress an uprising in Hungary, one of her dependencies. Worrying not just for Britain, but for the West as a whole, was that the Russian action in Hungary attracted nothing like the condemnation from 'world opinion' and even some domestic opinion as did Suez.

From Suez onwards, an enforced reappraisal of Britain's role began. It proved to be a reluctant reappraisal for many on most parts of the British political spectrum. Events, not least in the insistent form of economic calamities, pressed change on to even the most unwilling individuals and groups, who were by no means necessarily always Conservatives. To the extent that the reappraisal was domestically generated, the Conservative Governments led by Eden's successor as Prime Minister, Harold Macmillan, pointed some of the way, but, of course, not unerringly.

The general discontent with Britain's defence capabilities that the Suez adventure fostered made for an atmosphere conducive to changes in defence policy and organization. The form that the changes in policy took was less radical a departure from existing plans than it was presented as being by Duncan Sandys, Macmillan's Minister of Defence. After the Sandys White Paper of April 1957, the British armed forces remained as before committed to taking part in a confrontation with the Soviet Union, if needs be with nuclear weapons, and they were also expected to deal with counter-insurgency in the colonies. What the Sandys White Paper did was to emphasize the independent nuclear deterrent and to abolish conscription. An impetus for change was the hope of saving money in what had become a period of economic difficulty. It was thought that the nuclear deterrent would be relatively cheap to maintain; and there was the same expectation too about small volunteer forces as opposed to larger, mainly conscript ones. The abolition of conscription had the added political attraction for the Conservative Government that it pre-empted similar and it was assumed popular initiatives by the Labour Opposition. The size of the volunteer army was determined by the actual estimates of the numbers likely to be recruited, and not the numbers likely to be needed to fulfil commitments.6 What the Sandys White Paper did not do was to cut Britain's commitments that involved conventional forces, and these commitments remained in excess of her ability to meet them whether in NATO or East of Suez. Moreover, even when it was found that volunteer forces were more expensive than expected, there was no going back. The abolition of conscription was not only a bold move; in normal political circumstances it was an irreversible one too. Behind the rationalizations of defence organization that culminated in the creation of a unified Ministry of Defence in 1964 lay two related and unavoidable realities. These were that Britain tried to police a large part of the world without the conventional forces to meet her commitments, and without the economic resources to sustain the role.

Britain's abilities to maintain modern weapons systems in general and her independent nuclear deterrent in particular were also called into doubt within a very few years of Suez. The cancellation of the Blue Streak missile in 1960 marked the end of an era in British military policy. Until then, as in the Second World War, Britain met her major weapons needs through national military production. The cancellation of Blue Streak, and the decision to rely on the American Skybolt air launched ballistic missile to augment the range and penetration of Britain's V-Bombers, meant that Britain was dependent for the first time on another country for her weapons. The American cancellation of Skybolt in 1962 and its replacement by Polaris submarines took dependence a stage further. The V-Bombers were British weapons developed nationally. Skybolt was to be an extension to their range and strategic longevity. It was an increment to the national system. At Nassau in December 1962, the Americans agreed to provide Polaris missiles for British nuclear submarines, which were themselves American in design. Britain's continued participation in strategic nuclear weaponry was dependent on continuing grants of American technology and hardware. Britain's cancellation of the TSR-2 bomber in 1965, and the announcement of the hoped for replacement by the F-111, an American aircraft, carried dependence a stage further. Britain, now relatively economically weaker than ever was almost entirely dependent for her national security on the USA. How reliable was this ally in the face of the continuing Soviet threat to Britain ? When Britain declined to send troops to Vietnam to support the American intervention there, Secretary of State Dean Rusk's bitter response contained a warning: 'All we needed was one regiment. The Black Watch would have done. Just one regiment, but you wouldn't. Well, don't expect us to save you again. They can invade Sussex, and we wouldn't do a damned thing about it'.7

The Anglo-American alliance had been patched up after Suez. Things could never be quite the same again after Britain's public humiliation; but, down to the advent of Kennedy in 1961, President Eisenhower did his best to respect Britain's susceptibilities. Just as Eden for Britain had attended the Geneva Summit Conference in 1955, so did Macmillan attend the Paris Summit in 1960. Eisenhower allowed Macmillan to play the role of 'honest broker' in a search for detente between post-Stalin Russia and the West. Macmillan certainly played a part in securing the nuclear test ban treaty ratified in 1963. Kennedy said of Macmillan that his 'steadfastness of commitment and determined perseverance made this treaty possible'. Macmillan enjoyed the closest personal relation- ship with Kennedy of any foreign leader. Yet, it was a private relationship. Publicly, Britain was excluded from the meeting between Kennedy and Krushchev at Vienna in June 1961. Publicly, Britain played no part in the Cuban missiles crisis of October 1962 when Kennedy outfaced Krushchev. Britain in fact was the first of the Americans' allies to learn of the crisis, through her Ambassador, David Ormsby-Gore. The British Ambassador actually helped to suggest which aerial photographs of the Russian missiles should be released in order to convince sceptics of their existence. It was also Ormsby-Gore who suggested that the Russian ships carrying the missiles should be intercepted nearer Cuba than previously planned, so that Krushchev would have more time to climb down.8 Publicly, Britain was excluded from the settlement of the Cuban missiles crisis. It was this crisis which at last seemed to convince most of British domestic opinion - in a way that Suez did not seem to - that Britain's days as a major power were finally over.

This did not mean that the realization of diminished status was popular. Indeed, there was a public outcry when a former American Secretary of State, Dean Acheson, said in December 1962 that Britain's role was 'played out'. Macmillan privately thought that the violent reaction in Britain was not a good sign: 'we ought to be strong enough to laugh off this kind of thing'. Nevertheless, he felt the need to make a public reply which said that 'in so far as he appeared to denigrate the resolution and will of Britain and the British people, Mr Acheson has fallen into an error which has been made by quite a lot of people in the course of the last four hundred years, including Philip of Spain, Louis XIV, Napoleon, the Kaiser, and Hitler'. However, it was not the nobility of Britain's past that was at issue, it was her present and future role. As Acheson put it: 'Great Britain has lost an Empire and has not yet found a role'. Being Head of a Commonwealth with no political structure, or unity, or economic strength was no substitute. Playing the militarily weak broker between East and West was no long term substitute either, Acheson said. Like many Americans, Acheson felt Britain's future lay in Europe.9 That commonplaces of this kind caused a political sensation in Britain betrayed a hostility to change that Macmillan rightly found disturbing.

The Conservative Government under Macmillan had come to see that a choice had to be made - if one was still available - between the Churchillian circles of the Commonwealth, the Atlantic Community and Europe. The Macmillan Government made haste with the dismemberment of the remaining colonial empire, beginning with independence for Ghana in 1957 and for Nigeria in 1960. Rhodesia proved more difficult to dispense with. Macmillan chose to sail with the 'wind of change' rather than to try to frustrate it. Most Conservatives recognized the significance of Suez and the loss of the empire of oil. The liberal Colonial Secretary, Iain Macleod bore the brunt of the criticisms of others. That the emerging New Commonwealth clashed with the Old was soon evident with the expulsion of South Africa from the Commonwealth in 1961 because she pursued policies of apartheid or institutionalized racial dis-crimination. Only traditional Conservatives mourned South

Africa's passing. Others wondered which country it would be next. If it was another dominion for her 'White Australia' policy, what would the Commonwealth amount to then ? The New Commonwealth predictably aroused most enthusiasm with the District Officer element in the Labour Party. This was clear when Gaitskell led the Party in opposition to the Commonwealth Immigration legislation of 1962. The Conservatives, persisting with the policy of Civis Britannicus sum, continued to allow unrestricted Commonwealth immigration in the 1950s. Britain thereby imported a racial problem. In 1961, in response to massive popular pressure, the Macmillan Government belatedly imposed restrictions. It was not the belatedness of the restrictions that Gaitskell opposed, but the whole notion of restrictions. When Labour returned to office in 1964, under different leadership, it did so with a pledge to maintain immigration controls and eventually had to tighten them.10

If the Commonwealth was of diminished utility, then, if only by default, Britain had to opt for Europe. Developing the Atlantic Community, or membership of the USA, was not on offer. At their first meeting in 1961, Kennedy urged on Macmillan the need for a British application to join the European Economic Community. The application, although taken up with enthusiasm by a minority, had some of the hallmarks of a residual decision. Where else was there to go ? Some wanted to 'go it alone'. This attitude was most widely held in the Labour Party. When the Labour Government made its EEC initiative in 1966, Richard Crossman urged on Harold Wilson's Cabinet an 'offshore island' strategy. Crossman's vision was of Britain as a socialist jewel set in a silver sea. Unhelpfully for his case, however, he cited Japan – a citadel of free enterprise – as the example to follow. Crossman saw the Commonwealth as 'a dying concern'. As a 'Little England' man, he wanted Britain to shed the defence and foreign policy commitments implied in having a world role. This was different from Gaitskell's line in opposing the Macmillan Government's Common Market initiative in 1962. Membership of the EEC, Gaitskell argued, would mean 'the end of Britain as an independent nation state' – 'the end of a thousand years of history'. However, he dismissed what he called 'narrow nationalism'. Gaitskell believed that Britain still had the capacity to play a world role and one related to 'the modern Commonwealth'.11 It was difficult for Conservatives to match Gaitskell's level of conservatism, although some tried. The pro-European position, too, however, had its share of unrealistic romance, not least the notion that Britain could somehow run Europe once she was in. The argument that the EEC consolidated the defence of Western Europe was unconvincing. The threat remained the Soviet Union. As in Bevin's and Eden's time, Italy and France, with their important Communist minorities were scarcely reliable allies. There was the possibility that Germans on both sides of the Iron Curtain might stop a conventional Russian advance. A nuclear confrontation still required American participation. On this

basis, the continued presence of American servicemen in Europe
was to be welcomed on the grounds that the possibility of
American casualties offered some insurance, however slender,
that the USA would honour her NATO nuclear commitments to
Western European defence. As for the economic arguments for
Membership of the EEC, Britain's continuing decline was likely
to make her grateful for any spin-offs she could get from
Europe's 'golden triangle'. Those not blinded by idealism
could favour EEC membership, if only for the immediate future,
in order to establish a parasitic relationship with the German
economy. If the loss of two World Wars, and the division of
their country, could not stop the German economy, what could ?
Whether European membership could ever amount to more than this
remained to be seen. As it was, the Macmillan and Wilson
initiatives failed, and Britain was not able to join the EEC
until it did so under Edward Heath's leadership at the
beginning of 1973.

The quest for a role other than that of a Great Power was
one that Britain often pursued with marked reluctance. As late
as October 1966, Harold Wilson, as Labour Prime Minister,
insisted that Britain's frontiers were on the Himalayas.
Wilson seemed to have Churchillian cravings. In the curious
Anguilla episode in 1969, Wilson is said to have spoken in
Cabinet in terms suitable for the D-Day landing on the Normandy
beaches. He described the members of the Metropolitan Police
who landed initially on the West Indian island as the 'First
Wave'. Wilson's comparison of the Rhodesian crisis with Cuba –
and the paraphernalia of the Tiger and the Fearless talks –
betrayed longings for a grander role than any British Prime
Minister could hope to play by the latter half of the 1960s.
So did Wilson's entirely unsuccessful Vietnam initiatives.
These served to incense the American President, Lyndon Johnson,
who came to despise the Labour Prime Minister. The most that
Johnson could muster for Britain was general sentiment: 'it
may be an itty-bitty place, but that is where mother came
from'.12 In practical terms, the 'special relationship' was
over. So was the world role. The reluctance to face this
was eventually overcome by the effects of the continuing
relative decline of the British economy. These resulted in
attempts having to be made to rationalize the organization of,
and expenditure on, defence and external relations, and the
historic withdrawal from East of Suez. It seemed that only an
'economic miracle' could reverse the downward path on which
Britain was travelling, and expunge what was by the 1960s a
pervasive sense of defeat.

II NO ECONOMIC MIRACLE: THE SEARCH FOR ECONOMIC SUCCESS

It was the sense of victory in the Second World War, and
victory over the economic and social evils which were believed
to have preceded it, that, for a decade afterwards, encouraged
a dangerous complacency about the British economic and social

13

order. The British economy had been in decline relative to its major international competitors since the 1870s. The concern about 'national efficiency' displayed in Fabian and other circles between the turn of the century and 1914 had been shown to be justified by the British economy's performance in the First World War, even if some of the remedies offered were less obviously correct. The First World War began with Britain as the world's largest creditor, and ended with her as the world's largest debtor. The Second World War left Britain with the world's largest balance of payments deficit, and with a problem of sterling balances she was still trying to solve thirty years later. Whatever the damage done by the two total wars in accelerating Britain's economic decline, it was to the problems of the mass unemployment society in between them that the main thrust of British reformist effort was directed. This was true of the Beveridge Plan, and of Keynesian economic management theory. The Attlee Government's nationalization measures established a substantial public sector in a mixed economy after 1945. That Labour Government, like its immediate predecessors, also greatly extended State social provision. The resulting Managed Economy Welfare State - the Positive State - that emerged inevitably took a form generally related to past government activity. What was novel was the scale of State activity. The new economic and social order had its merits, not least in that it made Britain a more compassionate society than before. Nevertheless, however much, for years afterwards, the British stood back to admire parts of the edifice, the new order had one gross demerit. It proved not to be an order that could deliver sufficient economic growth to halt Britain's relative international economic decline.

The Attlee Labour Government at least started as if it knew what it was doing. Hugh Dalton, Attlee's ebullient first Chancellor of the Exchequer later recalled: 'by the end of the 1945-46 session we had passed Acts of Parliament nationalizing the Bank of England, the Coal Industry, Civil Aviation, and Cable and Wireless; two Finance Acts embodying my first and second Budgets, and my Borrowing (Control and Guarantees) Act; a National Insurance Act, substantially increasing pensions and other benefits; a National Insurance (Industrial Injuries) Act; an Act establishing, at one blow and in full plentitude, a National Health Service; a New Towns Act, and a Trade Disputes and Trade Unions Act, a straight repeal of vindictive and objectionable Tory legislation. This was assuredly a record legislative harvest, of which we might feel proud'. For the Labour Government, Dalton said, '1946 was an Annus Mirabilis'. The fuel crisis of the second winter after the war, however, made 1947 into Annus Horrendus. 'It was certainly the first really heavy blow to confidence in the Government and in our post-war plans', Dalton recalled. 'This soon began to show itself in many different and unwelcome ways. Never glad, confident morning again !'13

The Attlee Government of so many of the talents proceeded

to reel before a succession of blows. It was as if life was a cumulative punishment at the hands of a Rocky Marciano. In the end, in 1951, the Labour Government staggered demoralized from the scene, the victim of a technical knock out. It just gave up. This performance requires an explanation, and one that goes deeper than the tiredness of Labour leaders who had already served in the Coalition. The crucial reason why the 'confident morning' of the Attlee Government was so short lived lay in the nature of the Labour Party from which it was formed, and that Party's inadequate preparations for office in the long night before in Opposition in the 1930s. This did not matter so much in the sphere of social welfare where Beveridge and the wartime Coalition had laid much of the groundwork. Aneurin Bevan added the massive achievement of the actual establishment of the National Health Service to the earlier Coalition commitments to the principle. In the economic sphere, the Coalition Government's commitment to peacetime full employment had the support of Keynesian ideas, as did the Attlee Government in implementing it. Where the Labour Party had the opportunity to make a distinctive socialist contribution was in the spheres of economic planning and nationalization, in which it was found wanting.

For what was ideologically distinctive about the Labour Party was that alone of the major British political parties it was formally committed to socialism. Harold Laski was wrong about a great many things, but right when he said that the Labour Party was essentially different from the Liberals and the Conservatives. These older parties were like wings of the same party. They had their differences, sometimes fierce ones; but the Liberals and the Conservatives were agreed that the private ownership of the means of production could not be legitimately called into question. As Laski said in 1938, the rise of a Labour Party committed to socialism had so called the private enterprise system into question. The Conservatives' commitment to private ownership had not stopped them from experiments with State control: most notably, Baldwin's establishment of the Central Electricity Board in 1926. Their adherence to Protection was another indication of the Conservatives' ambivalence towards the free market. Nevertheless, a commitment to democratic socialism was something different. It was incumbent on those so committed to plan how such a socialist system would work. It was also required of them to plan how a mixed economy would operate, given that the socialist goal might well have to be approached in stages. Indeed, inherent in the Fabian approach - the dominant approach in the Labour Party - was the inevitability of the gradualness of the advance towards democratic socialism. Moreover, as the strength of the Fabians lay in pragmatism and machinery rather than theory, it was reasonable to expect that the Webbs and their followers and successors had detailed, practical plans for the running of the public enterprises they had advocated establishing, and also for the running of the mixed economy

created when those enterprises were established. Such
essential preparatory work was never done either by the
Fabians in particular or the Labour Party in general. That
this was so was obscured by the colourful intellectual life of
the Labour Party and the Left generally in the 1930s. This was
the supposed Golden Age: the Left Book Club flourished,
Strachey popularized, Tawney preached, Cole lectured, and Laski
predicted. These were exciting times for socialists. After
all, what Laski was predicting was a British Revolution.
Abroad, there was not just the Spanish Civil War and the rise
of international Fascism to distract and become emotional about.
There was the apparent success of the Russian experiment.
That overshadowed the contemporary Swedish essay in social
democracy and egalitarianism. Even for many of the
democratically inclined in the Labour Party, Russia seemed to
point the way. After a brief visit to the Soviet Union in 1930
in company with Strachey, Aneurin Bevan declared on his return
that 'whereas in Britain we were slaves to the past, in Russia
they were slaves to the future'.14 Socialism and slavery went
together in the Soviet Union, as the Webbs must have realized.
Many a Fabian heart must have fluttered with the belief that
the Russians had brought it off: they had shown that socialism
worked. Hence, the note of certainty to be found in the New
Statesman and other socialist literature.
    The mood of the Labour Party before assuming office in
1945 was caught by the eloquent Bevan: 'this island is almost
made of coal and surrounded by fish. Only an organizational
genius could produce a shortage of coal and fish in Great
Britain at the same time'. This, apparently, won Bevan the
loudest laugh of the 1945 Conference. Economic planning was
supposed to be easy, and nationalization was a panacea. In
practice, Herbert Morrison, on whose derivative ideas Labour's
nationalization measures were based, was only too pleased to
inherit economic planning machinery from the Coalition.15 Even
in 'confident' 1946, there was trouble.. The day after the Coal
Industry Nationalization Act received the Royal Assent, bread
rationing had to be introduced, something which had been
avoided at the height of the Battle of the Atlantic. In the
circumstances of the time, there was little else that John
Strachey and the Ministry of Food could have done. It was a
dubious proposition that the bread shortage could have been
planned away: but excessive hopes led to excessive disenchant-
ment. Similarly, the fuel crisis of 1947, although possibly
exacerbated by Emanuel Shinwell's complacency at the Ministry
of Fuel and Power, was largely unavoidable, given the severity
of the weather and the level of coal production. Nevertheless,
Bevan - or rather the Government of which he was a member - had
its 'shortage of coal' and from a newly nationalized coal
industry too. Such did its 'organizing genius' seem to be, in
relation to expectations, that had it charge of the fishing
industry too it might manage the concomitant shortage of fish
deemed impossible under planning by Bevan. 'Starve with

Strachey and shiver with Shinwell' was an easy gibe for the
Conservative Opposition to make. It was one that could only
strike home against a Government which had an exaggerated
faith in planning in the first place.

By 1948, the Attlee Government had nearly completed its
nationalization programme. In addition to the measures listed
by Dalton, electricity, transport and gas nationalization
legislation was on the Statute Book. Steel nationalization,
although delayed by the House of Lords, was inevitably going to
follow. The third anniversary of the 1945 Election victory -
July 5th 1948 - was chosen by the Labour Government as the
date on which the National Health Service was inaugurated, and
the various social insurance schemes came into operation. The
National Assistance Act of 1948 was the final part of the
Beveridge scheme to be passed into law. So, in three years,
the Attlee Government had gone as far as had been envisaged in
1945. Where did it and the Labour Party go from here ?
Morrison, who had tried to evade the commitment on steel
nationalization, was all for 'consolidation'. This meant what
it implied: administering the new order, the Managed Economy
Welfare State - the Positive State. The alternative was to go
on. Bevan was for this. He recognized that 'a mixed economy
is what most people in the West would prefer'. What mattered,
of course, was the balance between the public and private
sectors. Bevan insisted that 'in the society of the future ...
Private property should yield to the point where social
purposes and a decent order of priorities form an easily
discernible pattern of life'. Where was this pattern to be
found ? Russian behaviour in Eastern Europe - culminating in
the annexation of Czechoslovakia in 1948 - had destroyed the
faith of many democratic socialists in the Soviet example.
Stalin's Russia was a tyranny. Bevan himself described Soviet
Communism as the 'running mate' of Fascism. Nevertheless,
without the Russian example to follow, another socialist model
had to be found, or one constructed. This was not an exercise
that Bevan had any taste for. He continued to choose the path
of oratory. 'The language of priorities is the religion of
socialism', intoned Bevan. 'What is national planning', he
asked, 'but an insistence that human beings shall make ethical
choices on a national scale ?' National planning, in practice,
had proved difficult for the Attlee Government. It was only
really persisted with on the insistence of the Marshall Aid
authorities, who wished for evidence of some strategy as to
where their money was going.16   What Bevan could not
demonstrate was that socialism as extensive as he envisaged
was compatible with political democracy. What was to be the
fate of those who neither subscribed to 'the religion of
socialism', nor spoke its 'language of priorities', nor agreed
its 'social purposes' ? Attitudes inimical to socialism were
widely present in the electorate. Even in 1945, the Labour
Party could not take a majority of votes on a low poll and
there was no guarantee that Labour voting meant concurrence

with socialism, especially among marginal voters. Morrison, and then Gaitskell, were prepared to come to terms with this. At least at this stage of his political career, Bevan was not prepared to play the moderate, and denied the need for the Labour Party to do so. Bevan resigned from the Attlee Government in April 1951 over the proposed introduction of Health Service charges; but, as he soon made clear, his overriding concern was with what was to be Labour's strategy. The Attlee Government itself resigned six months later, following a narrow electoral defeat.

As the Conservatives had been dominant in the wartime Parliament, and had shared in the commitments of the Churchill Coalition Government, the changed economic and social order that they came to preside over in 1951 was partly of their own making. The Managed Economy along Keynesian lines had begun with the Budget of the Conservative, Kingsley Wood, in 1941. The Keynesian inspired Employment White Paper followed in 1944. The Butler Education Act was passed in 1944. In that year too, the Welfare State commitments to the social insurance schemes of the Beveridge Report, and to the principle of the National Health Service had been made. It is even difficult to believe that if they had been elected in 1945, the Conservatives would not have engaged in acts of nationalization, not least in industries such as electricity and coal mining where they had gone half the way before. Nevertheless, while the origins of the Positive State established by 1948 had a long history, and one to which the Conservatives had contributed, its modern authorship was mainly that of the renegade Liberals, Keynes and Beveridge, and its enactment had been largely the work of a Labour Government. A sea change had taken place in British society in the 1940s. The political world of Neville Chamberlain, and the economics that went with it, had not long survived his death in 1940. The experience of a second total war within a generation had removed popular acceptance of the need for 'economy' in public expenditure. Most people no longer believed that the money was not there to enable the State to do this, that, or the other. If the money could be found for the needs of war, then it could be found for the needs of peace. Keynesian ideas gave the new prejudices intellectual respectability. The old response to proposed government expenditure still to be heard from the Treasury remained 'where will the money come from ?' The Keynesian reply was 'from the Bank of England printing works at Debden'.17 After the experience of the 1930s, unemployment rather than inflation was deemed the greater enemy. Indeed, overfull employment was almost a condition of governmental electoral survival. Overfull employment gave the trade unions a bargaining advantage that was emphasized by the creation of a large public sector in the economy, a more developed social security system, and by the knowledge that public money was always there. The trade unions retained the legal privileges of their period of relative weakness. The 'vindictive and

18

objectionable Tory legislation' of 1927 that Dalton recorded
being repealed in 1946 had been mainly aimed at diminishing
the links between the trade unions and the Labour Party. These
links persisted. Schooled in the wartime situation, the trade
unions had been very co-operative with the Attlee Government,
not least during Sir Stafford Cripps's wages policy of 1947-50.
Nevertheless, a Conservative Government was potentially a
different matter, and particularly one led by Churchill, an
old adversary of the trade union movement. Would the trade
unions act towards the Conservative Government of 1951 as the
House of Lords had done towards the Liberal Government of
1906 ? In the event, the clash was postponed for twenty years.
    The Churchill Conservative Government of 1951-55 was left
alone to pursue its simple but effective economic and
political strategy. This was essentially a combination of
quietism and a mild dose of economic liberalism. Quietism was
assured by the maintenance of the new economic and social
order, apart from the partial de-nationalization of road
haulage and iron and steel. It was assured too by the mildly
inflationary wage settlements which appeased the then
moderately led trade unions. Walter Monckton, as a benign
Minister of Labour, poured oil on barely ruffled waters.
Churchill, determined to erase his earlier combative reputation
with organized labour, gave Monckton powerful Prime Ministerial
support. The Conservatives demonstrated in office that they
would maintain the full employment Welfare State. Moreover,
they gave the existing dispensation a colouring of their own,
by launching an ambitious housing drive guided by Harold
Macmillan as the relevant Minister. The target of 300,000
houses a year was met, and with increased provision for private
ownership. The Conservatives had made a move in the direction
of their aim of a 'property owning democracy'. They had also
staged a considerable political coup. The Conservatives also
gave some substance to their familiar Opposition war cry of
'set the people free'. This clarion call usually means that
the Party is short on policy, but the Churchill Government gave
it some meaning with their determined abolition of the
rationing and controls associated with Labour's era of
austerity. The period of the Churchill Government was when
the British consumers began to get their first taste of the
world of the consumer durables, soon to be advertised on
commercial television which the Conservatives legislated for.
It was the prospect of a more prosperous world that liberal
Conservatives such as the Chancellor, R A Butler, anticipated
with relish. Butler pursued policies of economic expansion
and reduced levels of taxation compared with those inherited
from his Labour predecessor at the Treasury, Hugh Gaitskell.
Nevertheless, Butler's continued use of Keynesian economic
management tools made for talk of Butskellism, or of
Tweedledum and Tweedledee. Butler himself wished to give
Conservative economic policy a sharper definition by
implementing official plans - called the Robot scheme - to

float the pound. However, he could not carry the Cabinet with him. Sterling remained fixed at the level which Cripps had devalued to in 1949. It was a balance of payments crisis in 1955 - after Churchill had gone, and Eden was Prime Minister - that brought the Conservative 'dash for freedom' to an end. The balance of payments deficit concerned was later revealed to be less than £100 million. By then, it was too late. The restrictive measures that Butler felt forced to impose knocked on the head the investment boom of 1954-55 that brought Britain as near as she was ever to get to an 'economic miracle'.18

This may not have been very near. That sterling had been put first in 1955 tended to be deflective from what was at the root of Britain's economic problems. Britain's role as the holder of an international reserve currency, like that of world banker and her desire to police much of the globe and also to govern part of it, imposed burdens that, had they shouldered them, might well have impeded the European rivals who were to pass her by. That Britain no longer had the economic strength to sustain this role was made painfully clear in the Suez fiasco. What did not follow was that shedding the world role would leave Britain economically strong. The British economy had been losing ground relative to the country's major international competitors since the 1870s. British society still bore the marks of the nineteenth century compromise between the landed interests and the leaders of industry and commerce. The latter had been peacefully integrated, but at the price of the ideal of the social elite still remaining the country gentleman as educated amateur. 'Trade' in all its forms was deemed socially inferior, an attitude bound to be deleterious to the long term economic performance of what had to be a trading nation. What was useful was deemed inferior to what was less directly useful. If there had to be science, then let it be pure rather than applied science. The educational system, certainly at its most prestigious centres, was oriented towards the production of amateurs. Macaulay had advocated amateurs as the best men to run India. This was to be translated into the belief that amateurs were the best men to run anything British. Amateurism infected the industrial and commercial leadership, combining unhealthily with the 'practical man', workshop mentality that reflected the stage of economic development at which Britain had experienced her Industrial Revolution. Britain had never acquired the system of economic organization and technological education that Germany had armed herself with. America's business was business, and Britain's had to be too for her not to continue to fall behind in the relentlessly competitive world economy. It was difficult not to believe that, without some great gift from God, Britain's relative decline was going to persist, unless there was substantial, relevant change in her society. Optimism about the results even of this could not survive knowledge of another legacy of the Industrial Revolution – the British working classes. Divided among themselves, not least on the basis of skill, and organized into a mass of conflicting unions, who were literally lawless, what was widespread among those classes was antipathy towards employers. As the nationalizers had found to their surprise, this meant any employers. The trade union leaders were associated with the Labour Party. So were most of their members whose votes dominated that Party's structure, and, together with their families, that Party's electoral base. This did not mean that the working classes were for socialism, although many union activists were. With that exception too, it did not necessarily follow that those classes were specifically against private enterprise, especially on their own account. What they were for was themselves. Otherwise, they were against. They were particularly against change, while also coming to expect as of right the affluence that only change could bring. This was a self defeating position, and the British working classes played their part in bringing their country to something akin to self defeat.

The Butler boom was the last time that Britain scented economic victory. That boom had been a brave attempt to bounce the British economy of the 1950s on to a higher growth path, and one which would have been comparable with the growth records of the countries who were to pass Britain by. What the end of the Butler boom meant for the Conservatives – who had been electorally confirmed in office during it – was that their 'market philosophy' had not met with the success that they had predicted. The reaction of some Conservatives to this was to argue that there was a need for an even more marked emphasis on economic liberalism. A further sterling crisis in 1957 brought this reaction to the forefront. Prime Minister Harold Macmillan and his Cabinet were faced with advice from the entire Treasury political team that economic recovery depended on cuts in public expenditure. Peter Thorneycroft, the Chancellor of the Exchequer, Nigel Birch, his Economic Secretary, and Enoch Powell, his Financial Secretary, wanted to give priority to stable prices. The conventional wisdom that pervaded the Managed Economy Welfare State was that such price stability could be easily combined with full employment, perennially rising real incomes and expanding social services. All that was supposed to be needed was enlightened Keynesian management of the economy. Thorneycroft and his team implicitly denied this. They wanted the control of the money supply and the defeat of inflation made the overriding priority, and advocated cuts of £50 millions in government spending. These cuts included the abolition of family allowances, a social benefit which, as the alarmed Macmillan pointed out, the Conservatives had played a leading part in introducing. In January 1958, rather than face a Budget on these lines, Macmillan accepted the resignations of his entire Treasury team. Whereas Thorneycroft, Birch, and

Powell hankered after the economics of the days of Neville Chamberlain, Macmillan's memories of the 1930s were less rosy. He had at one point resigned the Conservative Whip in protest against the high level of unemployment, the results of which he saw only too clearly in his constituency of Stockton. When he was Chancellor and then Prime Minister in the 1950s, his officials were said to have kept a tally of the number of times Macmillan mentioned Stockton in any one week. So, Macmillan's inclination was to gamble on expansion, even if this meant inflation, rather than with employment. In this gamble, he was probably in harmony with the mass of the electorate, certainly those in the trade unions, who, like him, remained obsessed with the 1930s. The gamble came off, in the short run. One reason it did so was a piece of luck on the wages front. The policy of appeasement was finally called to a halt, but not before what were to be disastrous concessions to 'fair wages' and 'fair salaries' had been made in the public sector. The Macmillan Government decided to confront the London bus strike of 1958 led by Frank Cousins, the recently installed and decidedly immoderate General Secretary of the Transport and General Workers Union. The Government won. It went on to win the 1959 General Election too, mainly it seemed on the basis of greater prosperity as evidenced by the wider spread of material possessions, notably consumer durables. The economy soon proved to have over-reached itself. The Conservative Government was forced once more to bow to balance of payments difficulties, and to put sterling first. It seemed that the 1949 exchange rate was as near as could now be obtained to an ultimate economic symbol like the Gold Standard.[19] The Conservatives were driven to ponder whether there was a way of stopping this 'stop-go' manner of running the economy. Like the Fabians of fifty years before, they were looking for 'national efficiency', and like them too, among other places, the Conservatives looked across to continental Europe.

The Macmillan Government looked to membership of the European Economic Community to change the context in which the British economy operated. It looked to France for the example to follow of running a national economy successfully. The French had a well developed system of economic planning. In the same summer of 1961 that the application to join the Common Market was made, the Conservative Government announced its conversion to economic planning, and the setting up of the National Economic Development Council (Neddy). Macmillan recorded that this decision led to 'a rather interesting and quite deep divergence of view between Ministers, really corresponding to whether they had old Whig, liberal, laissez-faire traditions, or Tory opinions, paternalist and not afraid of a little dirigisme'.[20] Macmillan, probably crucially, was in the latter camp. He had written earnestly about the virtues of economic planning in the 1930s. With French planning one of the intellectual fashions of the early 1960s,

Macmillan was poorly placed to resist it. That France, another fading colonial power, had suddenly taken off economically after years of stagnation, doubtless provided some of the contemporary attraction of French planning. The attraction was all the greater for the Macmillan Government because the Federation of British Industries had come to admire French planning too. Moreover, economic planning was also approved of by the trade unions, provided it did not extend to their activities. At odds with the unions in 1961 over its attempts to contain inflation by a 'pay pause', the Macmillan Government may have felt the need to build bridges. Above all, planning appealed to the British taste for compromise. Around the Neddy table, reasonable men of all sides could find the middle way out of Britain's troubles, and one which preferably minimized change.

Like the Fabians in the early years of the twentieth century, the search for 'national efficiency' took the Conservatives on to the paths of institutional and educational reform. The year 1961 witnessed changes in the methods of controlling public expenditure, and in the financial and economic obligations of the nationalized industries. Most dramatic, though, was the appointment of the Robbins Committee on Higher Education. Its Report, published in 1963, proved to be a massive step in the wrong direction. The Robbins Report reflected the contemporary delusion that there was a direct relationship between the scale of provision of higher education and economic success. This remained, at best, not proven. Nevertheless, the Conservative Government proceeded to expand the existing universities and establish new ones. There was no serious attempt to ensure that the orientation of this expanded higher education system was relevant to the needs of the economy. There was no effort made to ensure that the expansion was dominated by science and technology, even by giving differential grants to students reading such subjects. The tradition of university independence ruled out close governmental control of development, even if this had been desired, which it did not seem to be. So, the expansion of university education was undirected, and much of it took place in subjects of no practical value. At the end of it all, Britain was still left without technological universities to compare with the best of the German and French higher education systems. The Conservatives would have done better to have kept to the spirit of their 1956 policy on technical education, and applied that to the universities, placing science and technology first and everything else very much second in university provision. Indeed, the Conservatives might have done better to have kept to their attitudes of the 1950s in other ways too, notably in continuing to emphasize economic liberalism, discarded after the 1957 Rent Act. If the Conservatives had to look to foreign examples, they should have looked beyond French planning to Western Germany. There Konrad Adenauer's Christian Democrats, their political

counterparts, had built an 'economic miracle' on the basis of
a social market economy. The Conservatives looked elsewhere.
They had lost their way.

There was little worthwhile guidance to be found from the
Labour Opposition. The Labour Party later liked to describe
the Conservative period of office between 1951 and 1964 as
'thirteen wasted years'. It was a better description of the
Labour Party's record in Opposition during that time. What was
never resolved was the question raised in 1948 of what sort of
party the Labour Party was supposed to be. Was it to be a
party of reformism, of 'consolidation' ? Or, was it to be a
party of socialism, primarily defined in terms of public
ownership ? The running war between the two sides took up the
Party's energies in Opposition. This made for good theatre,
not least while Bevan remained with the Left on the political
stage. The socialists were the great survivors. They
survived even Bevan's eventual defection, undertaken in the
vain hope of being the Foreign Secretary in the Gaitskell
Labour Government that never came. The socialists also
survived the big guns of the trade union moderates lined up
behind Attlee and then Gaitskell. They survived the Krushchev
revelations about Stalin's Russia in 1956, the same year that
they had to endure the Soviet repression of Hungary. These
events reduced the New Statesman to intellectual disarray.
With Russia tarnished, where was the model to follow ? The
Left went on their travels to unlikely havens such as Tito's
Yugoslavia, Mao's China, and, later, Castro's Cuba and
Allende's Chile. They never found another Russia. Yet, the
Labour Left survived. It survived too the slings and arrows
of what it deemed the outrageous revisionist thinking of such
as Anthony Crosland. When, in the wake of the Conservative
election victory of 1959, Gaitskell tried to end the commitments to wholesale nationalization made in Clause Four of the
Labour Party's Constitution, he was defeated. Crosland
lamented of the British working class movement that it would
be true of 'no other country in the world that a proposal to
rewrite a forty year old constitution should arouse such acute
suspicion and resentment'. He concluded that the rank and
file of the Labour Party had not been listening to what the
leadership had been saying for the previous ten years.21 They
may have been listening, but they did not want to hear. The
Left survived because socialism, as Laski had said, was what
made the Labour Party what it was, what made it distinct. The
Left could appeal to the Labour Party's heart. Crosland and
Gaitskell could only appeal to its head.

What re-thinking the Labour Party did in its long spell in
the political wilderness was largely done by Crosland. He
believed that the pre-war reasons for the Party's largely
economic orientation were steadily losing their relevance.
Crosland wrote in 1956: 'Capitalism has been reformed almost
out of recognition. Despite occasional minor recessions and
balance of payments crises, full employment and at least a

tolerable degree of stability are likely to be maintained. Automation can be expected steadily to solve any remaining problems of under-production. Looking ahead, our present rate of growth will give us a national output three times as high as now in 50 years - an increase capable of sustaining not only a generous rise in home living standards, but also a level of investment in under-developed areas fully as high as they can physically accommodate'. With the problems of economics supposedly close to a solution, the Labour Party was free to redefine socialism in other terms than those of blanket nationalization, and ones which Crosland believed fulfilled earlier and more fundamental socialist aspirations. Crosland wanted socialism to be re-defined in terms of equality, which he took to mean social equality, which was directly and intimately linked with the level of government social expenditure. Priority had to be given to educational reform, mainly meaning the democratization of the Public Schools and the development of comprehensive schooling. Crosland also stressed the need for social expenditure to be used to promote social equality 'by removing the greater handicap which poorer families suffer as compared with richer during sickness, old age, and the period of heaviest family responsibilities; and secondly by creating standards of public health, education, and housing which are comparable in scope and quality with the best available for private purchase'. Crosland tried to break away from the forbidding Fabianism of the Webbs. Before many others dared to, he called for 'a trace of the anarchist and the libertarian' in British private life'.22 This was heady stuff in 1956. The notion that socialism need not be dull had a more lasting novelty.

Crosland's work influenced a political generation in Britain. Indeed, only J K Galbraith's thesis about the contrast between public squalor and private affluence seriously competed with it for political influence. Yet, for all the elegance of its presentation, Crosland's work was superficial even at the level at which it was pitched. He believed that Marx had 'little or nothing to offer the contemporary socialist',23 whereas what Marx continued to offer was a theory and one capable of a variety of interpretations. All Crosland had to offer was a defective practice. For, at the core of his work was the defect that he assumed that Britain had achieved an 'economic miracle' when she had not. Keynes had not solved Britain's economic problems. British economic management was not just the enlightened flicking of the right Keynesian switches. Without the assured economic growth that Crosland had assumed, public expenditure on the scale that he had envisaged was not sustainable except at the grave risk of severe damage to the economy, which, in fact ensued when such spending was undertaken. To the reply that Crosland was simply unlucky in the timing of his work, there are two obvious responses. One is that Crosland was actually fortunate to publish in 1956, one of the best years imaginable for a

revisionist tract, given contemporary developments in international socialism. The second response is that, even in
Opposition, Crosland had ample time to adjust his thesis, as it
was almost at once clearly the case that his central assumption
was unrealistic. He was either unable or unwilling to do this.
Given that the private sector was the main engine of economic
growth in his model, it was unfortunate that Crosland never
later explained why British private enterprise, which had
failed to meet his aspirations in the favourable climate of
the 1950s, should do even as well in the more egalitarian
atmosphere that he proposed. Without economic growth on the
Crosland projection, it was not possible - except by inflationary means - to meet social expenditure on the scale that he
advocated at the same time that the consumer durables
revolution persisted. Yet, Crosland either would not or could
not adjust his thinking. As a guide to a successful Labour
Government's strategy, Crosland's unrevised revisionism was
clearly inadequate. It encouraged expectations that could not
be met. It encouraged too the belief in that section of the
Labour Party most likely to hold the majority of posts in
government that the necessary re-thinking of its position had
been done when it had not.
      The Labour Government of 1964 was a grossly inadequate
vehicle in which to pursue 'national efficiency'. Harold
Wilson, the incoming Prime Minister, had himself compared the
Labour Party to an old stage coach. If you rattle along at
great speed, he said, everybody inside is either too
exhilarated or too seasick to cause any trouble. If you stop,
everybody gets out and argues where to go next.24   Wilson
had opposed Gaitskell's attempt in 1959 to impose on the
Labour Party something like the Godesberg Programme in which
the German Social Democratic Party had renounced nationalization. The old stage coach was better left without specific
directions. Then the travellers, including the fellow
travellers, could all believe that the Labour Party was headed
in their particular political destination. This was a
convenient way of sustaining an Opposition. Wilson was right
too, unlike the Gaitskellites, in believing that an un-
reconstituted Labour Party could win office: but what to do
with it ? Wilson persistently blamed the balance of payments
deficit left behind by the outgoing Conservatives in 1964 for
the subsequent record of his Government. Yet, the deficit was
no secret, and did not matter until the Labour Government
itself took office.25   That such a Government, formed from a
Labour Party still formally committed to socialism, would be
viewed with mistrust by the international financial community
was scarcely surprising. By a variety of measures - most
spectacularly the July measures of 1966 - down to the
devaluation of sterling in November 1967, the Wilson Government sought to convince overseas bankers that it was not as
radical as it sounded. At the same time, the Government was
trying to convince the Labour Party that it was as radical as

26

it sounded, and the electorate that it would honour the generous pledges made to them. For the Conservatives had been ousted with the help of outbidding them in promises of still more material prosperity and still more social services. What was the mechanism that was to deliver the higher levels of economic growth needed to make these pledges a reality ? Nothing less than a National Plan combined with industrial reorganization: but the latter took time, and the July measures of 1966 forced the abandonment of the Plan. The problems of the economy having been found to be intractable, the Labour Government concentrated its search for 'national efficiency' on institutional reforms.

III THE POSITIVE STATE: THE NEED FOR RELEVANT MACHINERY

There were few hints of the Administrative 'Revolution' before it actually began to get under way. Indeed, as the first decade after 1945 progressed, so contentment with Britain's governmental arrangements seemed to grow. There were a few voices expressing disquiet, but they were generally disregarded. British government seemed to have proved itself in both war and peace. Complacency was the dominant mood in British political life in the early 1950s. It was as if syrup has been liberally spread over a country with an insatiable sweet tooth. The Coronation of Elizabeth II was reflective of, and encouraged, the mood. It even seemed as if God was on Britain's side, because on the very day of the event - June 2nd 1953 - there was news of a Commonwealth triumph. A message had been received from Colonel H J C Hunt, leader of the British Mount Everest Expedition 1953. It stated that E P Hillary - a New Zealander - and his Nepalese Sherpa guide, Tensing Bhutia, had reached the summit of the mountain, 29,002 feet high, on May 29th. The message added, 'All is well'. As for the crowning of the young monarch, The Times said: 'Today her people pray for her as they would pray for their own kin, that God may give her peace, health, and happiness and length of days. They know that it cannot be always summer weather, but they believe that the sunshine in the Queen's heart will sustain her and them through the clouded days. As she goes forth among them from Westminster Abbey, all the lights of the past will be glowing in her crown, and all the voices of the future singing her praise. The splendid trophy brought to her from the summit of the world's highest peak is the earnest of the hope of a new heroic age'. It was the natural hope of a conservative country that there would be a new Elizabethan Age in which Britain would recapture past glories, and with a minimum of change. Past glories were only too soon to be seen to be beyond Britain's capacities, diminished as they were by - among other things - her continuing relative economic decline. Did Britain really have the governmental institutions relevant to the era of the Positive State ? A more fundamental question was whether the

27

particular form that the Positive State took in Britain had become an agent of accelerating national decline. Such a question had little immediate appeal in a country with no taste for the tabula rasa. When the time for change could be postponed no more, institutional reform was seized on, almost gratefully, as the road to salvation.

The Attlee Government had its own formula for salvation - economic planning and nationalization - and it also had the task of fulfilling the Coalition commitments to the Welfare State. Unprepared to actually practise economic planning, the Labour Government tried various arrangements. These mainly consisted of persisting with the Coalition's wartime machinery. This was supervised at first by Morrison as Lord President. He later doubted whether the Treasury was subject to the machinery for economic planning. It was as early as November 1947 that the machinery for economic planning was made subject to the Treasury. The short lived reign of Cripps - formerly President of the Board of Trade - as Minister for Economic Affairs ended when he became Chancellor. He took with him into the Treasury the functions of his previous post, Sir Edwin Plowden, his Chief Planning Officer, the Economic Planning Staff, and the Regional Boards for Industry. Cripps had doubted whether Morrison really understood what economic planning meant, 26 an observation that might have been made about himself. Where Morrison more obviously fell short was in his preparations for nationalization. He had converted the Labour Party to public corporations as the preferred administrative means of running nationalized industries. What was conspicuously absent from his preparations were details of how to run the industries as public enterprises, or - as seemed likely from the outset - public enterprises and social services combined. Among the questions unanswered were what were to be the rules to determine levels of investment, output, prices and costs ? The analogy of the pre-war Central Electricity Board dressed up in Morrisonian clothes would not suffice. A large public sector was not the same as a small one. What was its relationship to be with the remainder of what had to be an internationally competitive economy ? Morrison had concentrated on administrative form to the neglect of operational substance.

That it created the large, cumbersome Morrisonian public corporations, however, did not mean that institutional innovation was a major characteristic of the Attlee Government. It was kept too busy actually doing things. It inherited a changed Civil Service that still had several former temporaries in its higher reaches, which gave the Service a less 'closed' appearance. The public corporations dominated the Attlee Government's contribution to economic machinery. Certainly, the Government's commitment to economic planning was met with the minimum additional machinery to that of the Cabinet, the Treasury, and the Board of Trade, consonant with its implementation. The honouring of the Welfare State commitments bequeathed by the Coalition were mainly met within the already established forms of governmental organization. Beveridge's call for a unified Ministry of Social Security 27 was disregarded, and bodies such as the Ministry of National Insurance and the National Assistance Board were created, including associated local office systems. Education remained administered by a central Ministry and designated local authorities. The Children Act of 1948 led to a new service, but one handled by the established central-local government administrative means. The National Health Service required a special structure of its own. This was not just to meet the radical demands of Bevan as Minister of Health, determined to nationalize the hospitals. It was also to meet the various interests of and within the medical profession. The profession's attitudes ensured that there was never any likelihood of more than part of the National Health Service being placed under the combined control of the Ministry of Health and local government. In practice, a tripartite structure was devised. Those parts of the National Health Service dealing with hospitals and non-institutional medical services were organized in terms of a relationship between the Ministry of Health and various local and regional bodies on which the medical profession was very well represented. The third part, dealing with auxiliary services, was left to local government.

The effect of the nationalization of hospitals and of gas and electricity undertakings on the role of local authorities was one of Herbert Morrison's few regrets about the British system of government as he found it in the first part of the 1950s. In fact, 'all is well' was not just the message sent back from the triumph on Mount Everest on Coronation Day: it was also Morrison's message sent down from the highest reaches of British government. Morrison pronounced the system very nearly perfect. Never a drawing room radical, he could speak warmly of the monarchy. The House of Lords merited an affectionate pat. The House of Commons demanded nothing less than love, and, Morrison implied, did not find him wanting. Constitutional conventions such as Cabinet collective responsibility and individual ministerial responsibility were reverently defined. Notions that there was any real need for bodies such as a House of Commons Select Committee on the Nationalized Industries were rejected. Ministers having been given a closer relationship with the public corporations than in pre-war times, the established procedures of the House were deemed more than adequate. Morrison took special delight in condemning an ill fated scheme of Churchill's using peers as supervising Ministers or Overlords. Morrison closed with a tribute to the Civil Service and its loyalty to the Government of the day. Indeed, the centenary of the famous Trevelyan-Northcote Report on the Civil Service, celebrated in 1954, provided further opportunities for such tributes. Attlee joined in. Looking back at the Labour Government of 1945-51 and probably with Laski in mind, Attlee recalled: 'there were

certainly some people in the Labour Party who doubted whether
the civil servants would give fair play to a socialist government, but all doubts disappeared with experience'.28   That
experience of having helped to make Labour's contribution to
the construction of the Positive State seemed to have drained
what radicalism they had ever possessed from the Labour
leaders. Morrison and Attlee had taken to regarding the
machinery of British government with that special indulgence
which English people normally reserve for domestic pets.
    That there was little cause for this level of complacency
about the workings of British government was demonstrated at
the time with the revelations of the Crichel Down scandal of
1953-54. Indeed, the British Constitution could never be quite
the same again after the exposure at a public inquiry of maladministration by Ministry of Agriculture officials and others
in the disposal of compulsorily purchased land at Crichel Down
in North Dorset. The resignation of Sir Thomas Dugdale, the
Minister of Agriculture in the Churchill Conservative Government, gave those with the duty of papering over the cracks
which had appeared in the Constitution something to work with.
The resignation was said to have confirmed the doctrine of
ministerial responsibility. Sir David Maxwell Fyfe, the Home
Secretary, took the opportunity in the ensuing parliamentary
debate to define ministerial responsibility to his own, and
Herbert Morrison's, satisfaction. Yet, the disquiet would not
go away. It was well founded. The Conservative MP for North
Dorset, Robert Crouch, had used the traditional means of
pressing his constituents' complaints against the civil
servants concerned - parliamentary questions and contacts with
Ministers - without success. That the Minister himself had set
up the public inquiry, and had chosen to have the resulting
report published, had been entirely matters for his own
decision. Far from confirming the effectiveness of the
conventional means of securing redress of grievances, the
Crichel Down case demonstrated their inadequacy. That Crouch's
socially well connected constituent had been able to obtain the
measure of redress that he did was largely fortuitous. Moreover, while Dugdale prepared to accept a peerage and to return
to farming in North Yorkshire, the erring civil servants were
simply moved elsewhere in the State bureaucracy. The Crichel
Down scandal gave substance to the sentiment that the machinery
of government was now too large to be adequately controlled by
traditional methods. This was despite the opportunities that
in this case Dugdale and his junior Ministers - who included
Lord Carrington - had to affect policy. It gave credence too
to the belief that civil servants enjoyed too much protection
in the exercise of administrative discretion, and that their
actions needed to be made subject to some kind of independent
review. The Conservative backbenchers, who had been pursuing
their own Government, had wanted the heads of the civil
servants to roll, not that of the Minister. Nevertheless,
Dugdale's resignation was sufficient at the time to de-fuse a

difficult political situation for the Churchill Government.
What was not so easy to erase was the memory of the Crichel
Down scandal, and what were seen as its lessons.29
    The Butler boom helped to ensure that Crichel Down did not
do more than slightly disturb the soporific atmosphere of the
times. The boom explained the political ascendancy which the
Conservatives established within two years of their return to
office in 1951. The Churchill Government itself was a curious
regime. Whether Churchill was too old (77 in 1951) and in too
poor health to be an effective Prime Minister was more a
subject for later rather than contemporary political
speculation. What was obvious was that Churchill, already
assured of a much sought after place in history, shared the
widely held view that he was larger than life, and continued
to act accordingly. Hence, Oliver Lyttleton learnt that he
was to be denied the Treasury from a cigar smoking Churchill
who was 'in bed, in a quilted flowered bed jacket, the garment
slightly reminiscent of Don Pasquale'. In this garb, and from
his bed, Churchill then favoured Lyttleton with what sounded
like a speech on the economic situation. Butler, actually
chosen as Chancellor, and in similar circumstances, proceeded
to display massive competence at the Treasury. So did
Macmillan at the specially renamed Ministry of Housing and
Local Government. They were departmental Ministers of the
highest calibre. Eden was also regarded as such, at least
outside the Foreign Office. The Churchill Government thought
that it knew where it was going, and institutional change had
no more than a minor part to play. This did not stop
Churchill from undertaking the Overlords experiment, which
Morrison was not alone in condemning. Churchill's idea seemed
to be that Lords Woolton, Cherwell and Leathers, free from the
pressures of the House of Commons and of running individual
departments, would co-ordinate related government activities.
Ideally, this was supposed to make for more coherent policies.
The scheme was easy to attack as being government by
Churchill's wartime cronies, which the peers concerned
certainly had been, among others. The Overlords experiment
did not survive the autumn of 1953. Churchill also insisted
that Butler should have an unwanted assistant at the Treasury
in Sir Arthur Salter as Minister of State for Economic Affairs.
Churchill told his Chancellor that Salter was 'the best
economist since Jesus Christ'. Butler, however, found
Salter's 'numberless minutes in green ink', penned over
thirteen months, to be not very helpful. Butler also had the
unwanted assistance of a Treasury Ministerial Advisory
Committee - including Woolton - until it was absorbed into the
regular machinery of the Cabinet. As Churchill was not
particularly interested in machinery of government, the
various forms of assistance given to Butler possibly reflected
his distrust of a former political opponent in the pre-War
struggles over India and over Appeasement. Churchill certainly distrusted the Treasury itself, the scene of his

controversial Chancellorship of 1924-29. Butler's only regret
about the various arrangements made during his own Chancellorship seemed to be about the fate of Sir Edwin Plowden, at the
head of the Planning Staff. Plowden acted as Butler's 'faith-
ful watchdog-in-chief'. His role was 'to interpret and give
practical edge' to the advice given by 'the less voluble and
extrovert' Sir Robert Hall, the Government's Chief Economic
Adviser. Butler said that Plowden's departure for private
industry in 1953 'undoubtedly weakened my position and that of
the British economy'.30   To the outsider, it seemed that
Plowden was squeezed out of the machinery of government. It
was not very long before he was invited back to indicate what
the deficiencies of that machinery were.
     What changed the political atmosphere was the end of the
Butler boom and its consequences. These were the critical
developments which set in motion the Administrative 'Revolution'. The Crichel Down affair caused a few worried glances at
the structure of the Positive State, and the eventual appointment of a British Ombudsman can be seen as one of its long
term consequences. Suez was important for more than the
changes in defence and foreign policy making arrangements which
followed from it. Nevertheless, had Britain proceeded to
experience an 'economic miracle', the loss of Great Power
status and the end of Empire would have mattered much less.
Britain would have been good at something: running a successful modern economy. Moreover, sustained economic growth at
the level that Western Germany proceeded to achieve would have
made it possible at one and the same time to meet the investment needs of the economy, the demands of mass consumption,
and increased State social expenditure. The 'miracle' did not
occur. Britain remained a low wage, low productivity economy.
Full employment, in practice, tended to be defined in terms of
everybody having a job, not in terms of them being fully
employed doing it. The fashion for Anglo-American productivity
teams spelling out the details of this situation did not
survive the early 1950s, but this did not mean that the
problems had gone away. So, when Britain embarked on becoming
what in her case was misleadingly called an Affluent Society
she did so without an economic base which, in the long term,
could sustain the style of life of mass consumerism, at least
when accompanied by the scale of public expenditure currently
deemed politically desirable. What was widely unappreciated
at the time was that the Keynesian economic theory then ruling
the intellectual roost had no answer to Britain's fundamental
economic problems. It was a macro-economic managing theory
which rested on entirely unrealistic micro-economic assumptions.
The British economy had been in relative decline since the
1870s. That this decline was continuing was masked during
much of the era of the so-called Affluent Society by Britain's
sharing in the contemporary and sustained boom in international
trade. This boom was the major source of the prosperity of the
time, not Keynes's ideas, to which several countries did not

subscribe. Even domestically, Keynes's Grand Design for the mass unemployment society of the 1930s was not obviously relevant to the full employment society of twenty and more years later. Indeed, it was damaging to the extent that it encouraged the belief that all economic problems were remediable by topping up the economy with public expenditure. Whether it was perennially increasing real incomes, improved social services, full employment, or stable prices, the Positive State was always thought to be able to deliver, long after it was clear that it could not.

The demise of the Butler boom left the British political system without a party resistant to the growth of the State. The Conservatives, especially under Macmillan's leadership, acted as if their essay in economic liberalism had been a failure. Those Conservatives, like Enoch Powell, who persisted in the worship of the market, found themselves doing so in the wilderness, from which they were only allowed to return on the understanding that they would not practise their creed. Whatever its importance for the future, the establishment of the Institute of Economic Affairs in 1957 could hardly have taken place at a more inopportune time. Views of the kind associated with Friedrich von Hayek seemed even more out of touch with contemporary reality than when that scholar had denounced increasing collectivism as the road to serfdom in 1944. Indeed, writing in 1960, Hayek emphasized the divisions between himself and a British Conservative Party which subscribed to the sentiments of Macmillan's Middle Way.31 Such notions of intellectual purity ignored the lack of an alternative political home. The small Liberal Party could not oblige, once Jo Grimond had become its leader in 1956. Grimond's strategy was for the Liberals to replace Labour as the main electoral opponents of the Conservatives. Whether or not this was a wise strategy, it was certainly one that was persisted with. Meanwhile, the Liberals settled for being a party of protest in which role it enjoyed success of a kind. The number of Liberal revivals an elector experienced eventually became a way of telling his or her age, rather like counting the rings on an oak tree. One casualty of Grimond's approach was any close relationship between the Liberal Party and economic liberalism. With the Liberals and the Conservatives in retreat from the world of ideas, the intellectual initiative passed to the Progressive Establishment, and particularly to the Fabians, who believed in looking to the State for economic and social salvation, and who deemed reform to be 'a good thing'.

The Conservative Governments of the period from the 1950s onwards deemed some reform of the machinery of government to be a necessary thing: the Positive State had to be made to work. Having turned away from economic liberalism, the Conservatives increasingly turned to the State to provide the impetus for the level of economic growth needed to meet the various demands on the economy and - without extra taxation -

of the Welfare State too. The natural place to start was the Treasury, responsible for the management of the Managed Economy. Butler was said to have found wanting the quality of the official advice submitted to him in the critical year of 1955. In 1956, Macmillan, his successor as Chancellor, cast doubt on the relevance of the statistical information on which his Budget had to be based.32 The departure of Sir Edward Bridges in 1956 from the post of Permanent Secretary to the Treasury and Head of the Civil Service provided an occasion for change. Sir Norman Brook became Head of the Home Civil Service in addition to the Secretaryship to the Cabinet. He also became Joint Permanent Secretary to the Treasury, together with a newcomer, Sir Roger Makins, at the time the British Ambassador in Washington. The latter was placed in charge of the financial and economic work of the Treasury. It was unclear what was achieved in terms of greater economic expertise at the top of the Treasury by replacing one gifted intelligent lay administrator in Bridges by another in Makins.

This point did not elude the Civil Service's external critics, who were rarely in short supply, and who always included the indefatigable Fabian reformer, W A Robson. While others had celebrated the centenary of the Trevelyan-Northcote Report with lavish praise of the Civil Service, Robson had marked the occasion differently. He published a collection of essays by himself and by others, which contained criticisms of the Service's structure, and its arrangements for recruitment to, promotion into, and post-entry training in its leading, Administrative Class. Of course, there was no novelty in criticising the Civil Service - and particularly the Foreign Office - for disproportionately recruiting to its highest ranks Oxford and Cambridge graduates from relatively privileged social backgrounds. Similar criticisms had been made in another Robsonian collection in the 1930s. What the expression of such criticisms ten years after the Butler Education Act did was to suggest that the Civil Service was reluctant to come to terms with meritocracy. Moreover, when, reviewing post-war developments, Robson drew attention to the absence in the British Civil Service of anything comparable with the <u>Ecole Nationale d'Administration</u> in Paris, he was drawing attention to the persistence of the amateur tradition. What Robson pointed to with measured criticisms, another Fabian, Thomas Balogh was to do much more intemperately. For Balogh, what he called the dilettantes of the Administrative Class in general and of the Treasury in particular were nothing less than the main authors of Britain's national decline, which was occurring 'at a rate unparalleled since the crash of the Spanish Empire'. He believed that the 'jejeune amateurism' displayed by the Higher Civil Service made imperative change in a machinery of government that was a 'Mandarin's Paradise' and served only the interests of The Establishment. He did not expect that economic expertise itself would solve the problems of economic policy making. Nevertheless, with American experience in mind, he advocated the creation of a small and expert Council of Economic Advisers, responsible either to the Chancellor of the Exchequer or to the Cabinet, and charged with the elaboration of long term policies. Balogh also favoured the creation of a Ministry of the Budget, which would 'exercise continuous and expert financial control instead of the present fitful amateurish annual reviews of expenditure which only work on niggling points'. He wanted those civil servants with training in economics to be brought into the mainstream of administration. Knowledge of economics was also to be made a condition of service in economic departments, becoming an advantage in the recruitment process, and the subject of compulsory training on the French model. Balogh wanted the Headship of the Civil Service to be put into commission. He also proposed that departmental headships should be put into commission, making for a structure of specialized account-ability. He also wanted Ministers in charge of large depart-ments to be 'armed with private offices and experts recruited from outside and dependent on the Minister'. This last proposal made by Balogh in 1959 found a place in a report on the Higher Civil Service published in 1964 by a Fabian group of which he was a member. The report was similar in tone and content to Robson's critique of the Civil Service, while making more of such proposals as the removal of control of establish-ments from the Treasury.33

The Treasury seemed to be under fire from all sides from the mid-1950s onwards, not just for the quality of its manage-ment of the economy, but also for its handling of its traditional role of controlling public expenditure. A critical report from the Select Committee on Estimates on the latter subject led to the appointment in 1959 of a committee under the chairmanship of the by then ennobled Sir Edwin Plowden to examine the arrangements for such control. The Plowden Report, published in 1961, proved to be one of the milestones of the Administrative 'Revolution'. This was not mainly because it led to a further and important reorganization of the Treasury and to other organizational developments. Much more important than this was that after Plowden the Treasury changed from an annual money based approach to the control of public expenditure to one supposedly related to real resources and planned over a period of years. Ministerial proposals for public expenditure were to be related to national income, and ordered in relation to each other. So, Lord Plowden had re-visited the machinery of government, and having recommended that public expenditure had to be planned and, given that it could not be planned in isolation, had helped to restore planning itself. What remained of the old Plowden planning machinery was absorbed into the Neddy organization, which began to take shape in the summer of 1961. However, neither the Treasury's conversion to planning, nor the eclectic Macmillan Government's various initiatives in planning and in promoting regional development, served to satisfy those economists who criticized British government as somehow having rejected certain obvious clues to economic success. Indeed, the two popular contemporary histories of British economic policy were written in the manner of detective stories, with the economists casting themselves as Humphrey Bogart easily unravelling the mysteries of painless economic growth.34 The apparent success of Keynesian methods since the 1940s had given economists such confidence in their art, that it was only a short step to the revival of the belief that economic planning was easy. When instant success was not forthcoming, this was blamed on the supposed inadequacies of the Conservative Government and of the Treasury. A Labour Government and a special economic planning department were expected to do better.

The demands of the Welfare State were an important reason for the Macmillan Government's increasingly purposive search for a higher rate of economic growth. With the aid of full employment, and in the absolute, Victorian terms of Seebohm Rowntree, the Welfare State had abolished poverty, as a further survey of York had demonstrated.35 Nevertheless, there were demographic pressures at either end of the age scale which ensured that social expenditure was bound to increase. That, for example, the Guillebaud Committee was able to tell the Conservative Government in 1956 that the National Health Service was providing value for money was only partly re-assuring. It still left the problem to be solved of where to find the resources not just to maintain the Service in the face of the forces of demography; but also to meet the demands caused by the increasing sophistication of medicine. In addition, and in common with other social services, the National Health Service also faced the demands caused by the rising qualitative expectations of the public. There was an insistent inducement to find ways of making more efficient the use of resources in the National Health Service and education and the other social services, including the local authority personal social services. Offering as it did, the possibility of rationalization, institutional reform was bound to have its attractions for politicians. It also carried the risk of bureaucratic imperialism, which may have encouraged the Macmillan Government to make haste slowly, if not with London government, then with local government reform.

That the Macmillan Government's taste for institutional reform did not run to the establishment of a British Ombudsman was surprising, at least at first sight, given the Tory Party's alarm about bureaucratic powers at the time of Crichel Down. Then, the Labour Party had tended to defend the Civil Service, seeming to fear some kind of assault on the Positive State. Few people in, and connected with, the Labour Party had seriously thought about the risks entailed for personal free-dom in the creation of mass bureaucracies. Such fears were usually left to be expressed by supposedly reactionary lawyers, as in Lord Hewart's famous outburst against the New Despotism in the 1920s. An exception to this Fabian neglect was, once more, Professor Robson, for administrative law was one of his many targets for necessary reform. In 1956, and significantly for the future, Richard Crossman showed himself to be one of the few Labour politicians who even recognized the problem. Meanwhile, Maxwell Fyfe, for the Conservative Government, had set up a committee to review administrative justice, under the chairmanship of Sir Oliver Franks, like Plowden, one of the administrative figures of the age. When it was published in 1957, the Franks Report made some valuable recommendations; but none which would have made any difference in the Crichel Down type of case, as this was precluded from the Committee's terms of reference. Some lawyers and others believed that nothing less than the British counterpart of the French Conseil d'Etat was necessary to ensure adequate judicial review of executive discretion, and said so. Indeed, they continued saying so even after the success of another campaign conducted by lawyers and others for a British equivalent of the Scandinavian Ombudsman, or, as he was to be called, Parliamentary Commissioner for Administration. This campaign was launched in 1957, and most effectively conducted by an all party organization called 'Justice'. A committee of 'Justice', under the chairmanship of Sir John Whyatt, published a report in 1961, which advocated a British Ombudsman, and which attracted considerable attention and support, not least from Conservatives, including the then Solicitor-General, Sir Jocelyn Simon. The Whyatt Report was, in fact, a very cautious document. It envisaged Ministers being able to veto any proposed investigation by the Parliamentary Commissioner; and in such investigations that were permitted the Ombudsman had no assured access to internal departmental minutes. Nevertheless, the Macmillan Government declined to proceed to establish an office of Parliamentary Commissioner, and it was left to a Labour Government to pass the necessary legislation in 1967. One suspects that the Macmillan Government thought that however modest the Ombudsman's powers were to start with, they would then prove to be merely the base line for more agitation for further powers. Experience tended to bear this out. Even though Labour legislation was not as restrictive of the Parliamentary Commissioner's powers as the Whyatt Report, it was still criticized by reformers for not going far enough. Indeed, as a result, from its inception, the innovation of establishing an office of Parliamentary Commissioner was written down by many observers. Yet, from the first major case that was dealt with, it was clear that the Macmillan Government's belief that an Ombudsman's activities would be bound to be undermining of the doctrine of ministerial responsibility 36 was well founded, and that the office of Parliamentary Commissioner was an important constitutional innovation. Nevertheless, to appear to be more for the interests of governmental bureaucracy than the Labour Party - which did adopt the innovation - was a disadvantageous position for the Conservatives to put themselves in.

The Conservatives were destined to launch the Administrative 'Revolution' and later to govern during it: but the central and critical years of the Revolution belonged to the first Wilson Governments. Why the Conservatives lost their grip on office in 1964, when it seemed so secure as late as 1961, was afterwards to be a cause of much heart searching in Tory ranks. Scandals such as the Portland spy case, the Vassall affair, and, above all, the Profumo affair certainly damaged the carefully cultivated Conservative reputation for governmental competence and 'respectability'. Conservative morale was adversely affected too when Macmillan sacked no less than seven of his Cabinet Ministers in the famous purge of Friday the 13th of July 1962. De Gaulle's veto of the British application to join the European Common Market at the beginning of 1963 was a heavy political blow for the Conservatives. It may be that had Macleod and Powell agreed to serve under Lord Home, Macmillan's eccentric choice of successor as Prime Minister, the General Election of 1964 might still have been won. Even without the dissidents, some think that a fourth Conservative electoral victory in a row might have been possible had some kind of policy on land been found to take the edge off Labour's campaign on the subject. Nevertheless, the fact was that the Election was lost, and in the manner of a substantial Conservative decline compared with 1959. Maxwell Fyfe, one of the victims of the 1962 purge was not alone in attributing this decline to a revival of idealism among the electorate, and a revulsion against the 'never had it so good' philosophy of 1959. What the Tories needed, he thought, was 'a popular non-materialistic policy'.37 What such a policy would have consisted of remained unclear. What was clear was that the Conservatives had made a materialistic appeal in 1959, but they had literally failed to come up with the goods. Had they done so, they would have robbed the Labour Party of the main thrust of its own materialistic campaign of 1964: that it could manage the economy better than the Tories and finance all on the proceeds. Moreover, twenty years after the Butler Act, the Conservative unwillingness to make the Parliamentary Party more reflective of the educational revolution it had helped to promote, and of the social composition of its voters, was probably a disadvantage. The Conservatives still had a social edge. They still seemed to be run by what Macleod called 'the magic circle'.38 As The Establishment's traditional role was being undermined by the end of Empire and of the Great Power role, the close association of the Tories with it, if it was an asset was bound to be a diminishing one. It was easy for such as Harold Wilson to portray The Establishment as irrelevant to the economic challenges facing Britain, because this was substantially the case.

Unfortunately, the alternative, Progressive Establishment, allowed to dominate by the Tory decline, was also plainly irrelevant. It was very far from being some kind of previously

excluded class of managers, scientists and technologists fit
to compete on level terms with the Germans and the Americans.
The Progressive Establishment was well represented by the
academics, journalists, and school teachers, who were so
numerous among the 1964 and 1966 Labour parliamentary intakes.
They were not wealth creators. They were redistributionists.
Even the so called Labour moderates wanted nothing less than
an egalitarian crusade. It was a cause they were decidedly
immoderate about, and Crosland was no exception. One friend
later recalled about discussions in his own home: 'Tony
Crosland used to get so heated in these debates about egalitarianism that he once told my wife and myself that in any
event we would be on different sides of the barricades and he
would be able to shoot us first, because we had no war
experience as he had, and would not be able to handle a gun.39
Crosland's objective was to make Britain into what he believed
Sweden to be. This begged the question of the comparative
state of the British economy, the modernizing of which was
talked about by Fabians but treated as something readily
remediable by the very advent of a Labour Government. The
Fabian had little interest in soiling his hands with 'trade'.
This had little appeal compared with, say, making Britain into
what people like Crosland and Roy Jenkins called a civilized
society. This was supposed to be achieved by such measures as
abolishing capital punishment and reforming the law on abort-
ion, homosexuality and divorce. The working class MP who
complained that it was not measures of this kind which led
either him, or his father before him, to join and work for the
Labour Party was out of line with middle class, graduate
colleagues.40 The latter tended to talk of the working man
as Noble Savage, as if social distance lent enchantment. Yet
this taste for Ouvrierism stopped short of, for instance,
reflecting the prejudices of the masses on race relations: it
was idealized working men not actual ones that were lionized.
   The Fabians' faith in the improveability of human nature
was matched only by their belief in the improveability of
governmental machinery. The traditional Fabian view was that
'national efficiency' could be secured through State action
and promoted by the reform of its machinery. So, it was no
surprise that the period of Fabian intellectual dominance in
the 1960s and the first part of the 1970s was one characterized by administrative change. From the mid-1950s onwards, the
Conservatives had engaged in the reform of government as a part
of their attempt to make the Positive State work. Believing
that 'the machinery of government must be modernized', the
Wilson Labour Government elected in 1964 promised to go
farther and faster than the Tories. The Conservatives,
following Labour in 1970, promised to do the reforming job
properly. Reforming Parliaments, which were in some respects
willing to reform themselves, were encouraging of reforming
Governments. So was a 'public opinion', which deemed reforming the machinery of the State to be good in itself. In

addition, once the heady optimism of 1964 had passed, the
intractability of Britain's economic problems made institutional reform more attractive. It was not just the hoped for
savings of resources and gains in efficiency. Trying to reform
governmental institutions was something which politicians could
do. Moreover, given the electoral effects of what was defined
as economic failure, it was something which politicians could
do within what they expected to be a relatively short period of
office. Whatever the motives, tinkering with central governmental machinery and its manning took place on a substantial
scale - the Administrative 'Revolution'. Sometimes these
changes resulted from the activities of investigatory bodies -
Plowden, Fulton and the rest - and sometimes not. Few areas of
central government organization escaped change. The Foreign
Service was changed, and so was the Home Civil Service. The
office of Parliamentary Commissioner for Administration was
established. Governments found a variety of mechanisms for
establishing a presence in the economy, including economic
planning. At first sight, this activity constituted a remarkable level of change in the machinery of government. However,
on detailed consideration, of the kind which we will now give
to administrative change in British central government since
the 1950s, it is clear that what took place was all too often
superficial change.

References

1. Feiling (1946), p. 253; 360 H.C. Deb. 5s. c. 1502;
339 H.C. Deb. 5s. c. 373; Northedge (1974), p. 328.
2. Ibid., p. 146 (q.v. Dalton's remarks at Labour Party
Conference 1950); Kilmuir (1964), p. 193.
3. This was provocatively recognized by that honest, if
eccentric, socialist intellectual, Strachey (1959). Fieldhouse (1973) cast doubt on whether empires paid even before
1914.
4. Barnett (1972), p. 258; Northedge (1974), p. 185;
The Economist, 8.12.1945, p. 821; Dalton (1962), pp. 68-89;
Strang (1956), p. 289; Avon (1960), pp. 107-43; 175-88,
289-90. Dulles was certainly pleased at the Geneva Settlement,
not least where the partition line was drawn. 'The guy is
terrific', he told reporters afterwards: but he meant Mendes-
France, not Eden (Drummond and Coblentz, 1960, pp. 122-23). The
Geneva Settlement came remarkably close to the American seven
point memorandum (Gerson, 1967, p. 185). Why the Chinese acted
as they did, we shall probably never know. Although we have
the intelligent guesses of Hinton (1966), pp. 248-54.
5. Robertson (1965), p. 73; Thomas (1967), pp. 116,
164; Moncrieff (1967), pp. 44, 45; Nutting (1967), pp. 71,
167-68.
6. Avon, pp. 367-75; Martin (1962), pp. 28-9.
7. Rosecrance (1968), pp. 261-63; Heren (1970), p. 231.

8. Sampson (1967), pp. 235-36; Schlesinger (1965),
pp. 340-41, 699-70; Sorensen (1965), pp. 558-59.
9. The Times, 6.12.1962, 11.12.1962; Macmillan (1973),
pp. 339-40.
10. The Tory Home Secretary described the Immigration
legislation as 'one of the most bitterly fought Bills that I
have ever known' ('Lord Butler Looks Back', The Listener,
28.7.1966, p. 116).
11. Macmillan (1972), pp. 350-351; The Spectator,
14.4.1961, p. 499; Crossman (1976), pp. 30, 81-5, 104-5, 116,
182-83, 340, 406; Report of the 61st Annual Conference of the
Labour Party, pp. 154-65.
12. King (1971), pp. 323-24 (informant: Richard Marsh);
Heren (1970), pp. 182-83, 260.
13. Dalton (1962), pp. 93, 187, 203-5.
14. Laski (1938), pp. 90-5; Shinwell (1955), pp.172-73;
Martin (1953), p. 85; Foot (1960), p. 125. Cole (1935), p.408
even argued that economic planning would be easier to initiate
in Britain than it had been in Russia.
15. Foot (1960), pp. 503-4; 250 H.C. Deb. 5s. c. 55-7,
59; Morrison (1954), pp. 295-316.
16. Griffiths (1969), pp. 80-1; Donoughue and Jones
(1973), pp. 400-3; Report of the 47th Annual Conference of the
Labour Party, p. 132; Bevan (1952), pp. 118, 169; Report of
the 48th Annual Conference of the Labour Party, p. 172;
Mitchell (1966), pp. 74-120.
17. The Keynesian concerned being Brittan (1964), p. 92.
18. Woolton (1959), p. 379; Birkenhead (1969), pp. 274-
302; Moran (1966), pp. 394-95; Macmillan (1969), pp. 373-
460; Fisher (1973), p. 17; Butler (1971), pp. 154-82.
19. Macmillan (1971), pp. 342-74; Brittan (1964),
pp. 180-81.
20. Macmillan (1973), p. 37.
21. Crosland (1962), pp. 118, 120.
22. Crosland (1956), pp. 375-88, 518-20, 522.
23. Ibid., p. 20.
24. Smith (1964), p. 193.
25. The Bank of England recorded that it was not until
November 1964 that 'a severe crisis of confidence in the pound
developed' (Quarterly Bulletin, March 1965, p. 3) and Wilson
admitted this (702 H.C. Deb. 5s. c. 931, 933).
26. Dalton (1962), p. 241.
27. Cmd, 6404 (1942), p. 23.
28. Morrison (1954), pp. 45-52, 170, 255-62, 276-84,
344-36; Attlee (1954), p. 308.
29. Fry (1969), pp. 257-65.
30. Chandos (1960), p. 343; Woolton (1959), pp. 371-73,
377-78; Butler (1971), pp. 156-60. Churchill himself took
the departure of Lord Leathers in September 1953 to mark the
end of the Overlords (Moran, 1966, p. 467). Although Lord
Cherwell actually continued as Paymaster General for several
weeks afterwards. Sir John Anderson declined to become an

Overlord in 1951, telling Churchill that such a role had no place in the peacetime organization of government (Wheeler-Bennett, 1962. p. 352).

31. Hayek (1960), pp. 397-411.
32. Brittan (1969), pp. 122-23; 551 H.C. Deb. 5s. c. 867.
33. Robson (1954), pp. 299-307, 336-46; Balogh in Thomas (1959), pp. 83-126. Balogh's most amazing complaint was of the absence of a Progressive Establishment in Britain. Surely he was, and remained, a member ! The report referred to was The Administrators. The Fabian group was originally set up by Balogh at Wilson's request in 1963.
34. The books that I have in mind are Shonfield (1959) and, more particularly, Brittan (1964). Sadly, an 'economic miracle' proved more elusive than the Maltese Falcon.
35. Rowntree and Lavers (1951), pp. 37-49.
36. Stacey (1971), pp. 3-47; 666 H.C. Deb. 5s. c. 1125-26.
37. Kilmuir (1964), pp. 321-22. Sampson (1967), p. 257 was one of several others to take up this theme.
38. I. Macleod, 'The Tory Leadership', The Spectator, 17.1.1964, pp. 65-67. See also Enoch Powell's remarks about the need for a new style Tory Party made at the end of 1964 (Roth, 1971, p. 319).
39. Davenport (1974), pp. 105-6.
40. Simon Mahon of Bootle (McKie and Cook, 1972, p. 200).

Chapter 3

THE MACHINERY OF CENTRAL GOVERNMENT AND THE PURSUIT OF 'NATIONAL EFFICIENCY'

'Don't clap too hard - it's a very old building.' Archie Rice's advice to his audience in The Entertainer in 1957 was a comment on the general condition of Britain. The same comment could have been specifically directed at the machinery of British central government. For, it was from about 1957 on- wards that this machinery came to be seen as being in need of reconstruction. Although constructed on even older foundat- ions, the main framework of the 'old building' had been laid down in Victorian times, if not completed in many important ways until the twentieth century. What had been designed for an era when the prevailing ideology - if not always the practice - was laissez-faire, was unlikely to be suitable for a period when the role of the State was more positive. Late Victorian and Edwardian demands for changes in governmental machinery by Fabians in the name of 'national efficiency' had eventually led to the Haldane reconstruction plan of 1918. However, the design suited the architects - the Webbs - rather than more democratically inclined occupants. The estate of government was left to be developed largely unplanned, even when the functions of the State were vastly expanded following the commitments to the Managed Economy Welfare State of the 1940s. The public corporations which ran the nationalized industries were huge additions to the 'old building', and ones which were out of character with the traditional facade. The developments related to the Welfare State were accommodated more easily within a familiar structure. Such organizing principles as there were remained those of the original core of the machinery of central government. This was despite the running of the Positive State being a very different activity from that which the nineteenth century architects had anticipated. When the British economy began to get into perennial difficulties from the mid-1950s onwards, and with Britain's place in the world changing too, it was only to be expected that the machinery of government and its manning would be looked at critically. It was in character with the 'old building' that the subsequent reconstruction of British central government was done without anything resembling a

43

sustained overview. If British government was amateur when the
need was for professionalism, the recasting of its central
machinery was largely done in the amateur tradition. This
suited most politicians who were reluctant to examine their own
roles in the governmental process, thus robbing the reforming
activity of an important dimension. With coherent direction
the exception rather than the rule, the remodelling of central
administration often took on the appearance of change for
change's sake. 'National efficiency' was sought in an inefficient and importantly incomplete manner.

I   ATTEMPTING TO PUT THE 'OLD BUILDING' IN ORDER

The Administrative 'Revolution' of the 1960s and 1970s can be
divided into different phases, but one continuing theme was
that the recasting of the machinery of British central government was in some way promotive of 'national efficiency'.
Reorganization, rationalization, and reform meant different
things to different reorganizers, rationalizers and reformers.
For the Heath Conservative Government in its early years, it
meant associating administrative change with cutting back on
the role of the State, and with the better organization and
performance of the many functions that remained. The latter
part of the Heath era had more in common with the confusion of
the Wilson years of 1964-70. It was the exceptional phase of
the Administrative 'Revolution' in which administrative change
was directed towards identifiable and realizable objectives.
The machinery of British central government had 'just growed'
like Topsy, as some were given to lovingly remark. It was
reconstructed in a generally haphazard manner too.
    The earlier part of the Administrative 'Revolution' was
in some respects its most constructive period. In the aftermath of Suez, the Macmillan and Home Conservative Governments
of 1957-64 consolidated the arrangements for defence, and
began the process of rearranging those for external relations.
The economic situation led the Macmillan Government into a
Treasury reorganization, following the Plowden Report on the
Control of Public Expenditure; into the setting up of Neddy
and a supporting structure; and into the regulation of
incomes in the 'pay pause' and beyond through Nicky - the
National Incomes Commission. In addition, the Conservatives
effected the administrative change of establishing a Department of Education and Science. That department and the
consolidated Ministry of Defence were the first of the 'giant',
Jumbo, or 'federal' departments which were to be one characteristic of changes in central government structure. The Tories
also went in for departmental renaming activity, such as when
the Ministry of Works was translated into the Ministry of
Public Building and Works in 1963. Although, in the same
year, the Board of Trade kept its traditional name, despite
its President, Edward Heath exercising there wider
responsibilities as Secretary of State for Industry, Trade and

Regional Development. At least one Tory innovation was doomed
from the start when the trade union movement declined to
recognize Nicky. If an incomes policy was to be run through a
special institution another would have to be devised. The
Conservatives had involved the trade unions in the Neddy
structure, one on which their immediate successors could have
built had they had a clear idea of how to practice the economic
planning and interventionism that they preached. Some other
changes - notably those in external relations - needed to be
completed. To the extent that they involved staffing, they
had implications for the organization of the Home Civil
Service too. The changes in central government organization
made or begun under Macmillan and Home compared favourably in
effectiveness with those made in subsequent periods of the
Administrative 'Revolution'.

Administrative change played a much more conscious part
in the approach to governing of Labour under Harold Wilson
between 1964 and 1970. In Opposition one of the major themes
of Wilson's campaign for office was the need to modernize
British government. Nevertheless, some of the changes made
simply followed on from those indicated under the Tories: for
example, the merger of the Colonial and Commonwealth Relations
Offices in 1966, and their amalgamation with the Foreign
Office to form the Foreign and Commonwealth Office in 1968.
Wilson eventually followed the taste of his predecessors for
mergers in other cases too; such as his establishment of the
Department of Health and Social Security in 1968, and in his
anticipation of the setting up of the Department of the
Environment in 1970. By then, too, the Ministry of Technology,
a Wilsonian creation, had begun to take over some of its
fellow departments. At the outset, Wilson's approach had been
different. He had set up no less than five new, separate
government departments, including the Ministry of Technology.
The others were the Welsh Office, the Ministry of Overseas
Development, the Ministry of Land and Natural Resources, and
the Department of Economic Affairs. 'In the first twenty-four
hours of Labour Government in 1964', Wilson later recalled,
'we carried through the biggest peacetime revolution in
machinery of government for half a century'. What were the
results of this 'revolution' ? The Welsh Office established
itself as a permanent part of British central government. The
Ministry of Overseas Development survived in one form or
another as a replacement for the Conservatives' Department of
Technical Co-operation. This change proved to have little
point, given that, in real terms, less rather than more funds
were made available for overseas aid. The Ministry of Land
and Natural Resources, and the Department of Economic Affairs,
lasted for two and five years respectively. In both cases,
from the beginning, it was clear that neither department could
perform the role indicated for it. This was also true of the
Ministry of Technology, and not surprisingly so given that it
was charged with nothing less that the regeneration of British

industry. Nevertheless, as we have noted, the Ministry not
only survived: for a time, it grew. Other Labour creations
in the economic sphere included the Industrial Reorganization
Corporation, and - as a replacement for Nicky - the National
Board for Prices and Incomes. As Neddy, the Treasury - despite
surgery - and the Board of Trade survived too, there was some
confusion of responsibilities in this area. The frequent
Wilsonian reshuffling of Ministers, Ministries and departmental
responsibilities were confusing too. Although, together with
the plethora of committees and Commissions which were at work
investigating bits and pieces of government machinery, they
did give an impression of activity. Sometimes acts like
changing the National Assistance Board into the Supplementary
Benefits Commission seemed worth doing, if only marginally.
More often, they were cosmetic acts. One example of this
occurred when the then Prime Minister moved Barbara Castle from
the Ministry of Transport to the Ministry of Labour in 1968.
Mr Wilson found that 'in Barbara's case there was a psycho-
logical problem. The Ministry of Labour image, she felt, was
wrong'. He recalled, 'We discussed a title. She laid claim
to Labour and Productivity. I suggested that with a lady
Minister this might lead to bar room ribaldry. She took the
point and we settled on Employment and Productivity'.1   The
joke turned out to be on both Mrs Castle and the Prime Minister.
When, in 1969, they tried to pass industrial relations legislation, the trade union movement, already enraged by the
Labour Government's incomes policies, forced them to drop it.
     The Heath Conservative Government of 1970-74 came to
office with decided views about administrative change. These
were soon spelt out in a White Paper published in 1970 called
The Reorganization of Central Government. 'This Administration
has pledged itself to introduce a new style of government.
More is involved than bringing forward new policies and
programmes: it means resolving the issue of the proper sphere
of government in a free society; and improving the efficiency
of the machinery intended to achieve the aims it sets itself
within that sphere. This Administration believes that government has been attempting to do too much. This has placed an
excessive burden on industry, and on the people of the country
as a whole, and has also overloaded the government machine
itself ... The Government intend to remedy this situation.'
The Heath Government had immediately instituted a review of
central government organization, which was intended to differ
from the previous approach of piecemeal changes in the pattern
of departmental responsibilities. This review was involved
'not merely with departmental boundaries but with the central
mechanism by which public policy is made and carried out'. This
latter consideration led to the establishment in the Cabinet
Office of a Central Policy Review Staff, whose concern was with
the definition of government strategy. There were several
immediate results to show for the general review of departmental responsibilities. Two new 'giant' departments were

established: the Department of Trade and Industry, and the
Department of the Environment. Arrangements were indicated
for the future responsibility for defence procurement. Overseas aid administration was brought within the Foreign and
Commonwealth Office. There was yet another departmental re-
naming: the Department of Employment and Productivity simply
became that of Employment. The White Paper had a contemporary
air about it too in thinking in terms of establishing 'units
of accountable management', and of 'hiving off' various
governmental activities. Nevertheless, it was something new
for any British Government to even intend to subject 'every
activity, from the most traditional to the most recent
innovation ... to the same rigorous tests: is it relevant?
and does it have to be done by central government?' The
Conservatives anticipated that 'the product of this review will
be less government, and better government, carried out be fewer
people'.2

The attitudes to administrative change of the Heath
Conservative Government were based on more than hostility to
the experiences of the Wilson years. This hostility was
present, and it was one reason why, for example, the incoming
Tories soon abolished the IRC and the Prices and Incomes
Board. Of much greater importance was the Conservatives'
reaction to their own record in office between 1951 and 1964.
During the subsequent spell in Opposition, the view flourished
among the Tories that, apart from periods like 1952-55 and
1958-60, the Conservative Governments had not been on top of
their job. Private enterprise had not been put back on the
pedestal. There had been too little 'real' Conservatism. In
Edward Boyle's phrase, there was more than a 'death wish' among
many Tories in relation to the policies of the latter Macmillan
years. There was a 'murder wish'. Such were the origins of
Selsdon Man.3 The Conservatives committed themselves to the
rolling back of the State. Edward Heath, addressing the
Conservative Party Conference for the first time as Prime
Minister in 1970, proclaimed his Government's aim to be 'a
revolution so quiet and yet so total, that it will go far
beyond the programme for a Parliament to which we are committed
and on which we have already embarked; far beyond this decade
and way into the future'.4 What was envisaged was something
like the sea change which took place in and around 1945,
although in a different direction. The Tories scored a notable
electoral victory in 1970, but not one of those dimensions.
Their programme was not of an order which those opposed to it
would have to accept as electorally irreversible in the foreseeable future. It was always likely, for instance, that a
future Labour Government, under trade union instructions, would
have to repeal industrial relations legislation. The un-
romantic course in the situation of 1970 was to settle for a
version of the Churchill Government's approach after 1951: to
go for quietism and not a Quiet Revolution unlikely to be quiet
for long. The Heath Government took the other course. Long

before the Oil Crisis of November 1973 knocked it sideways,
the Heath Government was forced from this course, and into
expanding the role of the State again. Compared with 1970, the
Conservatives ended up in 1974 with more government, not
necessarily better government, and government carried out by a
similar number of people.

The return of another Wilson Labour Government in 1974
led to a further extension of the role of the State and of
public employment and expenditure. There was the usual spate
of departmental changes and re-namings and institutional
creations. It looked like more of the same. What forced
change was the repercussions of the Oil Crisis on an economy
still in relative decline. At best, these could be postponed.
The Labour Government postponed them until the sterling crisis
of July 1975. After that, there had to be a period of
adjustment. It proved to be too a period of reappraisal.
Into the reappraisal came the question of what had been
actually achieved by the recasting of government machinery
which had characterized the period since the 1950s. Much
time, effort, and resources had been devoted to renovating the
'old building'; but surveying its foundations had been
relatively neglected. It was not evident that British central
government was more 'efficient' in relation to its functions
than before. Indeed, in the economic and social sphere,
performance was such that it raised fundamental questions
about the Positive State.

II   THE POLICY 'GAP' AND THE NEGLECT OF THE POLITICAL
     DIMENSION

That the Administrative 'Revolution' of the 1960s and 1970s
was not concerned with fundamental questions about the role of
the State, and examining the foundations of central government
structure was very much in the British tradition. The Haldane
Report of 1918, the last act of the 'national efficiency'
movement of the earlier part of the century had been an
aberration. It had reviewed, and made recommendations about,
the organization of British central government from 'first
principles'. This excited administrative reformers but not
Governments. The Haldane Report was destined for the shelf
from the moment that it was published. The 'national
efficiency' movement of the 1960s and 1970s was different in
that it excited both reformers and Governments, and that a
considerable number of administrative changes resulted. The
classic criticism of the Haldane Report was that it neglected
the political dimension. This was deserved because, for
example, the Report defined the functions of the Cabinet
without reference to the fact that Ministers were party
politicians.5   Nevertheless, the Webbs and the other Haldane
reformers had squarely addressed themselves to the problem of
how to reconstruct a central machinery originally intended
for a primarily passive government into one suitable for more

active government. This could not be said to have been done in any sustained manner by the advocates of 'national efficiency' from the 1950s onwards. Their reforming activity was generally much more narrowly conceived. Moreover, they neglected the political dimension too.

The belief that British government at its centre was amateur when it needed to be professional was common to both Harold Wilson in 1964, and to the 'national efficiency' reformers of the earlier part of the century. Sidney Low reflected the earlier mood in an important study of the British Constitution published in 1904. 'English government is government by amateurs', he observed. 'The subordinates, in their several grades, are trained; the superiors, in whom rest responsibility and power, are untrained. Yet the necessity for trained intelligence and accuracy is greater than ever. The influence of government on all departments of national life has increased, and will continue to increase. We may not like this tendency, but we cannot check it ... The incessant and multitudinous activity of the State will grow, with the growing complexity of the social system, with the new wants, the new duties, the new dangers, which are constantly arising. A modern nation is running with all its motors at high pressure, and it will not run itself. The amount of skilled faculty required in every important business is greater than ever it was. But the greatest business of all - the business of government - is carried on by persons who have very often no special attainments, and as a rule no special training'. Low recognized that in their amateurism the Cabinet and its Ministers were reflective of the House of Commons whose members 'though generally upright, and sometimes able, are too apt to regard politics as a pastime, and the House itself as a club'. He recognized too that in the country there was 'no liking for the professional politician'. Nevertheless, Low believed, 'a different kind of leadership may be required in the future, and it may or may not be forthcoming'.6 It was largely not forthcoming in the form that Low wanted, and the massive change in the role of the State ideally required. That this was so, however, was not a major concern of the critics of British government of the late 1950s onwards. Their target was not Ministers. It was the Higher Civil Service, and the Administrative Class and the Treasury officials in particular, the apparent equivalents of the very people Low had seen as the trained subordinates of the untrained Ministers. This did not mean that Ministers were no longer amateurs in Low's sense, even though they were almost always now professional politicians of a kind. Their professionalism was usually that of parliamentary experience, and of other forms of public performance. The House of Commons retained many of the features of 'a club'. Spurs were still won on the floor of the House in Oxford Union style general debating. There was no necessary connection between success in such combat and the ability to run government departments. Indeed, any such

connection was likely to be fortuitous. In addition, few
Governments did not continue to include party worthies, whether
or not they were skilled parliamentarians. Ministers were
likely to be amateurs in relation to the now inevitably complex
subject matters of their departments.

Yet, the chief target of the modern 'national efficiency'
reformers was the Civil Service. This had changed considerably since Low's day and not always in the same direction as
the massively enlarged duties of the State seemed to require.
Most leading civil servants were certainly unlikely to be
thought of as trained subordinates. Their influence was widely
thought to be such that their subordination was seen by many as
being merely formal. In the opinion of their critics, the
leading civil servants were not considered to be trained, that
is, in the subject matters in which they gave advice.
Amateurism was the gravamen of Balogh's charge against the
Treasury, and of others against other departments. It was not
a charge that could have stuck so easily at the beginning of
the twentieth century, when Low wrote; or, for that matter,
during much of the nineteenth century. Amateurism was latent
but not explicit as it became during Warren Fisher's period as
Head of the Civil Service between the wars. It was then that,
for the first time, the Administrative Class was treated as one
for promotion purposes, and its members came to be seen as
supposedly interchangeable between not necessarily related
posts. This career pattern was not thought by those who
followed it to make the leading official into an amateur. The
leading civil servants saw themselves as professionals. Their
professionalism was in knowing their way around 'Whitehall',
and meeting the needs of the Minister, particularly parliamentary needs. Public administration was not thought to be
anybody's business. It could only be learnt 'by doing'. The
subject matters administered were supposed to be anybody's
business, anybody, that is , who had this special experience.
H E Dale, one of their number, wrote of the role of leading
civil servants in the inter-war period in this manner; and
C H Sisson wrote it up with similar elegance in the 1950s. Few
of those who criticized the Dale-Sisson administrators for
their attitudes, and who proclaimed them to be amateur,
recognized that Ministers also saw themselves as being
similarly versatile. The situation was that with the role of
the State more extensive and more complex than ever, and
growing more so, there was a double banking of amateurism at
the top of government departments. It involved both policy
initiators and the leading policy implementers - Ministers and
their major officials. By the 1960s, it was evident that
British central government was organized only to produce near
inertia.

Formal responsibility for policy making was clear enough.
The Cabinet was still the supreme policy making body, normally
bound by collective responsibility. The doctrine of
ministerial responsibility remained, as Low described it, 'the

main shaft and supporting pillar of the political edifice'.
Ministers were supposed to initiate policy, and the political
parties from which they were drawn had a responsibility for
undertaking the relevant research. Yet, the major parties have
usually given research activity a low priority. That the
Labour Party should have this attitude seems particularly
strange, at least at first sight, given the Party's socialist
commitment. Nevertheless, the Conservative Research Department, formed in 1929, has always seemed a more professional
organization than its Labour rival established eleven years
before. In a minor way, for some Conservatives the Department
has been a part of their career ladder. The Heath Cabinet of
1970, for example, had three former members of the Research
Department in its ranks. Political and intellectual stars
such as Enoch Powell, Iain Macleod, and Reginald Maudling
served in the Research Department aiding its head, Rab Butler,
in re-fashioning Tory policy after 1945. The Labour Party's
lack of serious research activity might be thought to be more
than made up by its support in intellectual circles, and
particularly that of the Fabian Society. However, for a long
time, the quality of the Fabian research output has been un-
impressive. Indeed, in 1977, a former General Secretary of the
Society, Shirley Williams, was honest enough to describe its
work as 'amateurism taken to its highest level'.7
     One of the few governments of recent times elected with,
if not necessarily because of, what appeared to be a carefully
constructed legislative programme was the Labour Government of
1945. In fact, as we have noted before, its nationalization
measures were ill prepared. Of Emanuel Shinwell's experience
at the Ministry of Fuel and Power, George Wigg, his
Parliamentary Private Secretary, later wrote: 'there was a
tragi-comic aspect to Shinwell's introduction to the job.
When instructed by Attlee to nationalize the mines, he
inquired at Transport House for the products of Labour thinking
over the years. After all, this was not a new subject. Coal
nationalization had been on Labour's programme for a quarter
of a century. Somebody must have worked out something at some
time. The archives were ransacked and revealed two copies of
a paper written by Jim Griffiths, one of them a translation
into Welsh !'8 So Shinwell was placed in a position of
extreme dependence upon his civil servants who, like the Civil
Service in general and the government departments they staff,
both were and are primarily organized around responses to
ministerial policy initiatives rather than providing such
initiatives themselves.
     When it came to strategy, the responsibility was clearly
that of the Cabinet. In normal peacetime conditions, the
Cabinet has rarely seemed effective in this role. With wartime experience in mind, and from Haldane onwards, proposals
have been often made for cutting down the size of the Cabinet,
and for reducing the number of questions presented for Cabinet
decision. These considerations were among the reasons why the

merging of departments was thought to have advantages. Before
coming to office in 1964, Harold Wilson anticipated having a
smaller Cabinet, but actually ended up with one of the same
size. Wilson was able to expand the Cabinet Office and
Cabinet Secretariat as he planned, but his expectation that his
Prime Minister's Office would become a 'power house' was
disappointed. Wilson said that he was going to restore Cabinet
Government as he understood it under Churchill and Attlee.
What he did practise, according to one of his Cabinet Ministers,
Richard Crossman, was a form of Prime Ministerial Government.
Wilson was portrayed as operating on a divide and rule basis.
His personal decisions were taken in consultation with an
inner private circle which included Marcia Williams, his
Personal and Political Secretary, and Sir Burke Trend, the
Secretary to the Cabinet, and hence, a civil servant. As for
the Cabinet Ministers themselves, Crossman recorded: 'we come
briefed by our departments to fight for departmental budgets,
not as Cabinet Ministers with a Cabinet view'. The Labour
Party had come to office without economic contingency plans,
and the Wilson Government still had none when the July 1966
crisis broke. Crossman lamented the absence in the Cabinet
structure of any domestic equivalent of the role played by the
Defence Committee in the defence and foreign policy sphere.
'We have', he wrote, 'no real instrument of central decision
taking for the home front'. Crossman said that this suited
the interests of the leading civil servants, who had no desire
to have a coherent policy making body imposed on them.9   This
latter assertion was not substantiated. Even if there was
Civil Service opposition, it would not constitute a veto.
Governments could have what Cabinet organization and committee
structure they liked. That the Wilson Government of 1964-70
operated without a coherent domestic policy was the responsibility of its political leadership.

In the 1970s, Governments of both political parties tried
to make institutional changes at the centre which would
facilitate coherent policy making. Two special units were
established in the Cabinet Office. The Heath Government set
up a European Secretariat in 1972 to co-ordinate policy
towards the EEC from the pre-accession stage. It continued to
play a coordinating role after Britain became a member of the
EEC in 1973. The subsequent Wilson Government set up a
Constitution Unit in October 1974 to coordinate work on
devolution policy and other matters related to the development
of political institutions. Earlier, in March 1974, a Policy
Unit was established in the Prime Minister's Office which,
among other things, provided him with general policy advice.10

The Heath Government made special institutional arrangements to try to ensure that it pursued a consistent strategy.
It thought that there was a need for 'a capability at the
centre for assessment of policies and projects in relation to
strategic objectives'. So, in February 1971, it established a
small multi-disciplinary Central Policy Review Staff, headed

by Lord Rothschild, and located in the Cabinet Office. Under the supervision of the Prime Minister, the Think Tank - as the Review Staff was to be known - was to work for Ministers collectively. Its task was officially described as threefold. First, it was to enable Ministers 'to take better policy decisions by assisting them to work out the implications of their basic strategy in terms of policies in specific areas'. Secondly, it was to aid Ministers in establishing 'the relative priorities to be given to the different sectors of their programme as a whole'. Thirdly, it was to help Ministers 'to identify those areas of policy in which new choices can be exercised and to ensure that the underlying implications of alternative courses of action are fully analysed and considered'. The Think Tank was accorded a place in the public expenditure process; and its work was said not to be intended as competing with policy analysis conducted in departments. The definition of the Think Tank's task which Rothschild himself preferred was that given by a colleague. He saw its role as 'sabotaging the over-smooth functioning of the machinery of government'; and 'providing a central department which has no departmental axe to grind but does have overt policy status which can attempt a synoptic view of policy'. He saw it as providing too 'a central reinforcement for those civil servants in Whitehall who are trying to retain their creativity and not be totally submerged in the bureaucracy'. The Think Tank's task was to 'advise the Cabinet collectively, and the Prime Minister, on major issues of policy relating to the Government's strategy'. It focussed 'the attention of Ministers on the right questions to ask about their own colleagues' business'; and it tried to devise 'a more rational system of decision making between competing programmes'. The Think Tank aimed to 'bring in ideas from the outside world'. Rothschild described the work of the CPRS under the Heath Government as mainly consisting of the preparation and presentation of six monthly reviews of the Government's strategy to the Cabinet, and separately to middle and junior Ministers; special studies requested or approved by the Cabinet; and collective briefs. The Think Tank consisted of between sixteen and nineteen staff, about half of them drawn from the Civil Service, and the other half from universities, industry, financial institutions, and international organizations. Most of the Think Tank's work was confidential and unpublished, such as, for example, a special study that it did of the Concorde aircraft project. When the Review Staff's work was published, it was often controversial, such as in late 1971 when the scientific community was predictably outraged by a report which advocated government research and development being put on a much more commercial footing. If Rothschild did not court controversy, he seemed to find it rather easily. In August 1973, on the same day as Prime Minister Heath was speaking in one part of Britain predicting a rosy future for the British economy, Rothschild was speaking elsewhere in the country saying the opposite. Rothschild was publicly reprimanded. To some outsiders, the Think Tank's prestige was never the same again. When Rothschild resigned in October 1974, he was succeeded by a much safer figure in Sir Kenneth Berrill. The publication of a much criticized report on overseas representation in 1977 even raised the question of what useful purpose the CPRS had come to serve. One of its early stars urged that the Think Tank should stop producing half baked reports, and go back to its original role of rubbing Ministers' noses in a strategic overview.11   Heath and his advisers had recognized the need for such a role. That they assigned it to a non-political body headed by a Labour peer in Rothschild was a curious act for a Conservative Government. For the point which was almost universally missed about the Think Tank was that in its role as governmental strategist, it was not just supportive of the Cabinet. It was doing work which the Cabinet should do, but which Ministers lacked either the time, will, or ability to perform.

That the existence of a policy 'gap' in British government was no more than partially recognized made importantly incomplete an Administrative 'Revolution' which was, in any case, characterized by piecemeal change. When a Royal Commission on the Constitution was appointed in 1969, it was not to provide an overview to an already much advanced process of institutional change. The Crowther-Kilbrandon Commission was a device used by the beleaguered Wilson Labour Government to de-fuse Scottish nationalism. The riches expected to flow from North Sea oil, much of it located off the coast of Scotland ensured that when the Crowther-Kilbrandon Report finally appeared in 1973, Scottish nationalism was rampant once more, threatening the unity of the United Kingdom. By that time, although some changes were to be made, and more were to be proposed, what had been de-fused was much of the previous enthusiasm for administrative change. For, the pursuit of 'national efficiency' through the reconstruction of machinery of government had yielded few tangible gains, as will be seen from the following chapters about the main changes made. In the end, the question of the ends sought as well as the means employed pressed more and more for consideration, and nowhere more so than with the management of the economy.

References

1.   Report of the 65th Annual Conference of the Labour Party, p. 166; Wilson (1971), pp. 521-22.
2.   Cmnd. 4506 (1970), pp. 3-9, 10-11, 13-15.
3.   Interview with Lord Boyle, 26.4.1977.
4.   Bruce-Gardyne (1974), p. 7.
5.   W.J.M. Mackenzie in Campion (1950), pp. 56-84.
6.   'Whitehall and Beyond', The Listener, 5.3.1964, p. 380; Low (1904), pp. 197-216, 304.
7.   Ibid., p. 136; Beichman (1973-74), pp. 92-113. Mrs. Williams made the remark quoted in an address to the Political

Studies Association on 5.4.1977.
    8. Wigg (1972), pp. 123, 125.
    9. 'Whitehall and Beyond', The Listener, 5.3.1964,
pp. 379-81, 396; 'The Prime Minister on the Machinery of
Government', Ibid., 6.4.1967, p. 448; Crossman (1975), pp. 275,
582-83.
    10. Dr. Bernard Donoughue, the Senior Policy Adviser to
the Prime Minister, and the head of his Policy Unit told me in
1978 that the Unit was generally about half a dozen in size,
although this varied from time to time. The Unit often used
part-timers, and also employed consultants, frequently from
among those who have previously worked in the Unit and
subsequently returned to their permanent occupations. The
Unit's basic work was to brief the Prime Minister on any policy
issues which concerned him. Donoughue said that this could
mean anything, and had meant most things; but tended to be
more in the domestic field than in the foreign (though the
Unit had briefed in foreign policy, especially on the EEC re-
negotiations). Donoughue's task was to direct the work of the
Unit and to brief the Prime Minister personally. He sat on
Cabinet committees and any official committees which seemed
appropriate. Members of the Unit sat on official committees
too. Donoughue also joined in briefing the Prime Minister for
parliamentary questions, accompanied him on some visits at
home and abroad, and occasionally assisted in speech writing.
Relations between the Unit and the CPRS were said to be good,
particularly since some members of the CPRS were old friends,
but there was no structured relationship. The Unit briefed
the Prime Minister. The CPRS briefed the Cabinet. The Unit's
advice might contain a political dimension. The CPRS's
normally did not. Other accounts include articles by G.W.
Jones, 'Harold Wilson's Policy Makers', The Spectator,
6.7.1974, pp. 12-13; and 'The Prime Minister's Men', New
Society, 19.1.1978, pp. 121-23.
    11. Cmnd. 4506 (1970), pp. 6, 13-14; Rothschild (1977),
pp. 89-95, 112-14; The Times, 27.9.1977 (the star was William
Waldegrave); H.C. 535-II (1977). pp. 603-6.

Chapter 4

TRYING TO MANAGE THE ECONOMY

After 1955, it was never to be said again of the British
economy that it had la puissance d'une idée en marche, as
R A Butler himself later remarked.1 The pervasive sense of
failure fostered a political and institutional climate in which
the institutional arrangements for economic management became
important targets for criticism and for change. These arrangements were uncomplicated in the mid-1950s. The Treasury, at
the centre of the Civil Service, was the government department
with the sole overall responsibility for the task of macro-
economic management. The Ministry of Labour and National
Service and the Board of Trade played a valuable supporting
role, providing the main institutional links with the trade
union movement and private industry and commerce. The Bank of
England had a semi-independent role, and one of sufficient
importance in economic policy making for it to share the blame
when things began to go obviously wrong. The Treasury received
most of the blame, and not just from extreme critics such as
Thomas Balogh. In the twenty years following the economic
climacteric of 1955, the Treasury was subjected to several
reorganizations and more changes. During that period, the
institutional arrangements for economic management were
generally made considerably more complex. This partly resulted
from the revival of economic planning, which led to the
establishment of the National Economic Development Council plus
a supporting framework, and then the Department of Economic
Affairs. It followed too from the return to prices and incomes
policies which led to the creation of a succession of bodies
that included the National Incomes Commission, the National
Board for Prices and Incomes, the Pay Board, and the Price
Commission. The last named body was reconstituted in 1977 by
which time all but Neddy of the others had gone. There was
also from 1974 a Department of Prices and Consumer Protection.
This was formed from part of the successor department to the
Board of Trade, which formally disappeared in 1970. A much renamed Ministry of Labour had survived as the Department of
Employment, together with a range of important hived off
agencies. The Treasury and the Bank of England still bore the

56

same names, and retained their responsibilities for economic management. What had been undermined was the credibility of the Keynesian macro-economic theory on the basis of which the economy had been managed.

The commitment of peacetime Governments to the Managed Economy was made by the wartime Coalition in 1944. That the commitment was made in a White Paper called <u>Employment Policy</u> was reflective of the overriding political concern that there must be no repetition of the mass unemployment of the inter-war era. That the commitment was made with such a public display of confidence owed more at the time to political necessity than any universal belief in government that Keynes had found the answer to the successful management of a modern economy. The political and intellectual tide was running strongly against the sceptics, and with those who believed that Keynes having shown <u>How to Pay for the War</u> had demonstrated in the <u>General Theory</u> how to pay for the peace. Indeed, for more than a generation after 1944, faith in Keynesian demand management proved to have few limits among most politicians, many of their official advisers, and the vast majority of professional economists in Britain. Yet, the <u>General Theory</u> had grave deficiencies as a guide to economic policy. This was more than a matter of Keynes's treatment of the role of money, which was later seized on by critics. Keynes's economic model was of a closed economy, which limited its relevance to the economic management of what had to be a trading nation, and one that was to be perennially plagued by balance of payments difficulties. Moreover, Keynes's macro-economic theory rested on a micro-economic base of perfect competition. Thus, the effects on macro-economic management of the activities of monopolistic organizations in both the public and private sectors, including trade unions, were assumed away. Keynes had only incompletely escaped from his Marshallian intellectual inheritance. In terms of theory, the Keynesian Revolution was not as revolutionary as it seemed.2

This did not stop the Keynesian Revolution from being revolutionary in terms of British economic policy. Keynes's policy prescriptions for the Britain of the 1930s had no necessary connection with the different situation after 1945. In his eagerness to promote counter-cyclical policies to lift the British economy from the inter-war Depression, Keynes had effectively undermined the authority of the Balanced Budget based on low levels of taxation and government spending. It was now as dead as the Gold Standard. To replace the latter, Keynes strived at Bretton Woods and in what little time he then had left to found a new international economic order. In commending the International Monetary Fund to the House of Lords in 1944, Keynes emphasized the freedom of action that Britain would have. He said that 'the experience of the years before the war has led most of us ... to certain firm conclusions. Three, in particular, are highly relevant ... We are determined that, in future, the external value of sterling

57

shall conform to its internal value as set by our domestic
policies, and not the other way round. Secondly, we intend to
retain control of our domestic rate of interest, so that we can
keep it as low as suits our own purposes, without interference
from the ebb and flow of international capital movements or
flights of hot money. Thirdly, whilst we intend to prevent
inflation at home, we will not accept deflation at the dictate
of influences from outside. In other words, we abjure the
instruments of bank rate and credit contraction operating
through the increase of unemployment as a means of forcing our
domestic economy into line with external factors.' Escape from
what Keynes called the 'old dungeon'3 of economic constraints
beckoned for the politicians. They believed that no longer
did they need to stand helpless in the face of economic events,
as, for example, their predecessors had done in 1931.
Keynesian tools enabled the economy to be managed. If
necessary, Governments could spend their way out of trouble,
and politicians thought that they had Keynes's authority to do
so.

Keynes had expected that his theory would be changed when
it was 'mixed with politics'. What was most surprising about
the New Economics was the extent to which the disciples and
converts who called themselves Keynesians were not restrained
by what the Master had actually said or written. It tended to
be glossed over, for example, that in 1937, with unemployment
still around 11-12 per cent, Keynes emphasized the dangers of
inflation. From that level downwards, Keynes had insisted that
unemployment must be dealt with, not by the general expansion
of aggregate demand by government, or by 'a further general
stimulus at the centre', but by 'a different technique',
meaning specific measures in the depressed areas. 'I am not a
Keynesian', Keynes had told Abba Lerner in 1946. Certainly,
Keynes had said that at full employment Neo-Classical Economics
came back into its own. This proved to be insufficiently
adventurous for the Keynesians, whose confidence in the New
Economics knew few bounds, even those recognized by Keynes
himself. The Coalition Government's commitment to the maintenance of 'a high and stable level of employment without
sacrificing the essential liberties of a free society' was
onerous enough. Beveridge, a Keynesian convert, led the way in
translating this commitment into one to full employment defined
in terms of a ceiling of 3 per cent unemployment, and a
permanent excess of job vacancies over applicants. For those
who did not share Beveridge's optimism about the behaviour of
the trade unions in this situation, his was a formula for in-
flation.4 Stable prices were just one of the perennial
benefits Keynesian economic weapons were supposed to have
guaranteed the means for; together with full employment,
rising output, and expanding social services. The General
Theory became the British economic bible, all the more
attractive for being very freely interpreted. That other
countries such as Western Germany passed Britain by while

practising another economic gospel did not deter the Keynesians. When Keynesianism did not work, the Treasury received the blame. It was in character with the Administrative 'Revolution' that institutional solutions were looked for when economic management failed to yield the expected results.

I   FROM CONSERVATIVE FREEDOM TO CONSERVATIVE PLANNING 1957-64

Such complacency as the Macmillan Government felt about the performance of the British economy did not long survive the 1959 election victory. The route to the Neddy experiment was a short one. When, in 1961, the recommendations of the Plowden Committee on the Control of Public Expenditure pointed in the direction of a revival of economic planning, its sentiments were in accord with what had become the dominant trend of opinion. By 1961, the Macmillan Government was politically vulnerable, and the Prime Minister certainly thought that it needed a new economic strategy. When he had accepted the resignation of his Treasury Ministers in 1958, Macmillan had gambled on inflation rather than with employment, believing there to be a choice. The reflation of the economy had brought a short term revival, but this had petered out by 1961 amidst balance of payments difficulties. The Conservative Government was heavily criticized by Keynesians, among others, for following the preferences of the Treasury and the Bank of England in giving priority to the maintenance of the 1949 exchange rate. Such 'sterling first' policies were deemed responsible for a 'stop-go' form of economic management, which was said to be stunting economic growth. In fact, the rate of economic growth attained in Britain in the 1950s had been, by her own modest historical standards, an impressive one.5   What Keynesians in particular were suggesting was that there was some painless way of lifting Britain on to a higher growth path, and that the Conservative Government was scorning opportunities to achieve this. Within a context of institutional change, and a conversion to economic planning and an incomes policy, the Conservative Government responded with a 'dash for growth'.

This 'dash' was led in 1963-64 by Reginald Maudling, who became Chancellor in July 1962. He came to preside over a Treasury much changed in structure compared with that of his predecessor, Selwyn Lloyd. The changes introduced in 1956 had only affected the top of the Treasury. The main structure of the department had retained its traditional pattern. The 1962 post-Plowden changes led to the abolition of the mixed divisions which had previously dealt with both the supply and establishment aspects of a department's activities; the amalgamation of Home and Overseas Finance; and a closer integration of the Economic Section with the administrative side. The appointment of Sir Burke Trend as Secretary of the Cabinet separated that post from the Permanent Secretaryship of the Treasury. The latter was made a joint post, held by Sir Laurence Helsby and Sir William Armstrong. The Treasury itself was divided into two sides and five groups. Helsby, who became Head of the Home Civil Service, was responsible for the management side, which comprised two groups. One was concerned with pay and conditions of service; and the other dealt with management services. Armstrong, the other Joint Permanent Secretary was responsible for the economic and financial side. This consisted of three groups: public sector (resources and expenditure); national economy; and finance. The new structure was not to be given a long, undisturbed period in which to be tested. In the meantime, Maudling's essay in 'fine tuning' the economy into sustained expansion proceeded on the basis of forecasts which as late as the 1964 Budget indicated that there would be no deficit in the balance of payments, whereas a substantial deficit did emerge.6

The Conservative 'dash for growth' was connected with the establishment of Neddy. In the post-Plowden atmosphere, 'planning like the French', as The Economist called it, became fashionable. Indeed, The Economist, a traditional advocate of liberal economics, had, by the early 1960s, itself come to follow this fashion. There were few dissenting voices to be heard when, in July 1961, Selwyn Lloyd, as Chancellor, announced that he intended to discuss urgently with both sides of industry means of pulling together the various existing processes of consultation and forecasting about the economy 'with a view to better co-ordination of ideas and plans'. The Chancellor said that he was not frightened of the word 'planning'. There was little reason why he should have been, given that the representatives of private industry and commerce were by now advocates of economic planning. So, with reservations, were the trade unions. Their representatives were present, together with those of private and nationalized industry, and the leading economic Ministers, when Lloyd chaired the first meeting of the Neddy Council in March 1962. Lloyd defined Neddy's task as being to examine the economic performance of the nation with particular concern for plans for the future in both private and public sectors of industry; to consider together what were the obstacles to foster growth, what could be done to improve efficiency, and whether the best use was being made of resources; and to seek agreement on ways of improving economic performance, competitive power and efficiency, in other words, to increase the rate of sound growth. It was decided that the Neddy Office, under a Director General, would have two divisions. One was concerned with broad economic questions; and the other dealt with particular industries and sectors of the economy. In December 1963, it was decided to establish Economic Development Committees, or little Neddies, for particular industries. They were to examine the economic performance, prospects and plans of the industry and assess from time to time the industry's progress in relation to the national growth objectives and

60

provide information and forecasts for the Council on these matters; and to consider ways of improving the industry's economic performance, competitive power and efficiency, and to formulate reports and records of these matters as appropriate.7

The establishment of the Neddy organization was widely acclaimed. The Economist, for instance, said that Neddy was something it had 'long advocated'. The journal went on to say that Neddy's first report was 'hearteningly likely to become' a 'five year plan' with 'a target rate of growth'. In February 1963, Neddy duly published a document called Growth of the United Kingdom Economy to 1966, which said that over the period 1961-66 a 4 per cent per annum rate of growth of the Gross Domestic Product was desirable. This target appears to have been set as early as Neddy's second meeting, and to have been submitted by the Office without previous detailed examination or discussion. It seemed to be assumed that the very existence of the Neddy Plan would provide a growth rate which was half as fast again as that which had occurred in the 1950s.8

The National Incomes Commission (Nicky), set up in October 1962, received none of the welcome that Neddy experienced. Its establishment marked a departure in the Macmillan Government's dealings with the trade unions. The Conservatives had not taken up ideas of the kind mooted in 1958 by the Tory barristers of the Inns of Court Conservative and Unionist Association, in a pamphlet called A Giant's Strength, for legislative curbs on union activity. They had preferred to humour the Giant, in the Monckton manner, with the occasional stand as over the London bus strike of 1958. In 1957, the Macmillan Government did establish a Council on Prices, Productivity and Incomes, the so-called Three Wise Men. This Council made periodic pronouncements about the state of the economy, which, at the time, tended to read like the stern edicts of a bygone age. They had the flavour of the Marshallian School of Neo-Classical Economics, the main target of Keynes's intellectual revolt. Indeed, Sir Dennis Robertson, the last disciple of Marshall's, was for a time a member of the Council, and may well have been responsible for its early advocacy of making the control of the money supply, and the containment of public expenditure, the cornerstones of economic policy. While such sentiments were hardly music to the ears of the TUC, their objection to the Three Wise Men was more fundamental. They wanted no interference - even of the kind limited to exhortation - with what they called free collective bargaining. The trade union leaders believed in economic planning, but only provided the process did not extend to wages. Hence, the TUC leaders joined Neddy; but, just as they had ignored the Three Wise Men, so they boycotted Nicky. The Macmillan Government's 'pay pause' was an unsuccessful incomes policy. The unions refused to be led by the Government's 'guiding light' in pay claims. Nicky was a largely function-less body. It was widely believed in the Treasury, and by academics such as Frank Paish and A W Phillips - of the famous

Phillips Curve - that there was a particular relationship between wage levels and unemployment. This ignored the power of the unions in the context of a large public sector. The very mention of unemployment in 1962-63 spurred the Macmillan Government on to reflate the economy. The trade union leaders applauded the Maudling boom, but did nothing to help the Conservative Government.9 Whether it was economic expansion in general, or real wages or regional policy in particular, the union leaders expected more from a Labour Government, certainly more than they were to receive.

II LABOUR, THE NATIONAL PLAN, AND THE ROAD TO STAGFLATION
    1964-70

Neddy and the Treasury survived the advent of the Wilson Labour Government in 1964, although Nicky was abolished. It was soon replaced by a National Board for Prices and Incomes, which inherited Nicky's staff and many of its objectives. The Labour Government's National Incomes Policy was described as one of 'a planned growth of incomes'. The Wilson Government wanted to break away from 'stop-go' economic management, not least to obtain the higher rate of economic growth needed to finance its promises for more public expenditure. As in 1945, the Labour Government was elected to office pledged to build a 'New Britain' by means of 'socialist planning'. Labour talked of, among other Plans, a Plan for the Regions, a Plan for Stable Prices, a Plan for Tax Reform, and, above all, a National Plan. These Plans did not seem to exist in a fully prepared form. Indeed, Labour's manifesto proposed the establishment of 'a Ministry of Economic Affairs' which would have 'the duty of formulating, with both sides of industry, a national economic plan'.10

The notion of having a Ministry, or as it came to be called, Department of Economic Affairs had been, apparently, under discussion for some time in Labour circles. Harold Wilson later recorded that he favoured the idea even before he became Leader of the Opposition. One of the Labour Government's economic advisers, Lord Balogh, has complained that 'Mr George Brown's memory of having founded the DEA in a taxi between the St Ermyn's Hotel and the House of Commons is fanciful. In actual fact a number of us were involved in discussion over a long period. All who thought seriously of these problems were convinced that so far as the machinery of government was concerned ... the establishment of a general economic department, separate from the Treasury, in charge of basically general (macro-) economic but not primarily financial problems, was essential'. Balogh's hostility to the Treasury was of long standing, but that department's association with 'stop-go' and 'sterling first' policies had led to a more general desire to clip its wings. A widespread Labour sentiment seemed to be that so long as economic planning was viewed as no more than the erection of a Keynesian superstructure for guiding fiscal controls, it could reasonably remain in the Treasury. Once economic planning was seen as an extroverted and dynamic process for transforming the economy, however, the style of action required became quite different. It no longer accorded with even the most exalted kind of house-keeping. The National Economy Group of the Treasury went to form the core of the DEA, which was divided into five parts. Two dealt with economic coordination, including prices and incomes policy; and the others dealt respectively with industrial policy, regional policy, and economic planning.11 The DEA was not, then, just concerned with economic planning in general or the production of the National Plan in particular. Nevertheless, the political reality was that the DEA's fate was inextricably bound up with the fate of the Plan.

The National Plan was launched in September 1965. According to George Brown, Secretary of State for Economic Affairs, 'the publication by the Government of a plan covering all aspects of the country's economic development for the next five years is a major advance in economic policy making in the United Kingdom'. In November 1965, Brown invited the House of Commons 'to welcome this Plan as a reasonable basis for claim-ing that at last Britain is on her way. The Conservatives did not oppose the motion 'that this House welcomes the National Plan'. Indeed, as the Neddy document of 1963 had been a Tory version of a National Plan, they could hardly honestly do so. The Labour Government's National Plan was a much more ambitious affair in style and content, and it was 'designed to achieve a 25 per cent increase in national output between 1964 and 1970'. In introducing the Plan, George Brown had written that 'the most serious economic problem facing us at the present time is the balance of payments'. The crisis of July 1966 and the severely deflationary measures thought necessary then led the First Secretary of State to be 'absolutely frank' with the House of Commons that these measures meant that 'the rate of growth we intended to get, and on the basis of which we predicted all other things for 1970, is no longer avail-able'. However, he insisted that 'we go on with the Plan'. In fact, ten months after its inception, the National Plan was dead. When George Brown told the House of Commons that 'for almost two years now we have tried to manage the economy in a way that no economy has been managed before',12 the remark did not receive the reception presumably intended.

The critical decision not to devalue the pound sterling, which its opponents thought condemned the Wilson Government to impotence by the summer of 1966, was taken within two days of Labour's return to office. Although the decision lay with Wilson, Brown, and James Callaghan, the Chancellor of the Exchequer, the Prime Minister's views seem to have been what really mattered. Wilson's commitment to the 1949 exchange rate was as firm as that of the Bank of England. His reasons were mainly political. He did not want the Labour Party to be seen as the Party of devaluation. He had 1949 in mind.

Perhaps a more appropriate analogy, given Wilson's own portrayal of the significance of the inherited deficit, was with 1931. Then, the National Government had effectively devalued when it had gone off the Gold Standard, and the blame adhered to its Labour predecessors. There was more to say in favour of Wilson's argument that 'devaluation was not an easy way out', if not for his belief that avoiding it obviated the need for deflationary measures. Wilson's case against devaluation did not include the more convincing arguments for this course. These were that lower prices might well not promote export led growth because the quality of British goods on offer and their delivery dates might well not satisfy the market. Wilson's case for having an over-valued currency was not argued for, at least in terms that international financial opinion found persuasive. James Callaghan later admitted that 'when I had been in office for one month I was approached by a very senior monetary authority in Europe, a person known to everyone concerned with this field, who spoke, as he said, on behalf of the Six. He said that he believed that we ought to devalue by between 10 and 15 per cent'. With international financial circles thinking this, speculation against the pound was inevitable, particularly when such interests anyway distrusted a Government formed from a Labour Party still formally committed to socialism. Whether or not as the result of the Wilson Government's own publicity of the potential gravity of the situation it had inherited, a financial crisis, or what proved to be a succession of crises, was sparked off in November 1964. Then the Labour Government anyway had to engage in various deflationary exercises which, despite their severity, unsurprisingly failed to change the financial community's unfavourable view not only of the performance of the British economy in general, but also of the future possibility of the 1949 exchange rate being maintained. Keeping sterling at 2.80 dollars seemed to become an article of faith with Wilson who, in conversation with Richard Crossman, saw himself as being like the Duke of Wellington using the equivalent of the lines of Torres Vedras to sustain the pound and to defeat advocates of devaluation. Memoranda proposing devaluation were said to have been destroyed. Devaluation became the 'great unmentionable' in the Labour Government. Although advocacy of it, or of floating the pound, surfaced from time to time, the authors often being economic advisers that Labour had specially brought into the machinery of government - Robert Neild, Thomas Balogh and Nicholas Kaldor. Wilson seemed to carry a majority of the Cabinet with him in the decision not to devalue during the July 1966 crisis, although the Labour Government was by then armed with a substantial Parliamentary majority.13   The pound was eventually devalued (by 14.3 per cent) in November 1967.

The July 1966 measures effectively finished off the National Plan. George Brown, having failed to persuade the Cabinet to devalue, threatened to resign, a threat which he soon withdrew, probably unwisely. Brown helped to pilot through Parliament the imposition of a statutory prices and incomes policy - the most controversial of the July measures - before moving on to the Foreign Office, to be replaced at the DEA by Michael Stewart. In August 1967, Prime Minister Wilson himself took overall responsibility for the DEA, with Peter Shore as his Secretary of State. This arrangement was terminated in April 1968, and Shore was left with ministerial responsibility for a department whose future was now in doubt. The confidence of the days when the National Plan had been launched had long since gone. When a DEA publication, The Task Ahead appeared in early 1969 it was felt necessary to carefully explain that this was 'a planning document, not a plan'. In November 1968, Wilson told Parliament that the DEA was 'a permanent, continuing and essential part of the machinery of modern government'. However, in October 1969, he announced his decision 'to bring the DEA experiment to an end, five years after it was set up'. The former Prime Minister subsequently wrote that he did not regret the original decision to establish the DEA. Indeed, he felt that 'something on DEA lines, however constituted, may have a permanent and central role to play in Britain's future machinery of government'. Wilson drew attention to the DEA's 'historic invention', the Industrial Reorganization Corporation. The development of regional policy was also, in his opinion, a 'significant achievement' of the DEA which was said to have pursued 'a policy for regional planning going far beyond the traditional Board of Trade responsibilities for industrial location'. As the result of what the Prime Minister called, George Brown's 'enthusiasm and drive', as early as February 1965 the appointment of Regional Economic Planning Boards and Regional Economic Planning Councils for the eight regions of England (Northern, North West, East Anglia, Yorkshire and Humberside, East Midlands, West Midlands, South West, South East) had taken place. Measures such as the Industrial Development Act 1966, the Local Employment Act 1970 and the Regional Employment Premium within the Selective Employment Tax were also introduced by the Wilson Government. Although for the country as a whole, 1967 was a worse year, the problem regions did not have such high levels of unemployment in the 1967 squeeze as they did in the 1962-63. To the extent that this resulted from regional policy, such progress as had been made had to be credited to the Macmillan and Home Governments too.14

The DEA experiment was surely doomed to failure from the outset. Short term considerations - the sphere of the Treasury - were by definition more immediate than long term needs - the sphere of the DEA - as well as being more easily identifiable. Wilson later said that Brown complained in July 1966 that the Labour Government had 'fallen back into the old Treasury position of past years'. A more convincing view was that the Wilson Government had never departed from that position, a situation emphasized by the refusal to contemplate

devaluation until forced to do so. As for what Wilson had
intended in setting up the DEA, Brown said that he thought that
the Prime Minister believed that 'a state of competitive existence between the DEA and the Treasury would keep everybody on
their toes'. Wilson apparently hoped for much more from the
'creative tension' between the Treasury and the DEA. As he
sometimes put it, 'the Treasury is too fine a machine; I want
to put some sand in it. If you put sand in an oyster it
produces a pearl'. Someone once replied 'but you know what
usually happens if you put sand into a fine machine'.15
    The DEA had relinquished responsibility for prices and
incomes policy eighteen months before its demise. For all its
condemnation of its Conservative predecessors' approach to
policies regarding wages and salaries, the Wilson Government's
National Incomes Policy, the key to its Plan for Stable Prices,
in fact proved to be a succession of policies, beginning with
a voluntary system. The trade union leaders were prepared to
join with employers' representatives and those of the Labour
Government to sign a Declaration of Intent on Productivity,
Prices and Incomes in December 1964. According to Wilson,
George Brown succeeded where Lloyd and Maudling failed,
because of his 'unique methods of persuasion'. The setting
for the signing of the Declaration, in 'the gilded salon of
Lancaster House', the Prime Minister thought was 'appropriate
to an international disarmaments treaty, but it was an
historic occasion'. As Mr Wilson added, however, 'the test
was to be its implementation'. By the autumn of 1965, Wilson
recorded, 'the voluntary procedures resting on the Declaration
of Intent were proving inadequate'. He also revealed that
Frank Cousins - in the Cabinet as Minister of Technology but
also still nominally General Secretary of the Transport and
General Workers Union - had 'repeatedly expressed considerable
scepticism about - indeed opposition to - what was still only
a voluntary policy. His life's work had been based on the
doctrine that a trade union leader's job was to get more wages
for his men; even a voluntary incomes policy seemed incom-
patible with that life long objective'. The Prime Minister
took encouragement from what he saw as the success of the
institutional expression of the incomes policy, the National
Board for Prices and Incomes, under the chairmanship of a
former Conservative Minister, Aubrey Jones. This Board was
comparatively small. It originally had nine members (including the Chairman), five of whom were full time and four part
time. From the summer of 1968 onwards it grew to fifteen,
though still with five full time members, employers' and trade
union representatives predominating. Its supporting staff
included seconded civil servants and others recruited from
universities. Explicitly the Board needed to do no more than
apply the rules laid down in successive White Papers on Prices
and Incomes Policy, and give its opinion on whether cases
referred to it came within the rules or not. While emphasizing speed in producing reports - in contrast with Nicky - the

Board did attempt to put its cases into a broader economic context. If its many reports had any one theme, it was the advocacy of productivity bargaining.16

Responsibility for the prices and incomes policies had been transferred in April 1968 from the DEA to what until then had been called the Ministry of Labour. This Ministry was renamed the Department of Employment and Productivity to please the incoming Secretary of State, Barbara Castle. The Labour Cabinet's links with the trade union movement were not as close as they had been following the resignations of Frank Cousins, who had gone even before the July 1966 measures; George Brown, who left earlier in 1968; and Ray Gunter, who left that summer. The trade union movement was seething with discontent about government restrictions on wage settlements. Committed socialists as opposed to Social Democrats succeeded to the leadership of the Transport Workers and of the Engineers in the shape of Jack Jones and Hugh Scanlon respectively. Moreover, the Seamen's Strike of 1966 was an early indication of an assertion of rank and file militancy, which, in his own union, Jones particularly chose to reflect. The Labour Government seemed to have shelved the issue of what to do about the trade unions by making their activities - together with those of employers' associations - the subject of investigation by the Donovan Royal Commission, appointed in 1965. When the Commission reported in June 1968, it was no surprise that the Labour Government took up a recommendation for setting up yet another institution - the Commission on Industrial Relations, established in March 1969. What was surprising was that, at the beginning of 1969, Mrs Castle went beyond the Royal Commission in proposals to regulate trade union activities contained in a White Paper called In Place of Strife and in an Industrial Relations Bill. Her ally in the Cabinet, Harold Wilson described the Bill as 'essential to our economic recovery, essential to our balance of payments, essential to full employment' and 'essential to the Government's continuance in office'. The Bill, which included provisions for penalties against unconstitutional strikers, was blocked by opposition within the Cabinet (led by the Home Secretary, James Callaghan); within Parliament on the part of some of the Government's normal supporters; and outside Parliament by the overwhelming hostility of the trade union movement. The Labour Government was defeated a year to the day after its surrender to the Labour Movement on June 18th 1969. In the winter of 1969-70, the incomes policy collapsed in a situation of inflation, stagnation, and rising unemployment.17

III THE UNWILLING REAPPRAISAL: THE HEATH GOVERNMENT AND
     BEYOND 1970-79

The events of 1969-70 tore a hole in Keynesian economic thinking that in the end proved impossible to hide. Inflation and substantial unemployment, which were not supposed to be able to characterize the same economy at the same time, had occurred together. The relationship between wages and unemployment was such too that the Phillips Curve plainly did not point in the direction of reality, and Paishite demand management theory did not match practice. Paish himself had the honesty to recant,18 but the Keynesians felt no such need. Monetarism might well be on the intellectual march; but the Keynesians still controlled most academic fortresses, the influential National Institute for Economic and Social Research, the Treasury, and they were even present in the Bank of England. Moreover, the notion that Governments could spend their way out of trouble was by no means dead not only in the academic mind, but among politicians and the public. The Heath Conservative Government was in trouble from the outset. This was partly because the outgoing Labour Chancellor, Roy Jenkins had not only bequeathed his successor a balance of payments surplus, as an adoring Press recorded. He also left behind a stagnant economy, steeply rising prices, a wages explosion, and increasing unemployment. The Heath Government compounded its difficulties by pushing through an Industrial Relations Act in the teeth of opposition from a trade union movement that was spoiling for a fight, and which seemed only too pleased to add Heath's scalp to that of his Labour predecessor.

For all its preparation for office, some of the Conservatives' commitments were not readily compatible. For example, at the same time as the Heath Government was trying to establish a legal framework within which it hoped industrial relations would be conducted, it was also attempting to abstain from overt intervention in wage determination. Hence, an early act was to abolish the National Board for Prices and Incomes. However, even without this institution, the Conservative Government had to have at least an attitude to public sector pay, because of the scale of employment involved and its cost. Hence, the so-called N-1 policy emerged under which the Heath Government appeared to aim to settle pay claims at levels at least one percentage point lower than the last settlement. The Conservative Government was more consistent in its ambitions to cut public expenditure and direct taxation at the same time. Although, in a context of inflation and the vested interests of the public sector, this was more easily proposed than achieved. Moreover, the Heath Government was committed to institutional change, which could acquire a momentum of its own, and which was rarely accompanied by reduced or even similar expenditure.

The Treasury survived the advent of the Conservatives unscathed, having earlier lost its establishment functions to the Civil Service Department in 1968, and having taken back the core of the DEA in 1969. Iain Macleod arrived as Conservative Chancellor with a fully worked out reform of the taxation system, which, after his death, was taken up by his successor, Anthony Barber. Like the Treasury, Neddy survived the Tory return too, as did the little Neddies whom Labour had made more numerous. Regional economic planning machinery, which, on the demise of the DEA had been transferred to the nascent Department of the Environment by the Wilson Government, remained there when that Department was actually established by the Conservatives in 1970. The Department of Employment and Productivity was renamed the Department of Employment, and, during the early disengagement policy of the Heath Government, its conciliation services were reduced. These functions of the DE were eventually revived as the Conservative Government changed course. Indeed, the DE became the subject of a succession of changes which altered its structure. Although there had been earlier hints of changes and some took place after it left office, the main changes were set in motion under the Heath Government. Pressure for change within the DE was supplemented by external criticism in an OECD Report, which related to the role of the Public Employment Service as an agent of economic policy. The form that the changes took was influenced by the Conservative Government's interest in 'hiving off' activities from conventional government departments to other agencies in an attempt to secure more accountable and effective management. The Employment and Training Act 1973 established the Manpower Services Commission to manage the employment and training services of the DE. The Employment Services Agency and the Training Services Agency had been established in 1972 within the DE. The Act took this process a stage further by making both of them separate statutory bodies reporting to the Manpower Services Commission, which was actually established in January 1974. The Training Services Agency was transferred to it in April 1974, as was the Employment Services Agency six months later. The Commission also became responsible for running the Professional and Executive Recruitment Service, which was inaugurated in March 1973.19

The Heath Government also established other institutions in the labour relations field, besides retaining, and developing the role of, the Commission on Industrial Relations. During their period in Opposition, the Tories had moved decisively in the direction of A Giant's Strength and, therefore, of legalism in industrial relations. The Industrial Relations Act of 1971 established a National Industrial Relations Court and a Chief Registrar of Trade Unions and Employers' Associations. 'With benefit of hindsight', Heath's Political Secretary later wrote, 'it was unrealistic of the Government to impose the Industrial Relations Act'. Given the contemporary mood of the unions, this was obvious to some others at the time. The dropping of promised legislation in the hope of driving a wedge between the political and industrial wings of the Labour Movement may well have been optimistic. Nevertheless, it was no more optimistic than the belief that major unions would meekly register, which they did not. The Act accorded the unions an almost American role as labour contractors and discipliners, which was at variance with their traditions. The Act offered the unions little in exchange for giving up many of their legal privileges. Forcing through the Act re-united the Labour Movement. While the Labour Party's largely synthetic anger in Parliament did not matter, the trade union opposition outside did. The ballot held under the Act in 1972 which, in effect, asked railwaymen to censure their own leaders for pressing for a higher wage settlement predictably ended in a result unfavourable for the Government. Then came a docks dispute - involving the Pentonville Five - in which the Official Solicitor'and then the Law Lords rescued the Government from the consequences of the operations of the NIRC.20 Within a year, the Industrial Relations Act was a dead letter, but Government-union relations had been more lastingly soured.

Indeed, 1972 also witnessed a humiliating defeat for the Heath Government at the hands of the miners. In the winter of 1970-71, the Government, with the aid of public support had defeated an electricity workers' strike only to lose any anti-inflationary benefits in the findings of the subsequent Court of Inquiry chaired by Lord Wilberforce. The Government then defeated a strike by the Union of Post Office Workers, only once again to lose out in the subsequent settlement. These partial successes served to encourage the Heath Government to persist with its de-escalation policy in relation to pay until in the winter of 1971-72 it was confronted by the National Union of Mineworkers. The miners, based on their tightly knit communities, were very different opponents from the postmen and even the electricity workers, not least in the level of popular support that they enjoyed. This factor inhibited any determined response by the Conservative Government to some ruthless picketing by the NUM most effectively, but not exclusively, directed at electricity generating stations. Soon, as one of the Prime Minister's aides put it, the Government was 'wandering vainly over the battlefield looking for someone to surrender to'. Lord Wilberforce was brought in to recommend another vast settlement, which the miners' leaders had to be persuaded to accept.21   It was for them sweet revenge for 1926.   Then they had been beaten by a Conservative Government after a seven months' strike. In 1972, the miners brought the Heath Government to its knees in seven weeks. The authority of the Heath Government was certainly never the same again after the miners and their allies humiliated the forces of law and order in the confrontation at Saltley coke works in Birmingham in February 1972.

The road to more inflation and another prices and incomes policy was paved with the good intentions of 1970. The Heath Government's inherited unemployment problem sapped its resolve to contain inflation. The first turning point probably was the Bromsgrove by-election of May 1971. Less than a year after its undistinguished period of office, Labour had comfortably won a Conservative seat. There was also, in November 1971, the famous incident when one of the few working class members left

on the Labour benches in the Commons, Dennis Skinner, melo-
dramatically flung on to the Prime Minister's lap an evening
newspaper announcing that unemployment had reached one million.
For a Conservative of Heath's generation, one million un-
employed was a significant statistic. One of Heath's aides has
since maintained that the Government and its advisers were 'at
all times more concerned about inflation than about unemployment'. The Government's behaviour suggested otherwise. When
the Treasury's confident predictions that unemployment would
turn down early in 1971 did not materialize, Anthony Barber,
produced a series of measures deemed minor by Keynesian critics.
Reflation had been 'too little and too late to reduce unemployment', Roy Jenkins intoned from the Labour benches, deriding
the Heath Government for its early concern about the rising
money supply. Jenkins conceded that Barber's March 1972 Budget
contained 'fairly massive reflationary measures'. In view of
later criticism of the Barber boom, one notes that, with the
exception of some Conservative adherents of monetarism,
contemporary comment was favourable, except in suggesting that
Barber had not gone far enough. The Barber boom was a Keynesian adventure. The Smithsonian Agreement of December 1971,
which undermined the Bretton Woods system, made possible the
removal of one constraint. In June 1972, Barber floated
sterling. For Keynesians, there was now no reason why, by
boosting public spending and stimulating purchasing power, the
Government could not promote greater economic growth and not
have to count the costs.22 The Heath Government strove to
oblige.

The Heath Government also soon felt forced to introduce a
prices and incomes policy. In the aftermath of the miners'
strike, the Prime Minister tried without success to negotiate
a voluntary policy with the unions. Although a statutory
prices and incomes policy was intellectually fashionable, the
Government had no illusions about its practical difficulties.
Nevertheless, with immense reluctance, from November 1972
onwards, the Heath Government took the statutory path. Two
special institutions - the Pay Board and the Price Commission -
were established in April 1973, with responsibility for rest-
ricting pay, prices, dividends and rents in accordance with a
pay and price code drawn up by the Government. In anticipation
of the incomes policy's fateful Stage III, the Pay Board was
instructed to prepare reports on anomalies and relativities.
Having cut productivity deals out of Stage II to avoid the
failings of the Wilson Government's pay policy, the Heath
Government wanted a formula to deal with the 'special case'.
The Prime Minister also tried to square the miners. Indeed,
Stage III was apparently built around what the NUM President,
Joe Gormley assured Heath the miners would accept. These
assurances were misleading. The oil crisis of November 1973
made the miners even more of a 'special case' than the events
of 1972 had done. Faced with another miners' strike, the
Heath Government introduced a three day week to try to conserve

71

coal stocks and, hence, maintain electricity supplies. Then, after much agonizing, the Conservatives appealed to the electorate, which declined to give them the necessary support.23

The Labour Government elected in February 1974, and narrowly confirmed in office the following October, introduced several institutional changes in the economic field. Some of them were designed to cement relations with the trade unions. The Industrial Relations Act was repealed. As a result, the NIRC, the CIR and the Registry of Trade Unions and Employers' Associations were disbanded in September 1974. In the same month, an independent Advisory Conciliation and Arbitration Service was established, initially on an administrative basis prior to the passage of the Protection of Employment Act. The Service took over the conciliation and arbitration functions of the DE, and also some advisory functions of both the DE and the CIR. Its management and development was planned by a Council, appointed by the Secretary of State for Employment and consisting of nine members drawn equally from employers, trade unions, and independent sources. Another area of the DE's work was hived off when a Health and Safety Commission and a Health and Safety Executive were established in October 1974 and January 1975 respectively. The Executive was formed mainly from existing government inspectorates covering factories, mines and quarries, and had powers to enforce statutory requirements on safety and health. Besides being responsible for the work of the Executive, the Commission had a research, educational and advisory role, and powers to prepare proposals for improving statutory provisions for health and safety at work.24

The Price Commission survived the change to a Labour Government – being placed under the Department of Prices and Consumer Protection, carved out of the remains of the Department of Trade and Industry – and Neddy and the Treasury survived too. However, following an internal management review, the Treasury was reorganized again in October 1975. Its work was re-grouped into four major sectors: the Chief Economic Adviser's Sector, the Overseas Finance Sector, the Domestic Economy Sector, and the Public Services Sector. In addition, a new Central Unit was set up. The Overseas Finance Sector was much the same as the Overseas Finance Group that it succeeded. As would be expected, it dealt with international currency questions, financial aspects of EEC membership, exchange control, management of the reserves, the balance of payments, and overseas aid and export finance. The Domestic Economy Sector inherited the functions of the former National Economy Group – except for the work of the Chief Economic Adviser – and also took over the former Public Sector Group's responsibilities for nationalized and private industry, with whom it was hoped to promote closer contacts. The Public Services Sector was made responsible for the control of public expenditure in the aggregate and for the management of the annual Public Expenditure Survey. Each of these Sectors was headed by a Second Permanent Secretary. There was also the Chief Economic

Adviser's Sector in which was concentrated those economists engaged on economic forecasting and the use of the Treasury's macro-economic model for the simulation of the effects on the economy of major options in economic policy. The Central Unit was designed to assist the higher reaches of the Treasury in the task of co-ordinating policy advice from all parts of the department. The achievement of better co-ordination was, indeed, one of the main general aims of the 1975 reorganizat-ion, together with simplification of the chain of command in the Treasury, and to change some demarcation lines between policy areas.25

What by 1975 had changed in the Treasury more than its structure was the position of the Keynesian economic thinking which had underpinned its style of economic management for thirty years. The change that took place was neither swift nor complete. For a time, Denis Healey, Labour's Chancellor between 1974 and 1979, urged his counterparts in the Western world to reflate their way out of the post-Oil Crisis recess-ion in the Keynesian manner. They did not take his advice. As with the Jenkins Chancellorship, the IMF brokers had to be called in to achieve a minor recovery in the British economy. With Keynesianism no longer commanding the field, there was more opportunity for other approaches to be aired. A New Cambridge School preached, among other things, an autarkic solution for Britain's economic management problem; one which was meant to appeal to socialists, but the implementation of a form of which might appeal in some circumstances to others. The monetarists also made ground: initially, at least. The words 'money supply' came as readily to the lips of Denis Healey in 1977-78, as they had done to those of Peter Thorney-croft in 1957-58. The economics of the Neville Chamberlain era seemed to be being revived. However, their practical application faced one massive obstruction not present in Chamberlain's heyday. This was a large public sector and the expenditure that accompanied it, reducing the scale of which was more easily advocated than achieved.

References

1. Butler (1971), p. 182. Butler, with acknowledgement, adapted a phrase from Macrae (1963), p. 41.
2. Fry (1979), p. 68-88.
3. 131 H.L. Deb. 5s. c. 844.
4. Harrod (1951), p. 462; Hutchison (1977), pp. 14, 65-73; The Times, 12.1.1937, 13.1.1937, 14.1.1937; Clark (1970), p. 53; Keynes (1936), p. 378; Cmd. 6527 (1944), p.28; Beveridge (1944), pp. 128, 194-201.
5. Deane and Cole (1962), p. 314; Knapp and Lomax (1964), pp. 1-24.
6. Chester (1962), pp. 419-26; Clarke (1963), pp. 17-24; Maudling (1978), pp. 118-19.

7.   The Economist, 28.10.1961, pp. 313-15;   645 H.C. Deb. 5s. c. 220;   Phelps Brown (1963), pp. 239-46;   Blackaby (1978), pp. 402-8.

8.   The Economist, 12.5.1962, pp. 537-38;   Blackaby (1978), p. 407;   Denton et. al. (1968), pp. 113-14;   Jewkes (1968), pp. 8-9.

9.   Moran (1977), pp. 54-6;   Blackaby (1978), pp. 364-65, 392-93;   Phillips (1958), pp. 283-99;   Maudling (1978), pp. 111-14;   Brittan (1969), pp. 129, 132, 171-86.

10.   Ibid., p. 165;   Craig (1975), pp. 229-46.

11.   Wilson (1971), p. 3;   Brown (1971), pp. 96-7;   Lord Balogh, 'Back to Square Two', The Guardian, 9.10.1969;   Self (1965), p. 39;   Roll (1966), pp. 1-11;   Allen (1967), pp. 351-59;   Blackaby (1978), pp. 409-12.   Lord Balogh told me that in a Memorandum that he wrote at Wilson's request in 1963 on the Civil Service he recommended the establishment of the DEA (and, for that matter, the ODM): see also Balogh (1963), p.34.

12.   Cmnd. 2764 (1965), p. iii;   718 H.C. Deb. 5s. c. 1064;   Jewkes (1968), pp. 12-13;   732 H.C. Deb. 5s. c. 1850, 1848;   Surrey (1972), pp. 249-68.

13.   Wilson (1971), pp. 5-7, 256-57;   754 H.C. Deb. 5s. c. 946-47;   Brown (1971), pp. 100, 114-15;   Brandon (1966), p. 43;   Brittan (1969), pp. 187-89;   Hutchison (1968), pp. 219-22;   Blackaby (1978), pp. 311-13;   Crossman (1965), pp. 71, 305-6, 573-77.

14.   The Economist, 2.9.1967, p. 773;   762 H.C. Deb. 5s. c. 1586;   788 H.C. Deb. 5s. c. 42-3;   Wilson (1971), pp. 710, 64;   McCrone (1969), pp. 271-72.

15.   Wilson (1971), p. 257;   Brown (1971), p. 114;   Brandon (1966), pp. 35-6.

16.   Wilson (1971), pp. 63-4, 132-33;   Mitchell (1970), pp. 57-67.

17.   Cmnd. 3623 (1968);   the articles by D.J. Robertson, J.R. Crossley, G.L. Reid, G. Grunfeld, W.R.C. Keeler, and H.A. Turner in British Journal of Industrial Relations, 6 (1968), pp. 287-359;   Cmnd. 3888 (1969);   Beckerman (1972), pp. 300-24;   Wilson (1971), pp. 640-45, 648-49, 653, 655, 657;   Jenkins (1971), pp. 139-68;   Crossman (1977), pp. 438-39, 442, 444-45, 474-75, 479-80, 497-510, 525-29;   Blackaby (1978), pp. 373-78.

18.   Paish (1971), p. 73.

19.   Showler (1976), pp. 26-51;   Steel and Stanyer (1975), p. 248;   'Role of Manpower Services Commission', Department of Employment Gazette, 81 (1973), pp. 1227-28;   Cassels (1979), pp. 74-85.

20.   Blackaby (1978), pp. 579-97;   Thompson and Engleman (1975), pp. 33-37, 97-124;   Hurd (1979), p. 105;   Moran (1977), pp. 54-76, 77-96, 124-48.

21.   Wigham (1976), pp. 165-69;   Hurd (1979), p. 103;   Harris and Sewill (1975), pp. 47-50.

22.   Blackaby (1978), pp. 205-7, 315-16;   Harris and Sewill (1975), pp. 10-11, 36-46;   833 H.C. Deb. 5s. c. 1523-

26; Hurd (1979), pp. 89-90; Pringle (1977), pp. 34-9, 52-3.
    23.   Harris and Sewill (1975), pp. 51-3; Steel and
Stanyer (1975), p. 247; Cockfield (1978), pp. 3-25; Hurd
(1979), pp. 103-5, 113-36; Blackaby (1978), pp. 378-85.
    24.   Steel and Stanyer (1975), pp. 248-49; 'Machinery of
Government in Great Britain', <u>Management Services in Government</u>,
30 (1975), pp. 167-68. Michael Foot later alleged that the
implementation of the Robens Report (Cmnd. 5034, 1972) had been
delayed by a 'Whitehall war' (871 H.C. Deb. 5s. c. 1287).
    25.   'Treasury Reorganization', <u>Economic Progress Report</u>,
No. 67, (October, 1965), pp. 1-2.

Chapter 5

FAILING TO CONTROL PUBLIC EXPENDITURE

'The system of control of public expenditure depends upon the attitude to public spending both of Parliament and of public opinion', the Plowden Committee observed in 1961. 'In former times, there were strong external pressures on the Government to reduce both expenditure and taxes, and every Minister who wanted to spend had to run the gauntlet of severe criticism from his Cabinet colleagues, from Parliament and from the public. The system was then effective in keeping expenditure down. This was the instrument, indeed, by which an austere discipline was maintained throughout the public service for generation after generation up to World War I in marked distinction to many other countries' experience. In the inter-war period, although attitudes were changing, there was still a strong body of critical opinion which served as a check on the growth of public expenditure'. The Plowden Committee believed that the social, political and economic changes of the twenty years down to 1961 had created a new situation. 'First, the scale of public expenditure is far greater. Supply expenditure is now 22 per cent of the Gross National Product, compared with 12 per cent in 1930, 6 per cent in 1910, and 4 per cent in 1870. In addition, there has been the expansion of local authorities' spending and the bringing of the fuel and power and transport industries into public ownership. As a consequence of these changes the public sector of the economy as a whole now employs about one-quarter of the total labour force. The total of public expenditure of all kinds ... represents about 42 per cent of the Gross National Product. Second, public expenditure has become more complex including, as it does, the cost of the most advanced technological projects and of scientific research; the financing of commercial risks that the private sector cannot take; aid of many different kinds to a variety of underdeveloped countries; and social insurance schemes of unprecedented scope. All of these activities involve commitments, contractual or moral, extending several years ahead. Third, there has taken place a great change in economic thought; the Keynesian Revolution in the role of public finance and its relationship to the national economy as a whole. The Budget is seen, not as a simple balancing of tax receipts against expenditure, but as a sophisticated process in which the instruments of taxation and expenditure are used to influence the course of the economy'. The Plowden Committee concluded that these factors and above all 'the fact that the main weight of Parliamentary and public pressure, central and local, is for innovations or improvements which cannot be brought about without increases in public expenditure, have created a situation in which ... the traditional system of decision making can no longer be expected to be effective in containing the growth of expenditure within whatever limit the Government have set. If, as must be expected, these changes are permanent, the system needs to be reconstructed accordingly'.1 The traditional system of Treasury control of expenditure was reconstructed along the lines that the Plowden Committee recommended. What we shall call the Plowden Revolution took place. What did not follow was that public expenditure was brought under effective control.

The factors which the Plowden Committee identified as leading to the growth of public expenditure were among those that proved to be too strong for the system it designed to regulate that growth. The other factors at work included modern Ministerial ambitions; electoral considerations, including indirect bribery; the lack of incentives for economy in a developed bureaucracy; and the urgings of pressure groups both within and outside the machinery of government. In the period of the Crosland-Galbraith ascendancy, indeed, public expenditure was widely regarded, at least among the politically active, as a unique force for social good. Governments were rarely short of advice from outside pressure groups advocating that they should spend more. In this political climate, a Minister's reputation was made in many government departments if he did well in securing more resources from the Treasury.2 Taxpayers and their interests were not directly represented in such duels any more than they were, for instance, in the Whitley system of industrial relations which, unsurprisingly, only flourished in the public sector. Public sector employees were - and became increasingly - highly unionized. In effect, they were pressure groups insistent for more public expend-iture to be spent on themselves. Their perennial quest was for parity of pay with the private sector. Claims for 'fair wages' and 'fair salaries' were pressed on employers - the Govern-ment - with a special ability to 'find the money'. They printed it. When, for example, the Conservative Government of the day implemented the Priestley Commission's recommendation in 1955 that Civil Service pay should be based on 'fair comparisons' with outside salaries, ascertained by 'pay research', this proved to be a massively expensive long term commitment.3 Moreover, in return for this kind of commit-ment - and acknowledging that some individuals or groups acted differently - neither Civil Servants, nor others working in

77

other parts of the central government bureaucracies, had much
incentive to organize work in an economical manner. Any money
saved would not accrue to them personally. From the bureau-
crats' point of view, the larger the bureaucracy the better in
many respects, because a well developed hierarchy would mean
enhanced general career prospects. From the politicians'
standpoint, the larger the number of public employees, the more
they represented an electoral interest which Governments had to
humour. The commitment to full employment also meant that
Governments were generally inhibited from cutting back on
public sector employment. To sustain full employment, Governments of all political colours 'topped up' the economy from
time to time with public expenditure, in effect bribing the
electorate with its own money. The 'topping up' was done in
the name of Keynes, the advocate of certain circumstances of
the unbalanced Budget. What was forgotten was the concern that
Keynes expressed - for instance, in concurring with Colin
Clark's famous dictum about taxable capacity - about the
inflationary effects of the high taxation that, however
belatedly, followed substantial State activity, and, hence,
spending.4   It was inflation that finally emphasized the
failure of the post-Plowden system to control public expenditure, and ensured that system's modification.

I   THE PLOWDEN REPORT AND ITS BEGINNINGS

'The broadening of the functions of the Treasury from those of
a department concerned principally with good housekeeping to
one seeking to guide the whole economic trend of the country
must mean that it directs proportionately less of its attention
to ensuring efficiency and economy in departmental spending',
the Select Committee of Public Accounts observed in 1951. This
then prestigious Committee was unconvinced by Treasury
assurances that its control over public expenditure was more
effective than it had been thirty years beforehand. Even then,
of course, the Treasury was much more than a department at the
head of a group of government departments responsible to the
Chancellor of the Exchequer, including the Board of Inland
Revenue and the Board of Customs and Excise. The functions of
controlling public finance and Civil Service establishments
made the Treasury the central Whitehall department; a position
which was strengthened by its more recently acquired role in
relation to macro-economic management. The Permanent Secretary
to the Treasury was Head of the Civil Service, which, among
other things, meant that he advised the Prime Minister on
appointments to the posts of Permanent Secretary, Deputy
Secretary, Principal Establishment Officer, and Principal
Finance Officer in other government departments. Sir Edward
Bridges, the then Permanent Secretary, was clear that 'the
Treasury of 1950 was not ill-equipped to deal with its many and
varied tasks'. He maintained particularly that the Treasury
had successfully translated its role in control of public

expenditure from the Gladstonian era of 'the saving of candle ends' to the more modern approach in which Treasury control had become 'less concerned with the prevention of all public expenditure, and more concerned with ensuring the most prudent and economical spending of money on approved projects'. A distinguished American observer came to much the same conclusion in 1956, the year of Bridges's retirement; and a year marked, as we noted in Chapter 2 by changes in the top echelons of the Treasury. These changes, among other things, were designed to emphasize tighter control over public spending.5 This minor reconstruction of the Treasury proved to be the modest beginning of a process of change which led to the Plowden Revolution.

An important stage in that process was the publication in 1958 of a Report by the Select Committee on Estimates about Treasury control of expenditure. The Committee, normally over-shadowed by the Public Accounts Committee, and lacking support of the kind that the Comptroller and Auditor General and his staff provided, conducted a thorough investigation and produced a very critical Report. The Committee concluded that: 'It became clear early in the course of the enquiry that it is really an abuse of language to speak of a "system" of Treasury control, if by the word "system" is meant methods and practices that have at one time or another been deliberately planned and instituted. What is called "Treasury control" is better described as a complex of administrative practice that has grown up like a tree over the centuries, natural rather than planned, empiric rather than theoretical. The question here at issue is whether a "system", many features of which emerged in times when government expenditure played a relatively small part in the national economy, is appropriate to the middle of the twentieth century'. The Committee thought that the Treasury had neither entirely abandoned its old 'candle ends' approach, nor fully established a partnership with financially responsible fellow government departments. The Committee found cause for disquiet. First, it considered that the existing arrangements for Treasury control, while they scrutinized new policies, were deficient in that they did not include systematic reviews of established policies to see whether or not they should be continued with, modified, or even abandoned. Secondly, the Committee thought that the existing 'system' was prone to the under-estimating of the costs of policies and major projects. Thirdly, it believed that the existing presentation of annual Estimates and Accounts concentrated too much attention on the policy and expenditure proposals for the forthcoming year. This stultified forward planning. There was a need for a 'forward look' in all government expenditure of the kind already under-taken in defence spending. The Select Committee missed a few obvious targets, including the most obvious of all: why should the level of public expenditure be decided before the level of revenue, instead of the other way around ? The

Committee ended its Report with a recommendation that 'a small independent committee, which would have access to Cabinet papers, be appointed to report upon the theory and practice of Treasury control of expenditure'.6

The Plowden Committee which was appointed by the Macmillan Government in 1959, was ' small' but not 'independent'. It was an 'inside' job. Five of the Committee's members were serving Civil Servants (including Sir Richard Clarke), and the other four, including Lord Plowden himself, were former Civil Servants - 'outsiders' who had been 'insiders'. Like the evidence that it collected, the Plowden Committee's actual Report remained confidential. The published Report's opaque prose attracted comment. Nevertheless, the Committee's main recommendations were clear enough when made public in July 1961. The Committee favoured a reconstruction of the traditional system of control of public spending based on four elements. First, it recommended that 'regular surveys should be made of public expenditure as a whole, over a period of years ahead, and in relation to prospective resources; decisions involving substantial future expenditure should be taken in the light of these surveys'. Secondly, 'there should be the greatest practicable stability of decisions on public expenditure when taken, so that long term economy and efficiency throughout the public sector have the best possible opportunity to develop'. Thirdly, 'improvements should be made in the tools for measuring and handling public expenditure problems, including in particular major simplification of the form of Estimates, modernization and clarification of the Exchequer Accounts, and more widespread use of quantitative methods in dealing with these problems throughout the public service. These should serve both to improve the work inside the governmental machine, and to contribute to a better under-standing by Parliament and by the public'. Fourthly, 'there should be more effective machinery for the taking of collect-ive decisions and the bearing of collective responsibility by Ministers on matters of public expenditure'. The Plowden Committee anticipated that these various changes might lead to concomitant changes in parliamentary procedure. The Committee emphasized the importance that had to be attached to management in the Civil Service under the changed system it proposed. It also recognized the increased demands that would be placed on the Treasury by the new system, and suggested that it would be necessary for the Treasury to review its organization to meet them. As we saw in Chapter 4, such a reorganization did take place in 1962. If 'the function of the Treasury' under the traditional system was 'that of lay critic',7 something more sophisticated was expected in the post-Plowden era. Certainly, things became more complicated.

II   THE 'GOLDEN AGE' OF PESC 1961-1972

For more than a decade after 1961, the Plowden Committee was widely believed to have found the answer to what it had defined

as 'the central problem ... of how to bring the growth of
public expenditure under better control'. Arrangements which
had fostered 'piecemeal decisions' about public spending were
overshadowed and overridden by the post-Plowden system, under
which, in its authors' words, 'decisions involving substantial
future expenditure' were 'taken in the light of surveys of
public expenditure as a whole, over a period of years, and in
relation to prospective resources'. Cleared away with the old
annual cash limits approach were the former, often misleading
categories of the Estimates, excluding as they had done the
burgeoning area of local authority spending. The Plowden
Revolution seemed to many to have introduced a more rational
system. In the 1950s, in the opinion of Sir Richard Clarke and
Sir William Armstrong and other high ranking officials, the
Chancellor and the Treasury had lost their grip on public
expenditure. The appointment of a Chief Secretary to the
Treasury, a new Ministerial post, from October 1961 onwards,
mainly to assist the Chancellor to control government spending,
could be taken as an indication of political recognition of the
need for changed arrangements, which Plowden had ensured would
be matched administratively. In contrast with the 1950s, for
those impressed with the post-Plowden arrangements, the period
1961-1972 was a Golden Age when authority was restored. Yet,
the factors which had helped to make the 1950s into an era
supposedly of base metal remained important. Economic management was still the first call on a Chancellor's attention.
High levels of public spending were still associated with
similar levels of general economic activity and of employment.
If the economy prospered, the Government continued to expect to
politically prosper, as the Heath Government expected to when
it abandoned its short lived policy of containing public
expenditure. Ideally, under the Plowden arrangements, priorities in spending were supposed to be decided in Cabinet on an
ordered basis. In practice, and particularly under pressure,
decisions were probably as likely as ever to be taken on
'horse trading' lines, or in a cavalier spirit - as with the
commitment to Concorde. The post-Plowden system could be
undermined not just from above; but from below the level of
the high ranking Civil Servants of the type who had designed
it and who ran it. The lower reaches of the bureaucracy had
few incentives to economize. The appropriate attitudes could
only hope to generally flourish when the political and administrative climate was antipathetic to public spending. The
Public Accounts, Estimates and Expenditure Committees could
only hope to flourish in such a climate. Otherwise, they
patrolled the machinery of government in vain. There was no
such antipathetic climate in the years 1961-1972. As otherwise misled American observers commented, the Golden Age of the
Treasury remained the 1930s, despite the purrings of that
department's high officials about the wonders of the post-
Plowden mechanisms.8
    'The development and use by Government of long term

81

surveys of expenditure and resources is the core of our
proposals', the Plowden Committee had written. From 1961 onwards, regular annual surveys of this kind were at the core of
the system of control of public spending. The system became
loosely known as the PESC system, the initials standing for the
Public Expenditure Survey Committee, which had an overview of
the whole operation. The Committee was chaired by a Deputy
Secretary of the Treasury, and on it sat the Principal Finance
Officers of all the major spending departments. Public
expenditure was defined in the Surveys as comprising the
current and capital expenditure of the central government and
local authorities, other than expenditure charged to the
operating account of trading bodies, together with the capital
expenditure of the nationalized industries and other public
corporations, and their debt interest. The principles underlying the measurement of public expenditure in the Surveys
were essentially the same as those used in National Income and
Expenditure Accounts.9

The PESC system had seven main features. First, Surveys
covering the whole of public expenditure were conducted
annually; the prospective levels of expenditure were reviewed;
and if Ministers considered it appropriate to do so, expenditure programmes were adjusted. Secondly, the Surveys
included estimates of expenditure for each of the next five
years. While some major programmes required a longer period
than this for their planning - and account was taken of this -
it was deemed neither necessary nor practicable for the overall
management of public expenditure to have a comprehensive range
of estimates for more than five years ahead. Thirdly, the
figures for future years were estimates of the cost of the
Government's existing policies. In some instances, it was
thought, the figures themselves gave greater precision to
these policies in showing the scale of action envisaged, or
the pace at which specific aims might be achieved. What the
estimates did not do was to anticipate future decisions either
to introduce new policies or to modify existing ones.
Fourthly, the figures for both past and future years were
presented in terms of constant prices. In fact, there were
two constant price series which served different purposes.
They were described respectively 'in volume terms' and 'in
cost terms'. The purpose of the volume series was to show
changes over time in the volume of goods and services used by
the various public sector programmes, either directly in the
form of purchase of goods and services or indirectly through
transfer payments to other sectors of the economy. Such a
series was designed to show whether the scale of provision of
a particular service was being increased or reduced, and by
how much. The constant price basis of the volume series was
described as 'at Survey prices'. In general, Survey prices
related to the price levels ruling at around the time when
estimates were prepared at the beginning of the annual Survey
operation. Figures described as being 'at 1972 Survey prices',

for example, were based on price levels at the end of 1971 or early in 1972. What a constant price volume series could not measure correctly was either the relative costliness of an individual programme over time, or of different programmes at particular points in time, or of total public expenditure in relation to the GDP or its components. In order to allow for this Relative Price Effect, while continuing to exclude the effects of general inflation, the constant price estimates for future years were adjusted to take account of the relative price movement which could be expected to occur between Year 1 of the Survey and each subsequent year. The fifth main feature of the PESC system was that the figures were analysed by function or programme and showed the relative amounts spent, or proposed to be spent on, for example, defence, health, education, social security, roads. This was thought to provide a suitable basis for considering social and political priorities and possible changes in existing government policies. Sixthly, the figures were also analysed by economic category so that public expenditure could be considered in relation to prospective resources. The implications for the rest of the economy were the subject of separate studies. Seventhly, the figures were further analysed between spending authorities - that is, between central government, local authorities, and public corporations - because of the differing degrees to which their expenditure was subject to governmental and Parliamentary control.[10]

The annual timetable for the PESC system might vary slightly from year to year, but typically it ran as follows. In December, instructions on the conduct of the coming year's Survey were issued by the Treasury. At the end of February, departments responsible for blocks of expenditure sent returns to the Treasury, including their up-to-date estimates of the cost of existing policies for the coming five years. In the March-April period, the Treasury and the individual spending departments discussed these estimates, and the supporting information provided by the departments, in order to reach agreement on the policy and statistical assumptions on which the estimates should be based, and then on the figures themselves. In May, a draft report on public expenditure was drawn up by the Treasury, and agreed in PESC. In June, a report was submitted to Ministers. Between July and November, Ministerial decisions were taken on the aggregate of public expenditure and its allocation to the various programmes. In November-December, publication of the programme estimates embodying these decisions took place in the annual Public Expenditure White Paper. A statistical and administrative unit within the Treasury collated the material for the Surveys, carried out the necessary co-ordination with departments and other Treasury divisions, and with their help drafted the report. As submitted to Ministers, the report set out an inter-departmentally agreed, up-to-date, costing of all existing policies. Any disagreements over the costings were separately recorded. The report contained no recommendations on what the future level of individual programmes or of public expenditure as a whole should be. The report stated what was thought would be the level of public spending if present policies were pursued.11

That was essentially what the PESC system looked like by 1972, and the Treasury saw it as providing Ministers with a regular means of seeing where their existing policies would lead in public expenditure terms, and for considering this against the economic prospects and their own social and political priorities. In this way, the Treasury believed, Ministers could decide whether the demands upon resources likely to be made by the public sector needed to be altered, or left unchanged, and whether the allocation of these resources between the various programmes of expenditure should be varied. The PESC system was not, however, seen by the Treasury as imposing any rigid form on decision taking. The system was said to be able to be used as flexibly as the Government chose and circumstances required. The Treasury emphasized that the PESC system did not mean that decision taking on public expenditure issues was confined to a single cosmic operation which occurred once a year. Public expenditure decisions, while they were always taken against the background of the latest Survey figures, had to be taken as policy required. What the Treasury thought that the PESC system did was to impose the discipline of a regular full annual review of the whole of public expenditure. The results of this review, representing a snapshot of public expenditure estimated at that time, provided the basis of the annual Public Expenditure White Paper.12

While there had been intermittent White Papers before, these annual Public Expenditure White Papers began in December 1969. This followed an initiative by the Wilson Government and the recommendation of the House of Commons Select Committee on Procedure. While the Procedure Committee wanted the Public Accounts Committee and the Select Committee on Nationalized Industries to be retained, it successfully proposed that the Estimates Committee should be replaced by a Select Committee on Expenditure. Whereas the Estimates Committee only surveyed annual estimates of supply expenditure, the Expenditure Committee was to provide a machinery for scrutinizing the PESC system which involved all public expenditure. Under the Heath Government, the Expenditure Committee was established in 1971, as was the practice of an annual debate on the Public Expenditure White Paper. In 1972, the Expenditure Committee successfully proposed that the Treasury should publish its Medium Term Assessment, the economic forecast against which the cost projections of existing policies were compared.13   To judge from the quality of the annual debates on its operations, many MPs remained baffled by, and resentful of, the PESC system.

Resentment seems to have characterized much of the Wilson Government's consideration of PESC recommendations. Although the PESC system was initiated in 1961, it was under the Labour

Government in 1965 that the Cabinet was first closely involved
in its operations. After the conflicts that resulted, from
July 1965 onwards, the Prime Minister was reported as reflecting on whether PESC was not the master rather than the servant
of the Government. Nevertheless, the following summer, Richard
Crossman, a member of the Cabinet Committee concerned, seemed
to accept that 'the PESC meeting has become our regular July
exercise'. However, according to his account, the July 1966
measures, which included cuts in public spending, were prepared
in a chaotic rather than ordered manner. Crossman said that
'over the weekend the centralized mandarin machine had once
again been put to work, working out a desperate programme without Cabinet knowing about it'. When the Cabinet finally did
learn of the crisis measures, Crossman's reaction was that
'nothing had been adequately prepared. Nothing had been
thought out properly. We were fixing things once again,
horribly inefficiently, at the last moment'. A 'horse trading'
atmosphere also characterized the post-devaluation cuts of
1967-68. Although Crossman thought that Roy Jenkins, as
Chancellor, eventually got through his economy programme almost
intact. Earlier, in 1966, Crossman had noted how Jenkins as
Home Secretary had - despite the then incomes policy - secured
a special increase in police pay: 'he hadn't bothered to go to
PESC to make his point but he'd been allowed to make it direct
to Cabinet'. Crossman was premature when he wrote in June
1967: 'we seemed to have crushed the PESC exercise - the idea
of a group of Ministers sitting in judgment on other Ministers'.
For, in July 1968, he was complaining again about 'the fantastic abracadabra of rules and regulations' of the PESC system
being 'still enforced upon us'. According to his own account,
'the rules of the PESC game' were still being applied right
down to the end of his period in office.14
  The advent of the Heath Government led to PESC, which was
essentially an input budgeting system, being complemented by
PAR (Programme Analysis and Review) which was an output
budgeting system. Considerable interest had been aroused in
output budgeting because of the development of Planning,
Programming and Budgeting (PPB) techniques in other countries,
notably France, the USA and Canada. Among domestic developments had been work applying PPB in the former Ministry of
Education and on the police side of the Home Office. The
Ministry of Defence had also developed a system of ten year
functional costings as a basis for its long term planning of
expenditure. The Heath Government installed a group of
businessmen in the Civil Service Department, who were familiar
with the use of PAR in private business, and who were
commissioned to introduce it as widely as possible into government. The central feature of PAR was supposed to be that it
was an approach to decision making which used all existing
techniques of cost appraisal and measurement, and sought to
apply them to alternative methods of achieving determined aims.
The contribution made by PAR theory was believed to be that it

involved a higher consciousness of what was being sought than existed before, and a more deliberate search for options and alternatives. This was thought to be perhaps particularly true of studies of current as distinct from new policies, where a special effort was required to review established practices to see whether they were still justified or should be replaced. PAR studies divided themselves into two main types. One type was 'objective' PARs, which dealt with subjects capable of fairly clear definition, and with easily ascertainable available options. The second type was 'instrument' PARs, which were concerned with activities, organizations or institutions that existed to achieve certain ends, and which were sufficiently important to be studied in their own right. While individual departments themselves carried out PAR exercises, also involved in the process was the CPRS and the Treasury supposedly providing a strategic overview.15

The Treasury, however, was not the force that it had been. Some, like Crossman, continued to complain about the undue influence of the Treasury. 'One cannot overestimate this', he wrote in 1966. 'All the Civil Servants I worked with were imbued with a prior loyalty to the Treasury and felt it necessary to spy on me and report all my doings to the Treasury, whether I wanted them kept private or not. There was nothing I could do, no order I could give, which wasn't at once known to the Treasury, because my staff were all trained to check with the Treasury and let it know in advance exactly what each of them was doing. When this Treasury system is reinforced by PESC, you get a staggering centralized control which is being in no way counteracted by the existence of the DEA'. The DEA was not designed for that task. Nevertheless, the removal to the DEA for five years of economic management functions did for that time and in that area weaken the Treasury's position. Moreover, in 1968, the setting up of the Civil Service Department took away the Treasury's traditional control over Establishments. The Permanent Secretary of the CSD became Head of the Home Civil Service, presiding over the machinery for senior appointments. Sir Richard Clarke, writing in the early 1970s, encouraged the possibility of 'a critical weakening of the centre' of government following from having three bodies located there - the Treasury, the CSD and the CPRS. He thought that the large 'federal' departments of the kind created in the 1960s and 1970s might lead to the pressure for rationalization. Sir Richard also wrote of a Treasury Concordat with the enlarged Ministry of Technology in 1968 over control of expenditure, and seemed to think this to be a model to follow.16 Whatever fears Ministers needed to have of the Treasury, that department's relative position had changed vis-a-vis the other government departments. The Treasury of Warren Fisher and even of Bridges had no need of Concordats. Fisher's Treasury could hope to play the parts of both Mussolini and the Pope, and had the advantage over their modern counterparts that the official 'religion' was inimical to public spending.

If the climate for the serious control of public expenditure was unfavourable at the centre in the 1960s and early 1970s, it was unlikely to be generally much different lower down the bureaucracy. Given the lack of incentive, it would be an unusual Civil Servant who tried to ensure that the particular organization in which he worked was run as economically as possible. One who did try, and later published his experiences, was Leslie Chapman, who, from 1967, held a senior management post in what was then the Ministry of Public Buildings and Works, and what became the Property Services Agency, a part of the Department of the Environment. As Regional Director of the Southern Region of the MPBW, Chapman had little early success in introducing economies. Conventional investigation suggested that not a single penny was being wasted. Chapman's own cursory examination suggested otherwise, and he found unconvincing a report by specialists who discovered waste only in areas of expenditure in which they were expert. He established a special team which comprised a Building and Engineering Technical Officer, a Mechanical and Electrical Engineer, and an Executive Officer. Chapman said that 'the team's brief was comparatively simple. They were to go to a depot, spend as much time as was necessary to do their work thoroughly and examine every penny that was spent on maintenance by that organization. They were never to take either documents or statements on trust. They were, in no circumstances, to accept that because something had been done for years it was necessarily the right thing to do. They were not to accept documentary evidence that work was being done, but were to see for themselves all that was being carried out. There were two general propositions which they were to examine. Was the work essential in the sense that without it the customer department could not carry out its function ? Secondly, if the work was essential, was it necessary to do it in the way in which it was being done or could an acceptable result be achieved by spending less time or money ? The first team looked at the Royal Army Ordnance Depot at Bicester, Oxfordshire. They reported that immediate savings of approximately 30 per cent of the total maintenance budget, and between 40-50 per cent of the directly employed labour force could be made; and that with reorganization, further savings would follow. The economies proposed covered almost every aspect of the maintenance organization's activities. Less grass needed to be cut than was being cut, and what needed to be cut needed less painstaking cutting. Lawn standards were pointless for grass which stretched between store sheds and was criss-crossed by overhead pipes and cables. There was no useful purpose served in heating gigantic stores the size of aircraft hangars to normal office temperatures. The contents were quite safe at lower temperatures. When the staff concerned needed to go there, they could be adequately clothed for the purpose. The team also saw no point in maintaining a depot railway system of a

standard suitable for inter-city expresses and used only by
slow moving trains, when roads could serve either as well or
better at a fraction of the cost. On the strength of the
Bicester study, new teams were turned loose on the other depots
in the region. These teams, like the first, consisted of
volunteers prepared to work very long hours without extra pay
to achieve results. They found similar situations, sometimes of
comic proportions. In one small area around Aldershot alone,
Civil Servants were uneconomically operating a gravel pit, a
saw mill, a sign writing centre, a foundry, joinery and wood-
working shops, a machinery maintenance workshop, and a printing
business. Elsewhere, there were nurseries producing shrubs and
trees, and installations supplying domestic water, treating
sewage, and sweeping roads. None of these activities were
essentially ones that the department needed to do. For good
measure, Chapman's teams cut back on the Civil Service car
service in the Region; closed down all but three stores depots
at a saving of at least 80 per cent in costs; and chopped back
the mushrooming staff welfare service. Predictably, when
Leslie Chapman urged on his superiors the need to introduce
similar economies in other Regions of the Property Services
Agency, he was rebuffed.17
    The matter was plainly one for the Public Accounts
Committee to follow up with effective action: but, as we shall
see, that watchdog was now toothless. The old mechanisms for
controlling public expenditure were doomed to failure in a
climate so markedly conducive to the growth of such spending.
It was soon to be reluctantly recognized that this was true of
the newer mechanisms too.

III FROM PESC TO 'PESC PLUS' CASH LIMITS 1973-76 AND BEYOND

'After many vicissitudes we have evolved a system for managing
the public sector which despite many continuing deficiencies
is probably superior to that found anywhere else in the world.'
Thus, in 1972, wrote a leading Treasury official, Sir Samuel
Goldman, about the post-Plowden system of public expenditure
control. As with Treasury control in 1956, PESC attracted
American admiration. According to two American observers, no
nation in the world could match the sophistication or thoroughness to be found in the British process of expenditure
projection. PESC was supposed to be nothing less than the
major modern reform of the machinery of resource allocation,
whose success owed something to having been launched in a
climate of severe financial stringency. Yet, the period
between 1964 and 1974 - when the Americans' study was
published - was a decade of unprecedented peacetime growth in
public spending. Over that decade, on one measure, public
expenditure as a percentage of GNP at factor cost had increased
from 43 per cent to 56 per cent. Whatever measure was
taken, the pattern was the same: a steady rise from 1964 to
1968, then approximate stability to 1973, followed by a
massive rise in 1974, continuing into 1975. Sir Samuel

Goldman drew attention to the 'essential dynamism' of the system of public expenditure management and control. From 1973 onwards, the essential dynamism of the growth of public expenditure was evidently such that it undermined the credibility of the PESC system. In 1976, annual cash limits were introduced across a wide range of public spending in an attempt to contain its growth, the effect of the imposition of which was diminished by the exclusion of transfer payments, the main source of growth.18

The authority of PESC, like the hopes attached to PAR, had crumbled within a very short period. Writing in 1971, Sir Richard Clarke had seen the next 2-5 years as a transition period in which PAR and PESC and the conventional system of public expenditure control would continue 'going on at the same time'. In the end, however, it was his view that 'there cannot be two methods by which the thousands of decisions about spending and staff are taken, both operating simultaneously'. Sir Richard clearly believed that PAR and PESC could and should prevail and become the system of expenditure and manpower administration and control within the departments, at the centre, and between the two. Sir Samuel Goldman described PAR as 'the most important and hopeful field for further development of the present system'. While 'significant results' could not be expected in 'under five years' from PAR, Sir Samuel believed that this 'should not be allowed to weaken support for a new effort in a vital field the potential gains from which are very large'. Edward Heath's Political Secretary later said that PAR was 'a sophisticated attempt to question from the inside the scope of modern government. Across-the-board spending cuts at moments of crisis were familiar enough - and were to become familiar again. But they were haphazard. They hit the good programmes with the bad. It should surely be possible to look quietly and systematically at the work of each department, and to eliminate those activities which happened because they happened and for no other reason. A system was therefore devised to subject the continuing activities of government to the same searching scrutiny which, in theory at least, is given to proposals for new action. But in practice it was found that each examination of this kind lasted for many months. The arguments against abandoning any particular programme were fiercely sustained by people who, by virtue of their position, know more of the details than their critics'.19 The potentialities of PAR were never very likely to be realized. Among other things, PAR meant Ministers and their departments having to reveal their priorities for spending to their Ministerial and departmental rivals in a competitive situation. Few PAR exercises were undertaken, and the hoped for strategic overview of the process by the Treasury and the CPRS, therefore, could not materialize.

While PAR scarcely got off the ground, PESC was destined to fall from the pinnacle to which it had been raised. PESC's basic weaknesses toppled it, exposed as they often were by the

criticisms of a Cambridge economist and former Treasury
official, Wynne Godley. With others, he acted from time to
time as a Specialist Adviser to the House of Commons Expenditure Committee. The MPs themselves were like uncomprehending
spectators at a very specialized game. Godley, whether in the
role of Adviser or witness largely dictated the play. Godley's
belief was that the attempt to control public expenditure
programmes in terms of 'constant price' outlays as defined for
the purpose of measuring the 'real' national income was mis-
guided. The correct way to control public spending was in
terms of ordinary and not 'funny' money. Godley argued that
'the emphasis on trying to control expenditure in real terms
has meant that the control of the money has to a considerable
extent gone by default'. Financial control was absent from the
PESC planning system, and Godley said that this was its
Achilles Heel. He brutally demonstrated the inadequacies of
PESC in evidence to the Expenditure Committee in late 1975.
From this it was clear that, at 1974-75 prices, expenditure in
1974-75 was about £5.8 billion more than it had been planned
to be in the Public Expenditure White Paper of November 1971.
According to the Treasury, some 30 per cent of this increase -
about £1.8 billion - was due to intervening announced policy
changes. That left a £4 billion increase that did not result
from such policy changes. This corresponded to about 5 per
cent of the Gross Domestic Product. The Expenditure Committee
concluded that 'even allowing for unannounced policy changes,
the Treasury's present methods of controlling public expenditure are inadequate in the sense that money can be spent on a
scale which was not contemplated when the relevant policies
were decided upon'. However, this did not mean that Wynne
Godley, and, therefore, the Expenditure Committee, wished to
scrap PESC. Godley pointed out that there were two possible
ways in which PESC could be altered: 'One is to go ahead, to
go forward and make PESC work and to introduce a financial
control system into it and have a positive planning system.
The other thing is to go back and have ... control in the very
crude sense of having a Treasury which tries to keep expenditure down and which does not commit itself to real resource use
for years in advance'. Both approaches involved the re-
introduction of cash limits, which the Treasury had already
announced, and which Godley supported in his evidence. In the
event, what the Expenditure Committee chose to call 'merely
regressing to a solely cash system' did not occur, and what it
termed a 'PESC plus' system was relied on.20
    That something was called 'a positive planning system' did
not, of course, mean that it would function any better than a
regression to financial tradition. What it was more likely to
be, at least in the short run, was politically easier. In the
era of the Administrative 'Revolution', the only Government
which came to office determined to cut public expenditure, and
with it taxation, was that headed by Edward Heath. This Tory
Government introduced public spending economies as early as

October 1970, and balanced them the following March with a reduction in income tax. The Conservatives pressed ahead with the implementation of a blueprint for tax reform prepared for them in Opposition by Sir Arthur Cockfield, an industrialist and a former Higher Civil Servant in the Inland Revenue. These reforms, included, among other things, a deliberate switch from direct to indirect taxation in the form of Value Added Tax. In practice, the Tory tax reforms were submerged by inflation. The Conservatives found too that containing public spending was easier said than done in the grim economic situation that they had inherited. Brendon Sewill, Special Assistant to Chancellor Anthony Barber, later recalled: 'During the recession it became much harder to keep public expenditure in check. Treasury control of expenditure ... depends ultimately on the Chancellor's strength and support in the Cabinet. Where there is any dispute between the Treasury and a spending department the Treasury officials' only sanction is to threaten that in the last resort the matter will have to be taken to Cabinet. When it is obvious that there is a majority in the Cabinet in favour of increasing expenditure (as is likely when men and resources are lying idle) it becomes comparatively easy to call the Treasury bluff'.21   The Heath Government's resolve to control public expenditure was overwhelmed by the political need that it felt to make a Keynesian response to unemployment. The urgings of the Economic Establishment were only one influence. So was the advocacy by various often well meaning pressure groups of public spending as good in itself. Not in the slightest disinterested was the pressure on the Government exerted by the highly unionized public sector itself. Into the gap spectacularly torn in the Heath Government's defences by the miners, others stormed. The more observant found financially well rewarded Civil Servants within the walls already.

The continuing absence of a sustained climate conducive to financial discipline in the public sector was bound to be undermining of any system of control of public expenditure. The Crown Agents Affair, which blew up in 1977, may well have been exceptional in the lavish scale of the waste of public money involved. More mundane, but still important, was the negative reception that his own department gave to Leslie Chapman's revelations about the economies that his teams had effected in the Southern Region of the Property Services Agency. The reaction of another Regional Director was that 'if Southern could save a third of their budget they must have been very inefficient to start with. I would send my chaps out hoping that they would find little or nothing'. More seriously, when the Public Accounts Committee asked the Chief Executive of the PSA, Sir Robert Cox about Chapman's reforms in 1975 he mis-led it by saying that the greater economies effected by the Southern Region were the result of its disproportionate loss of military personnel in the relevant period. Actually, Chapman's major reforms were achieved in a civil establishment at Bletchley. Yet, when the Public Accounts Committee eventually, and belatedly, confronted Cox with his admitted misinformation, nothing, of course, happened. The only resignation was the earlier one of the frustrated Chapman.22 Forty years before, it is difficult to believe that there would not have been an angry debate in the House of Commons; but sentiments were now different, and Civil Servants had no reason to fear the modern Public Accounts Committee.

By the second half of the 1970s, there were superficial changes in the political climate in which public spending took place. For a time, at least, the introduction of cash limits seemed to moderate financial indiscipline; and, from 1974-75, the Treasury developed a Financial Information System to support cash control. To placate the International Monetary Fund, from whom they needed to borrow vast sums, the Labour Governments of 1974-79 made cuts in public spending. Although they were cuts in capital rather than current expenditure, which meant that they could be restored, and that public sector employment was largely unaffected. Moreover, they were not cuts in absolute terms, but in the projected rate of growth of public spending. With the weakening of the authority of the Keynesians, public expenditure had lost some of its intellectual cachet, although the public sector unions had lost none of their combativeness. It was more widely recognized that future prosperity mainly rested on the wealth creating propensities of the private sector. This recognition was offset, however, by the knowledge of the company sector's generally relatively poor performance in international competition, a situation which, as we shall see, substantial government intervention had not been able to change.

References

1.   Cmnd. 1432 (1961), p. 6.
2.   See e.g. Boyle and Playfair (1965), pp. 251-52, 260-61. To the extent that they differed, Boyle adheres to his position.
3.   Fry (1974), pp. 319-33.
4.   C. Clark, 'Public Finance and Changes in the Value of Money', Economic Journal, 55, (1945), pp. 371-89. Keynes was still the editor of the Economic Journal at the time the article was submitted, and he wrote (in a personal letter to Clark dated 1.5.1944): 'In Great Britain after the War I should guess that your figure of 25 per cent as the maximum tolerable proportion of taxation may be exceedingly near the truth. I should not be at all surprised if we did not find a further confirmation in our post-war experience of your empirical law'. Clark considered that this passage was worth quoting because so many so-called Keynesians had taken Keynes's name in vain as advocating, among other things, unlimited taxation (1970, p. 21).
5.   H.C. 241-I, (1951), p. 1; Bridges (1950), pp. 6-7, 23; Chester (1957), pp. 15-23. The distinguished American was

S.H. Beer, and his book, <u>Treasury Control</u>.
  6.   H.C. 254-I, (1958), pp. xxxvi-xxxvii.
  7.   Cmnd. 1432, (1961), pp. 6-12, 20, 28; Chester (1963),
pp. 3-15; H.C. 254-I, (1958), Evidence, q. 147.
  8.   Cmnd. 1432, (1961), p. 5; Pollitt (1977), pp. 127-
42; Diamond (1975), pp. 137-53; Heclo and Wildavsky (1974),
pp. 151-59, 203-4.
  9.   Cmnd. 1432, (1961), p. 7; Treasury (1972), pp. 5-6.
  10.   Ibid., pp. 4-5, 23-5; Rees and Thompson (1972),
pp. 18, 12-15; H.C. 549, (1971), pp. 18-19.
  11.   Ibid., p. 20; Treasury, (1972), p. 6.
  12.   Ibid., p. 7.
  13.   Ibid., pp. 7-8; H.C. 410, (1969), pp. xiii-xvii;
Silkin (1975), pp. 45-66; H.C. 450, (1972), pp. x-xiii;
Pollitt (1977), p. 137.
  14.   Crossman (1975), pp. 256, 274-75, 283, 285, 289,
403-4, 486, 512, 518, 555-56, 572-73, 578, 607, 615-16;
Crossman (1976), pp. 90, 99, 114, 129-31, 173, 193, 196,
390-91, 398, 407-8, 414, 422, 434, 460; Crossman (1977),
pp. 123, 136, 231-32, 394, 706, 826-27, 832-33, 871-72.
  15.   Cmnd. 4506, (1970), p. 14; Goldman (1973), pp.
45-51.
  16.   Crossman (1975), pp. 615-16; Clarke (1971), pp.
48-9, 117.
  17.   Chapman (1978), pp. 13-55.
  18.   Goldman (1973), pp. 53, 58; Heclo and Wildavsky
(1974), pp. 202-371; Sandford and Robinson (1975), p. 1242;
Wright (1977), pp. 143-69.
  19.   Clarke (1972), pp. 42-3; Goldman (1973), p. 51;
Hurd (1979), pp. 29-30.
  20.   Godley (1976), pp. 58-63; H.C. 69-I, (1975), pp.
v-vii, ix; H.C. 69-II, (1975), Evidence, q. 778, 781, 796 and
p. 224; Wright (1977), pp. 155-56.
  21.   Harris and Sewill (1975), p. 42.
  22.   Chapman (1978), pp. 67, 189-206; H.C. 502, (1975),
Evidence, q. 1318; H.C. 622, (1978), Evidence, q. 3252-57;
<u>The Economist</u>, 17.6.1978, p. 22; Ibid., 7.10.1978, p. 29.

Chapter 6

PICKING UP THE LOSERS?:   THE STATE AND THE PRIVATE SECTOR

'The great art ... to make a nation happy, and what we call
flourishing consists in giving everybody an opportunity of
being employed; which to compass, let a Government's first
care be to promote as great a variety of manufactures, arts and
handicrafts, as human wit can invent; and the second to
encourage agriculture and fishery in all their branches.'
Keynes quoted with evident relish this eighteenth century maxim
from the pen of Bernard Mandeville, whom he hailed as one of
his intellectual precursors.1   Certainly, in the Keynesian
era, all Governments consciously strove to keep the nation
'happy' with high levels of employment; all Governments
encouraged agriculture; and few Governments felt either able or
willing to leave industry and commerce to their own devices for
very long. Even in the Conservative Ascendancy of the 1950s,
there was intervention, not least to try to regulate restrictive trade practices, and to influence industrial location.
From the early 1960s onwards, with a brief interval of
intentional disengagement, both Conservative and Labour Governments engaged in detailed intervention designed to make British
industry more efficient. In the short run, at least, there
were few obvious beneficial results. Indeed, after a decade
and a half of such intervention, the private sector was far
from 'flourishing', especially when confronted by foreign
competition.
     The central government arrangements in relation to
industry and trade were complex even before the Administrative
'Revolution' began. This complexity was not lessened as that
'Revolution' progressed, even in its earlier phase between 1956
and 1964. One reason for its persistence was that some government departments outside the ranks of those normally placed in
the trade and industry category had sponsoring responsibilities,
and were seen as the production department for particular
industries. For example, the Ministry of Works (from 1962, the
Ministry of Public Building and Works) was the production
department for the building, civil engineering and building
materials industries. The Ministry of Health, given its
responsibilities in relation to the National Health Service was

inevitably closely concerned with the production and distribution of a wide range of surgical, dental and optical goods, and with the pharmaceutical industry. The General Post Office, as their largest domestic consumer, acted as the sponsoring department for the makers of telephone and telecommunications equipment. The Post Office was commonly classified as a trade and industry department. So was the Ministry of Labour and National Service (from 1959, Ministry of Labour), although it was a Ministry of Industrial Relations and Welfare and a Ministry of Employment and Manpower, and not a production department. Besides the Post Office and the Ministry of Labour, the trade and industry departments comprised by 1964: the Ministry of Agriculture, Fisheries and Food; the Department of Agriculture and Fisheries for Scotland; the Scottish Development Department; the Board of Trade, including the Export Credits Guarantee Department; the Ministry of Power; and the Ministry of Transport. Some would have added the Ministry of Aviation, formed in 1959 from the old Ministry of Supply and part of the then Ministry of Transport and Civil Aviation. However, despite its civil aviation responsibilities, the Ministry of Aviation was weighted towards defence in terms of personnel and expenditure. The Ministry of Transport had become in effect a Ministry of Inland Transport and Roads, and a Ministry of Shipping, Shipbuilding and the Merchant Navy. The Ministry of Transport, therefore, had some responsibilities in relation to private enterprise, and also nationalized industries. The Ministry of Power (until 1957, the Ministry of Fuel and Power) had dealings mainly with nationalized industries, but also with the privately owned oil companies. The merger of the Ministry of Agriculture and Fisheries with the Ministry of Food in 1955 had the advantage, in theory, that the latter department brought in a responsibility for the consumer that contrasted with what critics called its new partner's tendency to act as a client of the National Farmers' Union. The English arrangements were more closely paralleled in Scotland after 1960, when the Department of Agriculture and Fisheries for Scotland was formed from a merger between the Department of Agriculture and the Fisheries Division of the Scottish Home Department. In 1962, the Scottish Home Department also ceded its responsibilities for industry to the newly formed Scottish Development Department, the establishment of which reflected an intensification of governmental concern about regional economic imbalances.2

The Board of Trade was still the senior government department in the trade and industry group in the first part of the 1960s, by virtue of both age and its range of responsibilities. It was the main point of contact inside central government for all those industries not assigned to other departments. The Board was responsible for all aspects of commercial policy and for the promotion of trade, a duty in which it was aided by the Export Credits Guarantee Department. It was charged with the regulation of commercial practices and property; a duty in which it was aided by the Monopolies Commission and by the Restrictive Practices Court with a Registrar of Restrictive Trade Agreements. The Board of Trade was also, importantly, responsible for the implementation of distribution of industry policy. It was an incursion into the Board's jurisdiction when, in 1963, the Lord President of the Council and Minister for Science, Lord Hailsham was given temporary special responsibilities for reviving industrial activity in the North East. Hailsham attracted ridicule by appearing in the area wearing a cloth cap. Regional policy was by then in political fashion. Another fashionable subject was the relationship between government and science and technology. The Board of Trade had responsibility, for instance, for the National Research Development Corporation. Yet, the Department of Scientific and Industrial Research was the responsibility of the Lord President. The Office of the Minister of Science had been established in 1959. Its responsibilities and some of those of the DSIR accompanied Hailsham into the newly formed Department of Education and Science in 1964. By then, from the Opposition benches, the Labour Party advocated a separate Ministry of Technology to revivify British industry.3

The closer involvement of government with the private sector did not begin with Labour's return to office in 1964. It had been earlier, Conservative Governments who had directed the Ford Motor Company to Halewood, the British Motor Corporation to Bathgate, and Rootes to Linwood. The Local Employment Act 1960 marked an intensification of governmental interest in promoting industrial development, and an elaboration of inducements. The little Neddies were the microeconomic counterpart of the NEDC itself, and their establishment ushered in a period of detailed State intervention in the private sector, in which there was only one short, incomplete break. The period between 1962 and 1979 can be divided into three parts: the era of Planning, Mintech, and the Industrial Reorganization Corporation 1962-70; the interlude of Lame Ducks and of Disengagement 1970-72; and the Age of the Industry Acts and of the National Enterprise Board 1972-79. In the first and third periods, Governments, particularly Labour Governments, committed themselves to picking out the winners, in terms of both industries and companies, to support. At least as often, they seemed to end in picking up the losers. Even in its Disengagement phase, the Heath Government was forced to pick up the losers too. Before the end of the Administrative 'Revolution', it was conventional wisdom that, in the contemporary British political climate, State intervention in industry was bound to have largely negative returns. Yet, it is worth noting here, especially as we shall not return to the subject, that in the same political atmosphere, British agriculture had been heavily subsidized by the State, and had become, on some estimates, the most efficient farming industry in the world.

I   THE ERA OF PLANNING, MINTECH AND THE IRC 1962-70

The necessity for greater State intervention in private
industry to promote the Britain that was to be forged in the
'white heat' of the 'scientific revolution' was argued for by
Harold Wilson before coming to office in 1964. Institutionally,
nothing less than 'a full Ministry of Science' was needed,4 and
a Ministry of Technology was established. The Wilson Government did prove to be more avowedly interventionist in private
industry than its Conservative predecessors, an approach
typified by the creation of the Industrial Reorganization
Corporation. The Tories had attempted to secure greater
efficiency through more competition. Labour tried to combine
this approach with encouraging industrial concentration and
supposedly backing winners. There was continuity in the
spheres of economic planning - until the National Plan was
abandoned - and in regional policy. Labour added to the
number of institutions, increasing the number of little Neddies
and establishing the Regional Economic Planning Boards, at
first under DEA chairmanship, and Regional Economic Planning
Councils. Although surrounded by institutional change, threats
of more of the same, and experiencing the loss of some
functions, the Board of Trade survived down to 1970.
    Earlier, in 1963-64, the Board of Trade's position had
been strengthened when Edward Heath was not only its President
but also Secretary of State for Industry, Trade and Regional
Development, and a leading figure in the Home Government.
Heath drove through the abolition of resale price maintenance.
He anticipated too changes in policy regarding monopolies,
restrictive practices and mergers, some of which Labour legislation implemented in 1965 and 1968. The reputation of the
Monopolies Commission had never seemed to recover from its
earlier record. Then, on one estimate, its pace of work was
so slow that, if maintained, it would take the Commission
8,000 years to cover the whole of private industry. The Board
of Trade's reputation did not seem to rate highly with its
former President, Harold Wilson. He later complained of the
Board's laissez-faire attitudes, compared its work in regional
policy unfavourably with the DEA, and tended to take functions
away from the Board. In the autumn of 1969, for example,
Wilson transferred responsibilities for mergers and monopolies
to the DEP. He also transferred most of the industrial
sponsorship responsibilities that the Board of Trade still had
to the Ministry of Technology. The Board was left with what
Wilson called certain 'transcendental' responsibilities,
providing services to industry and commerce including company
law, insurance, patents and copyright, and consumer protection.
This was together with what he termed non-industrial 'industries' such as distribution, newspapers, printing and publishing and films. Otherwise, the Board was intended by Wilson to
concentrate on exports, shipping and civil aviation. The Board
of Trade's responsibilities for regional industrial policy also

went to the Ministry of Technology, thus bringing together the sponsorship of major industries and decisions affecting their location, whether in the development areas or elsewhere.5

The Ministry of Technology was established in 1964, because, according to Harold Wilson, he had long felt that government needed to undertake two functions which existing departments were inadequate to perform. The first task was that of a 'Ministry for Industry'. Starting with a relatively small number of industries, but taking on a wider and wider sponsorship, the Ministry of Technology was intended to have a very direct responsibility for increasing productivity and efficiency, particularly within those industries in urgent need of restructuring or modernization. The second task of the Ministry of Technology was to speed the application of new scientific methods to industrial production. Wilson saw the new Ministry as 'NRDC writ large' and placed that institution under its charge. The Ministry took over the technological work previously done under the aegis of the Lord President of the Council, together with the responsibilities for industrial technology previously undertaken by a department of the Board of Trade. Wilson said that he intended that the Ministry should in due course incorporate the aircraft production section of the Ministry of Aviation, including that department's responsibilities for electronics and avionics. He thought that this would take time. So would the transfer to the new Ministry of responsibilities for engineering, ship-building and related industries. However, in the case of the computer industry, Wilson believed that time was not on his side. 'When, on the evening we took office, I asked Frank Cousins to become the first Minister of Technology', Wilson recalled, 'I told him that he had, in my view, about a month to save the British computer industry and that this must be his first priority. He succeeded'.6

Whether or not this melodramatic behaviour was in fact justified, what remained unclear was the need for a Ministry of Technology at all, certainly in the forms in which it existed down to October 1969. Its first Permanent Secretary, Sir Maurice Dean later recalled that early on the Ministry was repeatedly asked what it had actually done in the last six months. There were many times, he said, when an honest answer would have been 'much of our time is taken up with answering questions about what we are doing'. Dean's successor, Sir Richard Clarke later doubted whether the establishment of Mintech in its original form was the best way to set about the immense task of modernization of industry to which the Labour Government was committed. If large scale direct State inter-vention was needed, then a powerful department was required to conceive the necessary action, to plan it, and to carry it out. In retrospect, it seemed to Clarke that any of three other possible courses in October 1964 might have been better. The first of these would have been to have made the Board of Trade specifically responsible for industrial modernization and technology, and to have ensured that it was Ministered, manned and organized accordingly. Eight years (and four major changes in the machinery of government for industry) later, what Clarke called a powerful Industrial Development Executive had been established in the DTI, which dealt with industrial, commercial and technological considerations alike. Could this have been reached in one operation in October 1964 ? Clarke, unlike the author, thought probably not. However, Clarke did ask whether it was really necessary to go round an eight year circuit of reorganization and change to get there. The second possibility envisaged by Sir Richard Clarke was the establishment of a technological wing in the DEA: he believed that it might have been advantageous to have set up one new central industrial and economic department instead of two. The third possibility was to give immediately to Mintech the responsibility and staffs for sponsorships of engineering and shipbuilding and perhaps the other manufacturing industries, with aircraft production to come after examination. Had the intention been announced and urgency displayed, Clarke believed that Mintech in its October 1969 form could have been created four years earlier. He thought that any of the three courses indicated might have stood a better chance of getting a major modernization effort moving by, say, the end of 1965.[7]

The Ministry of Technology as it actually developed took three different forms. For, it was involved in two major mergers with other departments: one with the Ministry of Aviation in February 1967; and the other with the Ministry of Power taking in also large elements of the Board of Trade and the DEA in October 1969. Each of these mergers involved a complete reconstitution of the Ministry's functions and structure. Sir Richard Clarke said that the merger with Aviation converted the Ministry of Technology (or first Mintech) into a Ministry of Engineering (or second Mintech) and the 1969 changes converted it again into a Ministry of Industry (or third Mintech). The merger with Aviation was viewed with apprehension by some officials within the first Mintech because of the problems of Concorde and defence aviation. However, the view which prevailed was that it was absurd to have a Ministry of Technology which had no say in the Government's biggest stake in advanced technology, aircraft and electronics. The conversion of Mintech into a Ministry of Industry except in name in 1969 followed from the allocation to it of sponsorship of textiles, chemicals and other manufacturing industries from the Board of Trade; regional industrial policy and investment grant administration also from the Board; the transfer of the whole of the Ministry of Power; and the acquisition also of some DEA responsibilities, including the IRC, with which body Mintech had been closely associated from the start.[8]

The Industrial Reorganization Corporation was established in 1966. The Labour Government acted on the assumption that there was 'a need for more concentration and rationalization to

promote the greater efficiency and international competitive-
ness of British industry'. It said that many production units
in Britain were small by comparison with the most successful
companies in international trade, whose operations were often
based on a much larger market. Given its belief that market
forces alone would not produce the necessary structural changes
at the pace required, the Wilson Government felt the need to
establish the IRC to fill what it identified as an institutional gap. It was the intention that, whenever possible, the IRC
was to work through the normal machinery of the market. It was
to be able to acquire a stake in the ownership of new groupings
or enterprises that it helped to create or expand. However,
the IRC was not to act as a general holding company, and it
would be able to dispose of its investments when the profits of
nationalization had been realized. The Government emphasized
that the IRC was to give 'priority to schemes of rationalization and modernization which offer good prospects of early
returns in terms of increased exports or reduced import
requirements', and it was to have regard to 'the regional
aspects of the Government's policies for economic development'.
The Government was clear that the IRC would not support
ventures which had no prospect of achieving eventual
viability.9
      These were brave words, and a former Director later
described the IRC's role in almost heroic terms. Apparently,
this role was 'active, initiatory, discretionary or dis-
criminatory, non-bureaucratic, commercially-oriented, change-
promoting, almost if you like, free-wheeling, wheeler-dealing
and buccaneering. The best of British merchant-venturing was
for once harnessed to the public interest above all else. The
IRC was also experimental'. Indeed, in practice, the accountability of the IRC was doubtful. While it had a close working
relationship with government departments, and particularly with
Anthony Wedgwood Benn, successor to Cousins as Minister of
Technology, the IRC had a large degree of independence. The
IRC was effectively a government merchant bank, and it had no
difficulty in recruiting the necessary executives from the
private sector to sustain what remained a fairly small
organization. However, of the major mergers that the IRC
promoted, in retrospect only that which by September 1968 had
led to the amalgamation of the General Electric Company with,
first, English Electric and, then, Associated Electrical
Industries seemed to make obvious commercial sense. Whatever
the justifications advanced in the other major examples of
intervention, economic nationalism and social factors seemed
more important than any 'buccaneering' pursuit of industrial
efficiency. Hence, the IRC's determined creation of a major
British owned ball bearings company in the form of Ransome
Hoffman Pollard; its interventions in the computer and
machine tools industries (notably, involving Alfred Herbert);
and the merger of British Motor Holdings and British Leyland
to form the British Leyland Motor Corporation. Less willingly,

the IRC was induced by the Labour Government to take a minority holding when Chrysler took over Rootes Motors in 1967. Rolls Royce received substantial financial support from the IRC in 1969, and the promise of more, although the company was already in difficulties because of its commitment to the manufacture of the RB211 engine. Social factors played their part in the aid given to Cammell Laird, the shipbuilding and engineering firm. The IRC described itself as 'a prod and not a prop'. It turned out to be both, and it was not immediately obvious whether the IRC's prodding had been in directions which promoted greater industrial efficiency.10

The same could be said of Mintech, which never had the resources to have fulfilled its original assignment of 'stimulating a major national effort to bring advanced technology and new processes into British industry'. Mintech became a large industrial-technological department, and one which Sir Richard Clarke described as having a more positive and less regulatory relationship with private industry than had been the normal practice. Important changes in industrial structure resulted, some generated by the IRC, and some following from the direct intervention of Mintech. The contentious Industrial Expansion Act of 1968 was in fact little used. Although it did provide the means by which, for example, the British Aluminium and Rio Tinto Zinc smelter projects were supported. It was the instrument used too, when, in mid-1968, the objective of establishing a broadly based British owned computer manufacturing company was achieved with the creation of International Computers Ltd, which became the only substantial indigenous computer firm in Europe. Mintech's involvement in advanced technology in the civil aviation field was dogged from the outset by the inherited problems of Rolls Royce and Concorde. Sir Richard Clarke later said that if in 1962 there had been in existence the system of financial and economic appraisal which Mintech developed, the Concorde project would have failed the test, as the European airbus did in 1969.11 With projects like the establishment of Upper Clyde Shipbuilders in February 1968, Mintech had its own record of prospective failures, besides British Leyland and Alfred Herbert. Mintech may have backed some winners, but it certainly left a legacy of losers behind it too.

II THE INTERLUDE OF LAME DUCKS AND OF DISENGAGEMENT 1970-72

Disengagement from private industry and an unwillingness to sustain its 'lame ducks' were the early watchwords of the Heath Government in industrial policy. The IRC was abolished. Mintech was absorbed into a newly formed Department of Trade and Industry.

The Conservatives were unhappy with the division of work between the Board of Trade and the Ministry of Technology existing in 1970. They believed that creating a unified Department of Trade and Industry would have several advantages.

It avoided what the Heath Government saw as an unreal dichotomy between the department responsible for export promotion and overseas commercial policy and the department responsible for the bulk of government relations with industry. It made possible an effective strategy for the delegation of executive tasks. It averted the division of responsibility for government relations with publicly and privately owned enterprises operating in the same sector which would arise if responsibility for nationalized industries and privately owned industry were separated from each other. (Actually they were largely unified under the third Mintech from October 1969.) The creation of the DTI was supposed to greatly simplify industry's contacts with government by ensuring that a single department was responsible over virtually the whole field (except for manpower questions) making possible clearer identification of responsibilities and better communication. General industrial and commercial services (company law, standards, patents etc.) would be the responsibility of the same department as were the Government's relations with specific industries; and both manufacturing and service industries would be part of the same field of responsibility. The allocation of public resources to industry, both public and private sector would, with few exceptions, fall within the responsibility of a single Minister, making possible both the formulation and the consistent operation of a single policy. The unified structure was supposed to have advantages in the context of membership of the EEC, although it was not stated what these advantages were. The Heath Government duly established the DTI which took over the functions of the Board of Trade and those of Mintech (other than its responsibilities for aerospace research, development and procurement), and also had transferred to it from the DEP responsibility for monopolies, mergers and restrictive trade practices. A Secretary of State for Trade and Industry was appointed, who also held the historic office of President of the Board of Trade. Supported by two Ministers with delegated functions, the Secretary of State's primary concern was supposed to be with strategic issues of policy and priority.12

As an instrument of government, the DTI may or may not have been a more efficient organization than its predecessors: but, in the political climate of the 1970s, what could not survive for long was the original strategy it was required to pursue. The first Secretary of State John Davies, a former Director General of the CBI, lacked parliamentary experience. The term 'lame ducks' was first uttered under Labour pressure in the House. Nevertheless, it was neither lack of debating skills, nor of commitment on the part of Davies and junior Ministers like Sir John Eden and Nicholas Ridley, that defeated the Tories. Disengagement was easier said than done. Investment grants could be scrapped and regional policy could be modified. The IRC could be abolished and Mintech could be absorbed elsewhere. What could not be as easily disposed of was the legacy of expectations that ailing companies would be supported and uneconomic ventures propped up. The failure of two inherited projects destroyed the 'lame ducks' policy. When the cost of the RB-211 engine overwhelmed Rolls Royce, the company was allowed to go bankrupt. Nevertheless, the damage that the demise of Rolls Royce would do to defence capability led to the bulk of the company being nationalized. Then, Wedgwood Benn's creation, Upper Clyde Shipbuilders was allowed to go into liquidation, only to be rescued in the face of intense local pressure, successfully led by a Communist agitator. To fears about unemployment was added the warning from the Chief Constable of Glasgow that unless UCS was rescued he would need another 15,000 police to control the situation. The Heath Government surrendered. By March 1972, the interlude of 'lame ducks' and disengagement was over.13

III THE AGE OF THE INDUSTRY ACTS AND OF THE NEB 1972-79

It was the doubtful privilege of John Davies to have to announce the Heath Government's U turn in industry policy. He received a standing ovation from the Labour benches. The regional development grants which he announced - and which were legislated for in the Industry Act 1972 - looked very much like Labour's investment grants that Davies had discarded. Davies himself survived as Secretary of State until October 1972 when he was replaced by Peter Walker. Eden and Ridley had departed six months earlier. Their ministerial replacements, Tom Boardman and Christopher Chataway, were sympathetic to interventionism. Chataway believed that 'to say that government had better leave it all alone because it is sure to get the answers wrong is a counsel of despair in the modern world, for all governments are bound to be involved'. Chataway was made Minister for Industrial Development in April 1972. Under the broad direction of the Secretary of State for Trade and Industry, this Minister had special responsibility for private sector industry generally, and for industrial development in assisted areas. The Minister took charge of an Industrial Development Executive, which included the divisions of the DTI concerned with regional development and small firms, and the DTI's regional offices. The Minister was assisted by a Permanent Secretary, and a Director of Industrial Development appointed from the private sector. Within the Executive a Development Unit was also set up to help with the appraisal and implementation of industrial development needs. The Executive recruited staff from the City and industry to provide it with a range of financial, industrial and administrative experience. The Minister was advised by an Industrial Development Board, composed of representatives drawn from industry, banking, accounting and finance, and international industrial investment. The Board was to advise generally on industry-wide problems and priorities, and to consider specific major cases for selective assistance. In addition, Regional Industrial Directors and Regional Development Boards were appointed to work alongside the existing regional economic machinery.14

The Heath Government's essays in institutional change in the sphere of industry policy did not stop there. The Price Commission, for example, was established in April 1973. In the following November, the Government created an independent office, the Director General of Fair Trading, and a statutory committee, the Consumer Protection Advisory Committee. They received formally greater powers than were previously available in the area of consumer protection. The Fair Trading Act of 1973 also abolished the office of Registrar of Restrictive Trading Agreements, and renamed the Monopolies Commission as the Monopolies and Mergers Commission. The establishment of a Department of Energy in January 1974, in the wake of the Oil Crisis, marked the partial dismemberment of the DTI. The whole of the Industry Group of the DTI, apart from the Industrial Development Executive and the Iron and Steel Division, was transferred to the new department, which became the sponsoring department for the nationalized energy industries and the oil industry.15

The remainder of the DTI was broken up into Departments of Industry, of Trade, and of Prices and Consumer Protection, when Labour returned to office in March 1974. The Department of Industry was made responsible for general industrial policy, both national and regional, and for the sponsorship of individual manufacturing industries, including iron and steel, aircraft and shipbuilding. It also provided common services for the other former parts of the DTI. The Department of Trade was made responsible for general overseas trade policy, commercial relations, exports and tariffs, for civil aviation and shipping policy, and for the oversight of such matters as company legislation. The Department of Prices and Consumer Protection was responsible for the retained Price Commission; for work connected with monopolies, mergers and restrictive practices; and for the activities of the Director General of Fair Trading.16 These institutional changes did not mask the continuity of industrial policy between the latter Heath Government and its successor. For example, it was Christopher Chataway who, in March 1973, first tried to rescue the British motor cycle industry from its commercial fate, even if it was Anthony Wedgwood Benn who flamboyantly supported the workers' co-operative at Meriden with public money. More generally, in the eighteen months in which he was Secretary for Industry from March 1974 onwards, Benn made full use of the powers given him by the Industry Act of 1972. What mainly differed was the rhetoric, for Benn tended to appeal to the expectations aroused in the Labour Party in Opposition about the efficacy of planning agreements with leading private companies, and about the changes that would follow from the establishment of a National Enterprise Board.

To the extent that there was a practical model for this Board as originally proposed, it was the Italian Institute for Industrial Reconstruction (IRI) which dated from the Fascist dictatorship of Benito Mussolini. To some this seemed a strange choice, but not to those who remembered Mussolini's early socialist training. The National Enterprise Board which (together with a Scottish Development Agency and a Welsh Development Agency) was actually established in November 1975 was a different body from that originally envisaged. While the NEB did not lack formal powers for intervening in private industry, it was denied a strategic power and the funds that went with it. From the outset, the NEB's activities were dominated by the holdings transferred to it. British Leyland (nationalized in 1975 and later called BL) and Rolls Royce together contributed 92 per cent to NEB turnover in the first six months of 1978, 92 per cent to NEB profits in the same period, and had taken up nearly 94 per cent of loans made by the NEB. Transferee companies as a whole had taken up 98 per cent of the total loans made. The NEB was mainly involved with taking care of 'lame ducks'. Otherwise in the area of activity available to it, as the requirement made in 1977 that the NEB should look for a 15 to 20 per cent return on its capital by 1981 suggested, the NEB had tended to act more as a State investment bank operating on commercial criteria.17

The relative decline of British manufacturing industry, marked by what some saw as a falling rate of industrial profitability, had not been arrested by the institutional innovations and the greater interventionism that had character- ized the period since 1962. Indeed, some of the major problem companies were the creations of Mintech and the IRC. No sooner had the Labour Government launched its Industrial Strategy in November 1975 than the Chrysler car company demanded to be rescued. When interventionism had been begun in the early 1960s, the British motor car industry had seemed a growth industry; but, a decade and a half later, parts of it - certainly, the British owned part - were ailing. There was little likelihood of a subsidized BL and Chrysler both being viable in the foreseeable future. Yet, the Government of the day understandably shrank away from the consequences for employment of letting either company go under. From full employment to what was literally called Job Creation had taken less than a decade from 1966. British private industry was short of winners, but not of losers, some of the consequences of earlier State ventures. Some of the losers were little more than social services for those working for them, pre-empting resources that, ideally, might be better used elsewhere; for example, in the social services proper.

References

1. Keynes (1936), pp. 359-62, 371, actually slightly misquoted Mandeville's _Fable of the Bees_ (1714; 1924 edn., Vol. 1, p. 197) and certainly generally misinterpreted him. Mandeville was more obviously a precursor of Adam Smith - despite the latter's strictures.

2.   Grove (1962), pp. 84-5, 88-108;   Chester and
Willson (1968), pp. 353-63.
3.   Ibid., pp. 357, 368-72;   Grove (1962), pp. 85-8; 272;
Vig (1968), pp. 34-54.
4.   Report of the 62nd Annual Conference of the Labour
Party, pp. 137, 140.
5.   Cmnd. 2299, (1964);   Blackaby (1978), pp. 422-28;
Worswick and Ady (1952), p. 413;   Wilson (1971), pp. 5, 244-45,
269-70, 709, 710.
6.   Ibid., pp. 8-9. For another view of the origins of
Mintech: Lester (1973), p. 92.
7.   Dean (1966), pp. 43-60;   Clarke (1973), I, pp. 29-30.
8.   Ibid., pp. 29-30.
9.   Cmnd. 2889, (1966), pp. 2-3.
10.   McClelland (1972), pp. 23-42;   Beesley and White
(1973), pp. 61-89;   Blackaby (1978), pp. 431-39;   Young and
Lowe (1974), pp. 189, 231-36;   H.C. 286, (1969), p. 9.
11.   Clarke (1973), 2, pp. 137-62.
12.   Cmnd. 4506, (1970), pp. 7-9.
13.   805 H.C. Deb. 5s. c. 1211;   Bruce-Gardyne (1974),
pp. 30-7, 78, 155-56;   Blackaby (1978), pp. 420-21, 456, 466-67.
14.   Ibid., p. 480;   Bruce-Gardyne (1974), pp. 79-80;
Cmnd. 4942 (1972),pp. 5-6.
15.   Steel and Stanyer (1975), pp. 245, 247-48.
16.   Ibid., pp. 245-46;   Cmnd. 5710, (1974).
17.   Holland (1972), pp. 5-44, 56, 61, 220, 221;   Parr
(1979), pp. 51-62.

Chapter 7

STRIVING TO BE THE UNIVERSAL PROVIDER: EDUCATION AND THE
SOCIAL SERVICES

.

'The eyes of the world are turning to Great Britain. We now
have the moral leadership of the world and before many years we
shall have people coming here as to a modern Mecca, learning
from us in the twentieth century as they learned from us in the
seventeenth century.' Thus, Aneurin Bevan extolled the
virtues of the British Welfare State on the eve of July 5th
1948, the day on which the National Health Service and the
Beveridge social security schemes came into operation.   The
British Welfare State was one in which organized power was
deliberately used through politics and administration in an
effort to modify the play of market forces in at least three
directions. First, by guaranteeing individuals and families a
minimum income irrespective of the market value of their work
or their property. Secondly, by narrowing the extent of in-
security by contingencies (for example, sickness, old age and
unemployment) which would otherwise lead to individual and
family crises. Thirdly, by ensuring that all citizens without
distinction of status or class were offered the best standards
available in relation to a certain agreed range of social
services. Together with some smaller services such as child
care, the main categories of government provided or subsidized
services which led Britain to be described as a Welfare State
both were and are education, medical care, social security, and
housing.1 The realization of many of the aims of the Welfare
State was made easier by the attainment of full employment
for so long after 1945.   Similarly, the economic growth with
which the Managed Economy was also for so long associated
obviously facilitated finding the resources to improve
services. Nevertheless, the relative economic decline that
Britain experienced, despite this growth, helped to ensure
that she never became 'a Modern Mecca'. Some of her rivals,
particularly those with better economic records, had taken
the opportunity to develop social services on a more generous
scale than Britain's. The main worshippers at 'Mecca' tended
to be Britain's own citizens, especially academic authorities
led by Richard Titmuss. They displayed a remarkable insular-
ity, except when it came to importing Galbraithian notions to

support those of Crosland. The Welfare State never was the Universal Provider. The individual was always better placed - where this was at all practicable - when he was able to rely on family, friends or neighbours to sustain him, and voluntary societies persisted too. Yet, the public had - and were encouraged by Labour politicians particularly to have - expectations of universal State welfare; and not just expectations of more services but of better ones. In a context of relative economic decline, demographic pressures, and almost continuous scientific and medical advances, the gap between actual government provision and popular expectations tended to widen. The apparent economies offered by institutional reform were particularly attractive. Its focus was largely directed at the local level, the one at which social policy was mainly administered. There were important changes in the relevant areas of the central government machinery too.

In 1956, when the British Welfare State was still widely thought to be second to none, there were five government departments with responsibilities for the social services: the Ministry of Education, the Ministry of Health, the Ministry of Housing and Local Government, the Ministry of Pensions and National Insurance, and the Home Office. In addition, there was the National Assistance Board. There were also three Scottish departments with social administration responsibilities: the Scottish Education Department, the Scottish Home Department, and the Department of Health for Scotland. Over the next twenty years, it was the exceptional institution which escaped undergoing at least one of the processes of the Administrative 'Revolution': either re-naming, re-allocation of functions, or merger. The exception was the Scottish Education Department, which still retained the same name and similar functions. The Home Office still kept its name, while losing some of its social policy responsibilities and gaining others. The first of the general changes took place in 1962 with the establishment of the Scottish Development Department, and the merger which created the Scottish Home and Health Department. Down to 1970, no less than three 'federal' departments were formed which had social policy functions: the Department of Education and Science, the Department of Health and Social Security, and the Department of the Environment. In the meantime, the National Assistance Board had been re-named. Other bodies came and went, and not only in the controversial sphere of race relations. The notion that government could promote racial harmony was symptomatic of widely held contemporary assumptions about the efficacy of State action. The political belief, fostered by the intellectual dominance of Crosland, Galbraith and Titmuss, that there were few social problems which could not be cured by more public spending gave the period from the early 1960s down to 1973-74 a unity that makes a chronological treatment of administrative change in relation to social provision too repetitive. In this chapter, the main areas of administrative change are discussed separately.

I THE FORMATION OF THE DEPARTMENT OF EDUCATION AND SCIENCE

The actual provision of education was not the direct responsibility of the Department of Education and Science when it was
established in 1964 any more than it was of the Ministry it
absorbed. As far as education in State schools in England and
Wales was concerned, this remained the responsibility of the
local education authorities. The DES, like the Ministry of
Education before it, provided the legislative framework within
which the local authorities operated, together with some
central supervision and control. The main additions to the
central department's responsibilities made at the time of the
merger or shortly afterwards were those relating to civil
science, the universities, and the arts. The inclusion of
civil science was probably reflective of the contemporary and
potentially important debate, popularized by C P Snow, about
science being treated as the inferior of the 'two cultures'.The
debate might have been more usefully concentrated on the
relative standing of technology. There seemed to be a
political need by the early 1960s to be seen doing something
about the position of civil science. Leaving government
responsibility for it with Research Councils, the Department
of Scientific and Industrial Research, and (from 1959) a
Minister for Science was apparently not enough. The Trend
Report of 1963 on civil science had seen 'obvious advantages
in an arrangement whereby responsibility for higher education
and responsibility for civil scientific policy were vested in
one and the same Minister'. However, the Report did not
proceed to indicate what these advantages were. The lack of an
alternative as likely to be acceptable to the scientific
community was one. Further encouragement of any notion that
scientific research preferably should be impractical was an
argument against. The bringing of higher education within the
remit of the DES in any case gave it a broader role than the
Ministry of Education had performed. Although, in 1970, this
role was cut back once more when the Welsh Office assumed
responsibility for primary and secondary education in the
Principality.2
    Whether the creation of the DES structure made for a more
effective instrument of government than the Ministry of
Education had been under, say, Conservative Ministers such as
Sir David Eccles or Sir Edward Boyle was difficult to establish. The record of Anthony Crosland as Labour Secretary of
State for two and a half critical years from early 1965 was not
related to the structure. Crosland came to the DES armed with
his egalitarian creed, but with no plans for putting it into
practice. He scorned 'the melancholy waiters' who urged him to
wait for more research or to wait for some official Report.
So, for example, in his Woolwich Speech, which he later saw as
an 'appalling blunder', Crosland announced at once his policy
of developing the polytechnics as part of a binary system of
higher education. He seemed to act as if resources were

readily available, and that, in any case, what was done had to be undone. Resources were later more restricted: hence, following the devaluation of 1967, the Labour Government was forced to leave to its successor the task of fulfilling its commitment to raising the school leaving age. Margaret Thatcher, the Conservative Secretary of State between 1970 and 1974, was able to do this. She was not able to undo the Crosland legacy. This was certainly the case with the comprehensive schooling policy which Crosland urged on local education authorities in his famous Circular 10/65. Whereas in 1965 under 9 per cent of the maintained secondary school population of England and Wales were in comprehensive schools, in 1975 the figure was about 70 per cent.3   On the other hand, at the same time, the Public Schools Commission set up by Crosland in 1965 had proved ineffective in undermining the position of private education. So, what Crosland did may have been Progressive, but it less obviously represented progress in his own terms of securing greater equality of opportunity.

II   THE GENESIS OF THE DEPARTMENT OF THE ENVIRONMENT

The genesis of the Department of the Environment set up in 1970 was more complicated than that of Education and Science. It was a merger of no less than three important departments: the Ministries of Transport, Public Building and Works, and Housing and Local Government. The last named Ministry had its origins in the Ministry of Health formed in 1919. When the original Ministry was divided up in January 1951, a Ministry of Local Government and Planning was established. When the Conservatives returned in the following October, committed to the famous 300,000 houses a year target, the Minister responsible, Macmillan said that 'it was at once clear that the Ministry must be re-christened, in order to pin the Housing flag firmly to the masthead'. The title of Ministry of Housing and Local Government was misleading according to its later, famed Permanent Secretary, Dame Evelyn Sharp. This was because the Ministry had four main functions of equal importance, if not equal political interest, and only two were mentioned. The four were public health; housing; town and country planning; and the system, powers and finance of local government in England and - until the advent of the Welsh Office - Wales. Some blurring of departmental responsibilities took place after 1962 when the Conservatives translated the Ministry of Works into the Ministry of Public Building and Works. The changed Ministry was to have special responsibilities for the building industry, including that, for example, displayed in the operation of a swiftly enlarged departmental empire that embraced the bulk of the works responsibilities of the former Service departments. The Ministry of Housing directly ceded certain powers relating to the control of building. Under Labour, one reason why building for the Services was not transferred to the Ministry of Defence was that Denis Healey was persuaded by

Charles Pannell - one of his few personal political allies - that his prestige as Minister of Public Building and Works depended on keeping this role. His Prime Minister described Pannell as bringing 'a pugnacious energy to the somewhat placid Ministry of Works'. Nevertheless, this 'pugnacious' pilot was dropped immediately after the 1966 Election.4

A separate Ministry of Land and Planning would have been created in 1964 if Harold Wilson's original inclinations had been followed. Land had been an issue in the 1964 Election. Labour had committed itself to lowering the price of building land. The means of doing this included the establishment of a Land Commission. Dame Evelyn Sharp, whom he found 'a tremendous and dominating character', convinced the Minister of Housing, Richard Crossman, that his department had been 'sold down the river' by his having initially agreed to the new Ministry. Crossman would only be in titular charge of the Labour Government's promised housing drive if, on the one hand, Public Building and Works ran all the materials and labour side of housing, and, on the other, the new Ministry ran land and physical planning. As 'the whole basis of her department' was threatened, the Dame waged a 'Whitehall war' to keep physical planning in the Ministry of Housing. She succeeded. The new department was made the Ministry of Land and Natural Resources, and it was wound up in early 1967. Its role had been mainly confined to setting up the Land Commission, itself abolished in 1971 by the Tories. Following the July 1966 measures, the Land Commission was only given very limited funds. Dame Evelyn was probably right when she said that the Commission was doomed to ineffectualness anyway because of its lack of links with local authorities. Labour did not make the same mistake with the Community Land Act 1975: it was a municipalization measure.5

The end of the separate existence of Dame Evelyn's beloved Ministry was indicated when, in October 1969, Crosland was made Secretary of State for Local Government and Planning charged with - among other things - preparing a merger of the Ministries of Transport and of Housing and Local Government. Wilson later decided to add the Ministry of Public Building and Works. The 1970 Election intervened before these mergers could be completed, and the resulting Department of the Environment was actually established by the Heath Government. Except in Scotland and Wales where the Scottish and Welsh Offices continued to play the major part, the Department was made 'responsible for the whole range of functions which affect people's living environment'. The Government said that 'it is increasingly accepted that maintaining a decent environment, improving people's living conditions and providing for adequate transport facilities all come together in the planning of development. These are among the main functions of local authorities and are having an ever increasing impact on ordinary people, in town and country and especially in and around the larger urban areas. Because these functions interact, and because they give rise to acute and conflicting requirements, a new form of organization is needed at the centre of the administrative system'. This unification of functions was thought to place central government in a better position to deal with the reorganization of local government, then about to be embarked upon. The rationale behind the establishment of the DOE seemed to be similar to that which led to the creation of the first Ministry of Health in 1919. Then it was thought that if public and personal health were brought together in a big Ministry this would not only be administratively neater, but also the subject matters would receive the attention they merited. Environment might well be a 'horrible word' as Dame Evelyn Sharp said, but it was also a fashionable one in the late 1960s and early 1970s when the problems posed by pollution interested some of the politically aware. A specially created, big Department of the Environment had its political attractions. From an organizational point of view, it is difficult to believe that as far as central government was concerned much change was needed. The Ministry of Housing and Local Government had piloted through a Clean Air Act in 1956, and had established responsibilities in the field of pollution control. As Dame Evelyn herself said, essentially what the Ministry was concerned with was the environment: the physical conditions in which people live.6   If change there had to be it could have taken the form of adding to this Ministry the more recently acquired building industry responsibilities of the Ministry of Public Building and Works. The other functions of that Ministry could have been hived off to a Property Services Agency of the type actually created in 1972. However, to have retained a renamed, even expanded Ministry of Housing and Local Government perhaps would have been less politically dramatic than setting up a Department of the Environment including Transport. Its creation could be more easily presented as being indicative of governmental recognition of the importance of pollution and the environment.

The DOE including Transport was a conglomerate. Peter Walker, as Secretary of State between 1970 and 1972, felt the need to take special steps to coordinate a ministerial team that contained Ministers for Local Government and Development, for Housing and Construction, and for Transport Industries, as well as junior Ministers. Walker held a meeting every morning at the DOE (as he was to do at the DTI too) with all his Ministers. The meeting took place at about 08.45 hrs and normally ended between 09.15 and 09.30 hrs. There was no agenda and no minutes. There were no Civil Servants present. Any Minister could raise any topic he wished, and Walker found these meetings vital in controlling such large departments. On any major issue affecting the DOE, for example, the reform of housing finance and the reform of local government, Walker would ask all the Ministers to a meeting to agree the basic policy so that every Minister, no matter what his individual responsibilities, knew the strategy and contributed to it on the big issues. About once every five or six months all the

Ministers would go away for the weekend together from the Friday afternoon until Sunday evening, again without Civil Servants. These weekends were totally devoted to the long term strategy of the department. In addition, once a month Walker took the five Permanent Secretaries in the department to dinner, meeting at his office at 17.00 hrs and normally the evening finished around midnight.7   The DOE was associated with important reorganizations of local government and water authorities. Nevertheless, these measures were not ones which seemed to derive any obvious benefit from the existence of the DOE in its particular form. The DOE itself was the subject of reorganization in September 1976, when its transport functions were transferred to a new Department of Transport, headed by a Secretary of State with a seat in the Cabinet. At the same time, the number of senior Ministers in the DOE was reduced to a Secretary of State and a Minister for Housing and Construction. The structure of the DOE now resembled what it might well have been like if the simpler merger of the former Ministries of Housing and of Public Building and Works had been made in 1970.

III   THE ESTABLISHMENT OF THE DHSS AND OF THE SUPPLEMENTARY BENEFITS COMMISSION

Disparateness of responsibilities was a feature which the first DOE shared with the Department of Health and Social Security, formed in 1968. In the health and social security spheres, the Conservatives bequeathed to their Labour successors in 1964 central government administrative arrangements which consisted of the Ministry of Health, the Ministry of Pensions and National Insurance, and the National Assistance Board. Since the changes in its responsibilities made in 1951, the Ministry of Health had become largely a Ministry for the National Health Service. After Bevan, its Minister was not usually of Cabinet rank. Enoch Powell was one exception in 1962-63. Kenneth Robinson, the Labour appointee in 1964, was not. The Ministry of Pensions and National Insurance tended to be treated as a minor department after the merger which created it in 1953. Margaret Herbison was made Labour's Minister in 1964. Douglas Houghton, a member of the Wilson Cabinet as Chancellor of the Duchy of Lancaster and Chairman of its Social Services Committee, was made 'overseer, guide ... and philosopher' to the departmental Ministers whom, he explained, were to do the 'hard work'. Wilson, presumably with Churchill's experiment in mind, later stated that a system of Overlords was 'unworkable under our administrative parliamentary system'. Houghton, it seems, was just an overlord with a small 'o'. He was put in charge of a major review of social security. His Prime Minister described him as 'a most successful "half back"' in his role as social services coordinator. However, Houghton does not seem to have been the Blanchflower or Scoular needed. In February 1968, Richard Crossman complained that 'for nearly

three years we've been talking about the great review which
was being conducted by Douglas Houghton. Endless detailed
papers have been written, and I'd read many of them, but, under
Houghton there'd been no overall review of how the services
were working - whether the priorities were right, what
reorganization was required, what rethinking of basic
principles. Nothing of this had been done'.8   The failure to
produce a comprehensive plan for pensions was the most glaring
omission.

Well before Houghton left the Government in early 1967, it
was clear that Labour's promised Incomes Guarantee was never
going to appear. A proposal which had the then novelty of
linking the tax and social security systems, the Incomes
Guarantee was intended to provide selective benefits without
recourse to a detailed and stigmatizing means test.   The
proposal had to compete with other social security commitments
in a context of economic difficulty; and it was insufficiently
well prepared to be able to survive opposition from the Board
of Inland Revenue. The related ambition of reducing National
Assistance to Bevan's intended 'national scheme to assist
people in ... special circumstances' had to be abandoned. In
1966, National Assistance became Supplementary Benefits.   The
National Assistance Board was renamed the Supplementary
Benefits Commission. A Ministry of Social Security was formed
from a merger between the newly named Commission and the
Ministry of Pensions and National Insurance. Although the same
local offices and staff were used, it was hoped that the ending
of the clear distinction between contributory and non-
contributory social security would encourage those eligible to
be readier to apply for Supplementary Benefits than they had
been for National Assistance. At first, the evidence was
inconclusive, although take up rates did seem to improve among
the elderly. By the mid-1970s, a more general improvement in
take up rates could be discerned.

The Ministry of Social Security itself did not have a long
life. Its first Minister, Margaret Herbison, resigned in the
summer of 1967; her discontents including the unwillingness of
the Government to fully maintain earnings related National
Insurance benefits. In November 1968, the Ministry - embracing
as it did the Supplementary Benefits Commission - was merged
with the Ministry of Health to form the Department of Health
and Social Security. Richard Crossman at its head as Secretary
of State for the Social Services had earlier run into opposition to the new Department from Labour academics, Richard
Titmuss and Brian Abel-Smith. Crossman recorded that 'they
were nervous of a merger working right the way through from the
top to the bottom of both Ministries with transferability from
section to section and from job to job. They dislike this
whole notion because they believe that the jobs in the Ministry
of Social Security - the special work of the Supplementary
Benefits Commission, for example - are totally different from
the work of the Ministry of Health, and the kind of person who

is being trained in the old bureaucratic tradition of the
National Assistance Board and the National Insurance Office
would not be suitable for work with the doctors in most
sections of the Ministry of Health. Of course, as I pointed
out to them, what they were revealing was a very strong social
feeling - that the officials of the Ministry of Health felt
superior in every way to the officials of the Ministry of
Social Security. Richard Titmuss did not deny this but he
tried to prove his point by emphasizing the terribly low
standards of the Ministry of Social Security ... both he and
Brian led me to see that whatever I do I mustn't ruin their
splendid Ministry of Health by just mixing it up with the
vulgar Ministry of Social Security'. Crossman came to
appreciate the difficulties of the merger. Nevertheless, it
went through, and as Secretary of State, Crossman strove to
make up for the time which he regarded as lost by Labour. He
was involved with plans to change the structure of the National
Health Service, and with the introduction of a Hospital
Advisory Service. He gave his main attention to passing
comprehensive pensions legislation, an ambition which was
frustrated by the timing of the 1970 Election. Crossman's
energy and ability, like that of his Tory successor, Sir Keith
Joseph, tended to obscure the disparate nature of the formally
unified DHSS. A unified central government structure had been
welcomed by both major parties. It had also been favoured by
the Seebohm Committee on Local Authority Personal Social
Services to complement unification at local level. Child care
responsibilities and the respected Child Care Inspectorate were
transferred from the Home Office to the DHSS in 1971. Nevertheless, despite the gradual development of common services,
the DHSS did not cohere. The two Permanent Secretaries
continued to lead largely independent administrative structures.
Of the two, normally, health administration was a more policy
making and advisory activity, inevitably strongly medical in
content. Although large sums of public expenditure were
channelled to subordinate agencies, health administration
usually involved few direct managerial responsibilities.
Social security remained a large managerial operation, and its
headquarters responsibilities were mainly about the articulat-
ion of codes that could be applied uniformly throughout the
local office network.10 The continuing division of work within
the DHSS was given some recognition in September 1976 when a
Minister of State there was made Minister for Social Security
with a seat in the Cabinet.

IV   THE ADVENT OF THE DISCRIMINATION BOARDS

Although the Home Office lost functions to the DHSS, it gained
others in the field of race relations and equal opportunities.
These responsibilities were shared with other bodies: the
Equal Opportunities Commission, the Race Relations Board, the
Community Relations Commission, and the Commission for Racial

Equality.

The various pieces of race relations legislation did not
attract the controversy that had accompanied the Commonwealth
Immigration Act of 1962. Enoch Powell's 'rivers of blood'
speech in 1968 was certainly controversial; but it did not
destroy the largely by-partisan approach to race relations that
both the Labour and Conservative leaderships adopted once
popular sentiment was recognized. The Labour Party, with its
District Officer tradition, and a natural desire to corner the
immigrant vote, was more disposed towards anti-discrimination
legislation and supporting institutions. Shorn of rhetoric,
the arguments for this approach were two. First, limits were
set on the extent to which the indigenous population could
discriminate. The exclusion of the immigrants from housing and
employment opportunities and social gatherings was to be
prevented. Secondly, the legislation gave the immigrants hope
of a wider acceptance. Housing was the key thing. Mobility
would give access to better areas and the educational and
medical facilities and employment opportunities that went with
them. The Race Relations Board and the Community Relations
Commission were established in 1966 and 1968 respectively to
supervise the working of the legislation. They were merged
into a Commission for Racial Equality in 1977, armed with
stronger legislation, the powers within which bordered on
reverse discrimination.11

Trying to improve human nature by legislation has proved
to be a thankless task. Moreover, to the extent that it was
designed to punish those who incited racial hatred, the
legislation was superfluous. The Public Order Act of 1936
contained the necessary powers. It stated that 'any person who
in any public place or at any public meeting uses threatening,
abusive or insulting words or behaviour with intent to provoke
a breach of the peace or whereby a breach of the peace is
likely to be occasioned, shall be guilty of an offence'. The
most that may have been needed in addition was an amendment to
housing legislation. More ambitious race relations legislation
had the danger not only of creating unrealizable expectations,
but also of having the opposite effect from that intended. The
emphasis on the minority groups' separateness and the need for
special privileges might well create an appetite for more of
the same, thus making racial integration more unlikely. In
addition, once a bureaucracy was established, in the form of
the Race Relations Board and the Commissions, its growth was
assured, with those manning it having a vested interest in
racial problems remaining prominent and a cause for public
spending.

Discrimination against women differed from discrimination
against racial minorities in the sense that women actually
constituted a majority of the population and they were
indisputably resident. In the 1960s and 1970s, the antics of
the Women's Movement tended to obscure the fact that the
advocacy of equality for women had a distinguished intellectual

history dating from Socrates. In more modern times, this advocacy seems to have come chiefly from women with educational and professional qualifications - a middle class minority - who could expect to be the main beneficiaries. Meeting their more popular demands required legislation aimed at ensuring equal pay and conditions. Such monitoring as was needed could be - and to an extent was - done by the Department of Employment. Yet, an Equal Opportunities Commission was established in 1976, raising the same fears about bureaucratic imperialism and needless expenditure as the comparable bodies in race relations.12

The equal opportunities and race relations legislation was in keeping with the notion of the State as Universal Provider. As the Administrative 'Revolution' progressed, the costs of this general role were increasingly borne in on those paying for it, many of them intended beneficiaries. Every activity could not be a social service, and increasingly, parts of the economy seemed to be seen as such. For those who shared the views of The Guardian newspaper, the moment in 1969 when education passed defence as the largest single item of public expenditure was a welcome one. For others, it was one more mark of national decline.

References

1. Foot (1973), p. 237; Briggs (1961), p. 228; Titmuss (1963), pp. 1-11.
2. Cmnd. 2171, (1963), p. 46; Cmnd. 2154, (1963), pp. 238-56, 293-96; Cmnd. 4506, (1970), p. 12.
3. Crosland (1975), p. 206; Kogan (1971), p. 193; DES, Statistics of Education 1965, Pt. I, p. 44; DES, Statistics of Education 1975. Schools, I, pp. ix-x.
4. Macmillan (1969), p. 364; Sharp (1969), pp. 11, 21; Cmnd. 2233, (1963); Reed and Williams (1971), p. 235; Wilson (1971), p. 219.
5. Ibid., p. 9; Craig (1975), pp. 264-65; Crossman (1975), pp. 23-5. Dame Evelyn Sharp's views were expressed in a programme called Trial of Strength in the Granada Television series Inside British Politics shown on 19.6.1977.
6. Wilson (1971), p. 711; Cmnd. 4506, (1970), pp. 10-11; Sharp (1969); Hall et.al., (1975), pp. 371-409; Draper (1977), pp. 4-9.
7. Letter from Peter Walker to author dated 3.7.1978.
8. 701 H.C. Deb. 5s.c. 868; Wilson (1971), pp. 325, 711; Hall et. al., (1975), p. 435; Crossman (1976), p. 668.
9. Hall et. al., (1975), pp. 410-71; Cmnd. 6615, (1976), pp. 51-4; Cmnd. 6910, (1977), pp. 135-39; DHSS, (1978), pp. 1-7.
10. Wilson (1971), pp. 420-21; Crossman (1976), pp. 380, 774; Ibid., (1977), p. 21; Cmnd. 3703, (1968), pp. 194-95; Cmnd. 4506, (1970), pp. 11-12; Brown (1975), pp. 74-5.

11.   Cmnd. 6234, (1975); H.C. 448-I, II, III, (1975);
The Spectator, 20.9.1975, p. 363.
12.   Cmnd. 5724, (1974); Plato, Republic (trans. F.M.
Cornford), pp. 145-47, 150, 256; Davies (1975), pp. 86-92.

Chapter 8

SEARCHING FOR THE BEST FORM OF DEFENCE

'We were disembowelled' at Suez, Sir Oliver Franks said of
Britain to Churchill's doctor a few months after the 1956
fiasco. 'After the war we acted as a Great Power, though we
had not the resources. A kind of confidence trick. It came
off as long as the decisions we made were acceptable to the
other Powers. The trouble with these island empires has always
been the same: they had too few men. America and Russia can
afford a holocaust, we cannot.' Franks thought that the
consequences of Suez would be felt for many years after 1956.1
In fact, Britain's position in the world never recovered from
the humiliation of Suez. In the military sphere, changes
already under consideration were swiftly pressed ahead with by
the Macmillan Government, and less than six months later the
Sandys White Paper of 1957 outlined changes in defence policy.
These were radical in the sense that they abolished conscription and emphasized Britain's reliance on nuclear weaponry.
These changes did not make Britain any more credible as a
military power. British troops were rarely out of action for
long somewhere in the world - Brunei, Aden, and then Northern
Ireland. Nevertheless, their numbers were small, and the
quality and amount of equipment available to the Services
became a familiar target for expenditure cuts. Professional
Armed Forces, like nuclear weapons, proved to be much more
expensive than had been anticipated. Defence expenditure,
inevitably, had to shoulder a share of the consequences of
Britain's relatively declining economy. Equally inevitably, in
the era of the Administrative 'Revolution', the institutional
arrangements for defence were changed.

I   FROM SUEZ TO THE THORNEYCROFT-MOUNTBATTEN REFORMS 1956-64

At the time of Suez, there were five defence departments: the
War Office, the Air Ministry, the Admiralty, the Ministry of
Supply, and a small Ministry of Defence. Sixteen years later,
when the Procurement Executive was established in the Ministry
of Defence there was only one defence department - the Ministry
of Defence itself. The biggest step in this amalgamation

119

process was the establishment of a unified Ministry of Defence in 1963-64. That this change came when it did owed a great deal to the prestige of its main author, the Chief of Defence Staff, Lord Louis Mountbatten. The support of the Prime Minister, Harold Macmillan, was another crucial factor.

The central government organization for defence was not short of critics in the 1950s. This was certainly true of the Ministry of Supply. Reginald Maudling, the Minister between 1955 and 1957, recalled that 'it was a strange department, and the target of a good deal of criticism, much of it justified'. The Ministry was supposed to be concerned mainly with the supply of munitions to the three Services, and this was a large part of the routine work of the department. However, in addition, the Ministry had responsibility for the aircraft production industry generally. The relationship with the aircraft industry was a close one. The scale of modern projects and research expenditure ensured that the industry was largely dependent on government contracts and support, including the scientific and technical support provided by the Royal Aircraft Establishment at Farnborough, another of the Ministry's responsibilities. Relations between the RAF and the aircraft manufacturers were notoriously poor. The RAF was always demanding more from the manufacturers and complaining that they were not getting their requirements met. While the manufacturers were saying that they were doing all that was possible, and that the RAF was asking too much. There was cause for complaint. For example, once it was found that the Hunter fighters in their latest model experienced a complete engine stall when their guns were fired. Maudling concluded that the interposition of a third party between customer and supplier exacerbated argument. Relations between the Air Ministry and the Ministry of Supply were certainly strained. Maudling recommended the abolition of the Ministry of Supply, and, naturally felt unable to continue as Minister when asked to do so by Macmillan as incoming Prime Minister.2 The Ministry, however, survived, to have its name changed to the Ministry of Aviation in 1959.

Macmillan was otherwise determined to change the central organization for defence that dated from the Attlee Government's reforms of 1946. Macmillan had found being Minister of Defence in 1954-55 to be a 'bitter experience' one of 'painful frustration'. He explained: 'the Act of Parliament which established the Ministry of Defence after the war clothed the Minister with doubtful authority and gave him insufficient means to fulfil even the functions which he was supposed to carry out. A new Ministry, staffed not with the highest commanders but with subordinate, if devoted, officers, could with difficulty assert its will against the long tradition of the Armed Forces of the Crown. Their Lordships of the Admiralty, with their hierarchy of Admirals under the First Lord; the War Office with its Secretary of State and Army Council; even the later created Air Ministry, again with its

Secretary of State - it was in these historic bodies that
rested the real, practical control. Moreover, the responsibility of their political heads to Parliament had scarcely
been altered by the emergence of the Minister of Defence'. As
actual operations of any kind required a single command,
Macmillan was unconvinced of the virtues of these arrangements.
'When I became Prime Minister', Macmillan recalled, 'I was
determined to remedy the inherent weakness of the system. I
made many tentative approaches, always to come up against
strong and sometimes emotional resistance'. The traditions of
the three Services were the main barrier. Another major
obstacle was the argument that a strong Ministry of Defence
would be bound to take on the character of the Oberkommando
der Wermacht, still conventionally, if unconvincingly, held
responsible for the failures of German military direction in
the Second World War. The forceful behaviour of Duncan Sandys,
Macmillan's Minister of Defence between 1957 and 1959, did
little to quell such fears. A reorganization in 1958 did make
the Minister responsible for 'the formulation and general
application of a unified policy of the Armed Forces of the
Crown as a whole and their requirements'. This made the
Minister of Defence more than a co-ordinator, on paper. In
fact, Sandys had minimal success in securing institutional
recognition of the powers he wielded. When Sandys left to
take over the Ministry of Aviation in 1959, it was clear how
little his changes had affected the three most important
processes by which defence policy was formulated. Insufficient
had been done to establish the central control of programmes
and budgeting; the examination of, and allocation of resources
for, proposals by the Services for the procurement of expensive
weapons systems; and the construction of a general framework
of strategic policy against which the requirements presented
by the individual Services could be assessed.[3]

The changes of 1963-64 were designed to remedy these
deficiencies in the existing structures. Lord Mountbatten and
Sir Solly Zuckerman, the Chief Scientific Adviser from 1959,
were both dissatisfied, with the existing arrangements at the
Ministry of Defence. Zuckerman took the opportunity to put
his side of the Ministry in order after completing a report in
1961 on the management and control of research and development
that had been begun by his predecessor. Mountbatten pressed
for wider changes. That changes came perhaps owed something
to the imminence of the end of conscription. The prospect of
professionalized forces may have helped to limit the
opposition from the Services. Certainly, their advent
emphasized the need for a more economical use of manpower.
There was a generally increased awareness of the sheer cost of
defence in the context of continuing national economic
difficulties. This cost was underlined by a succession of
cancellations of defence projects. This increased public
scepticism about weapons systems to such an extent that even
very favourable deals were looked at askance. This was the

case, for example, with the Nassau Agreement of 1962 made with
the USA for Polaris missiles. Denis Healey, after six years
as Labour's Defence Secretary, admitted in 1970 that the
Agreement had been a brilliant achievement. It gave Britain an
effective and cheap deterrent. The cost of the five boat
nuclear submarine force did not exceed £400 million overall,
which was less than 4 per cent of the Defence Budget per year
for seven years. Yet, although he was to persist with the
Polaris project when he reached office, at the time Healey had
been hostile to the Nassau Agreement. Indeed, it had a
generally poor reception. The dominant inclination was to cut
defence. The Conservatives had cut it from 10 per cent GNP in
1951 to 5.5 per cent in 1964. There was pressure to cut it
still more, and one way was by administrative rationalization. 4

The reorganization of the Ministry of Defence which took
place in the autumn of 1963 was the responsibility primarily of
the incumbent Minister, Peter Thorneycroft, who took over the
office in July 1962. It was an open secret that much of the
initiative and many of the ideas came from Lord Mountbatten,
who had become Chief of Defence Staff three years earlier in
the summer of 1959. In January 1963, Macmillan invited
General Lord Ismay and Lieutenant General Sir Ian Jacob to
conduct an inquiry into the operation of the Ministry of
Defence. Their Report, produced the following month, although
not exactly what Mountbatten himself wanted, formed the basis
of the changes made later in 1963 and confirmed by legislation
passed in 1964. A single Ministry of Defence was established
under a Secretary of State. It absorbed the existing Service
Ministries, which subsequently existed as its Navy, Army, and
Air Force Departments. The Ministry of Defence was 'to ensure
effective co-ordination ... of all questions of policy and
administration which concern the fighting Services as the
instruments of an effective strategy'. Broad issues of defence
policy continued to be settled at Cabinet level. The Defence
Committee of the Cabinet was replaced by a Committee on Defence
and Overseas Policy, composed of Senior Cabinet Ministers,
including, of course, the Secretary of State for Defence. The
Service Ministers, who were reduced to Minister of State status,
attended this Committee only by invitation. While being
identified with the separate Services, their subordination to
the Secretary of State was supposed to be emphasized in the
general allocation of duties and the level of administrative
support, as well as in relation to Parliament. As will be
seen, in one notable case these arrangements did not work.
Ironically, given Mountbatten's pressure for reform, the
position of the Chief of Defence Staff and of the Chiefs of
Staff changed little, except that the mechanism for central
control of operations was strengthened. The constitutional
position remained that established in 1958. The Chiefs of
Staff Committee remained 'collectively responsible to the
Government for professional advice on strategy and military
operations and on the military implications of defence policy'.

The CDS tendered the collective advice of the Committee, and when their views diverged submitted the alternatives 'when they have been discussed and defined' to the Secretary of State. However, as principal military adviser to the Secretary of State, the CDS could¹ also 'tender his own advice to the Minister in the light of the views expressed'. The Permanent Under Secretary was made primarily responsible for the long term financial planning and control of the defence programme, and the allocation of resources between the Services. In the complex field of weapons procurement, the position of the Chief Scientific Adviser was strengthened to provide greater opportunities for the critical evaluation of projects. To establish a more independent framework in which they could be evaluated, a new body was created called the Defence Operational Requirements Staff.5

II   THE HEALEY REGIME AND AFTER 1964-79

Although the unified Ministry of Defence was established under the aegis of Peter Thorneycroft, the new arrangements received their first sustained test under Denis Healey, his Labour successor as Secretary of State from 1964 to 1970. Healey seemed to be ideally suited for the job. He had striven to master contemporary defence terminology. He allied specialized knowledge to a formidable intellect. If the new Ministry of Defence was supposed to be Britain's Pentagon, as some saw it, Healey could be portrayed as her equivalent of the then still fashionable figure of Robert McNamara. Nevertheless, Healey never matched his promise. That this was so was more than a matter of being required by the Treasury to operate within a Defence budget limited to £2000 million at 1964 prices. It followed from Healey's view of Britain's role in the world. Such realism as Healey had was more related to the world of 1951, when Labour had lost office, than that of 1964 and beyond. Healey failed to discern the reality of Britain's position in the American alliance, the reality of the Commonwealth, and the reality of Britain's resources in relation to her then commitments East of Suez. In short, he believed, with his Prime Minister, that Britain could play a world role into the 1970s, when economic and political realities indicated that her role would soon have to be confined to Europe and the North Atlantic. To stay East of Suez with any credibility, the Royal Navy had to have a new aircraft carrier, the CVA-01. This was denied in the Defence Review of early 1966. Britain could not afford both the carrier and the purchase of the American F-111 aircraft for the RAF. Healey backed the latter. Christopher Mayhew, the Minister for the Navy, had the honesty to resign. Mayhew himself could not see it being politically possible for 'white faced' Armed Forces to play a peacekeeping role on the Asian mainland and in the Middle East in the 1970s. However, he argued, if it was desired to play such a role, then the money should be found to meet the commitments

involved. The commitments should not be made without the
resources. A change of policy only came in the aftermath of
the devaluation of sterling in 1967. Although Healey himself
wanted a later deadline, the Labour Cabinet decided in favour
of withdrawal from East of Suez by the end of 1971. This was
announced in the Defence White Paper of February 1968 which
stated that 'Britain's defence effort will in future be
concentrated mainly in Europe and in the North Atlantic area'.6
    The aftermath of devaluation witnessed another defeat for
Healey. One of his earlier victories, when Roy Jenkins was
Minister of Aviation, had been to persuade the Cabinet to
cancel the TSR-2 aircraft in 1965. This was said to be
possible because of the availability of a low cost substitute
in the form of the high performance, multi-mission F-111, which
the American Government was prepared to sell to Britain. In
early 1968, in the context of the Wilson Cabinet's search for
post-devaluation economies, it fell to Healey to defend the
F-111 commitment from its critics. The skill in argument of
Jenkins as Chancellor of the Exchequer helped to ensure that
he failed. Richard Crossman recorded gleefully: 'Denis is
not a very successful speaker either in Cabinet or in the
House. He plays the role of the young McNamara - the man who
is briefed on all the top level secrets and who can mock and
deride any ideas put forward by his amateur colleagues. The
supercilious expert is always in danger in a British Cabinet
but Denis has a further difficulty. After all, he had already
presented us with no less than four successive defence reviews
and he had defended each as it came out with new facts, new
figures, new statistical demonstrations. Moreover I remembered
that he had sold the F-111 to us as an aeroplane essential for
defence East of Suez which would in fact be based East of Suez
and not used in Europe. Now he was defending it as essential
to European defence. I got the impression that he could
defend it just as brilliantly as essential to southern Irish
defence'. The F-111 had certainly played a variety of roles
for Healey, being an alternative to another aircraft carrier
and also the TSR-2. Now, the F-111 itself was dropped.
Healey was left without an aeroplane for either naval or RAF
purposes (the European MRCA and the Anglo-French Jaguar were
later supposed to compensate for this). Healey was tempted to
resign, but resisted the temptation.7
    The unified structure of the Ministry of Defence had
received a thorough testing under the Healey regime. While he
did show interest in cost benefit analysis and modern management techniques, Healey had little taste for administrative
reform. He thought that radical administrative changes on top
of far reaching changes in policy would damage the morale of
the Services. One experiment that was tried - presumably with
the Mayhew resignation in mind - was the replacement of the
three Service Ministers by two Ministers of Defence, one for
equipment and the other for administration. This experiment
lasted from January 1967 down to the fall of the Labour

Government in 1970, after which the Service Ministers returned. A more important change took place when the Heath Government brought defence procurement fully within the Ministry of Defence. The exclusion of the military work of the Ministry of Aviation from the 1963-64 changes was a curious decision. When the Ministry was wound up in 1967, Wilson gave its military functions to the Ministry of Technology. The Heath Government temporarily set up a Ministry of Aviation Supply in 1970, and appointed a project team under a businessman, D G Rayner, to examine the arrangements for defence procurement. As a result of the Rayner Report published in April 1971, a year later the military procurement functions previously both within and outside the Ministry of Defence were concentrated into a Procurement Executive within that Ministry in which it formed a parallel structure headed by its own Chief Executive.[8]

The reformers of 1963-64 never expected to achieve the changes that they thought necessary at a single blow. Nevertheless, it was a big gap in the changed arrangements that the Ministry of Aviation - the scene of the Ferranti and Bristol Siddeley affairs - remained outside the unified Ministry of Defence. This gap was only closed in 1972. It may well be that few would want to go back to the 1956 or 1958 arrangements: but then Britain's defence role was less ambitious even ten years later. That this was so, as we have seen, was more the result of the pressure of events than the use of any superior mechanism for framing defence policy. Healey complained in his first Defence White Paper that 'the present Government has inherited defence forces which are seriously over-stretched and in some respects under-equipped'.[9] Any of his successors could have made a similar statement without exaggeration. Neater organization charts could not hide the continuing decline in resources in relation to commitments, and, after Suez, doubts about the will to defend.

References

1.   Moran (1966), p. 726.
2.   Maudling (1978), pp. 60-1.
3.   Cmnd. 6923, (1946), pp. 5-10; Macmillan (1973), p. 409; Macmillan (1969), p. 562; Snyder (1962), pp. 123-37; Cmnd. 124, (1957); Cmnd. 476, (1958); Howard (1960), pp. 66-70; Howard (1970), pp. 9-11, 15, 55-6.
4.   Office of the Minister of Science (1961); Reed and Williams (1971), p. 157; Howard (1970), pp. 9, 12-13.
5.   Cmnd. 2097, (1963); Howard (1970), pp. 14-19.
6.   Cmnd. 2901, (1966), p. 10; Cmnd. 3540, (1968), p.2; Mayhew (1967), pp. 131-53; 725 H.C. Deb. 5s. c. 254-65; Reed and Williams (1971), pp. 166-246. The verdict of a British General with NATO rings true: 'Healey's basic misunderstanding of defence policy from the mid-sixties to the mid-seventies stemmed directly from his excessive interest in the Indo-Pacific area' (Ibid., p. 246).

7. Williams et. al., (1969), pp. 55-66; Crossman (1975), pp. 190-92; Crossman (1976), pp. 646-48; Reed and Williams (1971), pp. 176-84, 238-44. Lord Longford, Lord Privy Seal and a member of the Labour Cabinet, said that Healey had convinced him that Britain would be virtually naked without the F-111 (Ibid., p. 240). Presumably, Healey was convinced of this himself, but he did not resign as Longford did over education cuts.

8. Ibid., p. 276; Cmnd. 4506, (1970), pp. 9-10; Cmnd. 4641, (1971), pp. 7-58; Cary (1974), pp. 18-24.

9. Howard (1970), p. 34; Cmnd. 2592, (1965), p. 5.

Chapter 9

CHANGING THE GUARDIANS: THE REFORM OF OVERSEAS REPRESENTATION

When Britain signed the Test Ban Treaty in 1963, it was the
last time that she was to appear in international negotiations
as a Great Power.1   The question of what kind of overseas
representation Britain now needed had been already put by the
Prime Minister Harold Macmillan to the Plowden Committee, whose
report was published in 1964.   The Plowden Committee of 1962-63
proved to be only the first of three major inquiries into
overseas representation that were to be made within a decade
and a half.   The others were made by the Duncan Committee in
1968-69, and by the Central Policy Review Staff led by Sir
Kenneth Berrill in 1976-77.   In addition, there have been
several changes in the machinery of government for external
relations.   In 1966, the Colonial Office was merged with the
Commonwealth Relations Office to form the Commonwealth Office.
The Macmillan Government had rejected a recommendation from
the Select Committee on Estimates in 1960 in favour of a joint
department.   Nevertheless, in 1962, it had established a joint
Secretaryship of State for Commonwealth Relations and for the
Colonies.   In addition, in 1961, the Conservative Government
had transferred the day-to-day responsibilities for the
technical assistance aspects of colonial development, and the
staff of the Colonial Office concerned, to a Department of
Technical Co-operation.   In 1964, the incoming Labour Government replaced that Department with a Ministry of Overseas
Development.   The Wilson Government then carried through the
merger which created the Commonwealth Office, and in 1968 it
merged that department with the Foreign Office to form the
Foreign and Commonwealth Office.   The Heath Conservative
Government believed that overseas aid should become the
ultimate responsibility of the Secretary of State for Foreign
and Commonwealth Affairs.   So, in 1970, the separate Ministry
was converted into the Overseas Development Administration of
the FCO, with its own Minister.2   In 1974, the returned
Wilson Government re-established a separate Ministry and in
1975 partially put it back into the FCO again.
     While few areas of the machinery of government escaped the
attention of reformers during the Administrative 'Revolution',

there were fewer still who received as much attention as the machinery for overseas representation. It was to be expected that the end of Empire and the weakening of links with the Commonwealth would lead to changes in the relevant parts of the British administrative framework. Nevertheless, the setting up of no less than three high level bodies of inquiry into overseas representation within fifteen years was a remarkable level of investigatory activity, at least by British, if not American standards.3 Labour Governments, in particular, may have come to feel that the institutions concerned, especially the FCO were, however understandably, reluctant to change, and needed regular external stimuli to encourage them to change. The style and social tone of diplomats and other senior staff at the core of the machinery for overseas representation seemed to attract external criticism. The sentiment which Laski once expressed that the Foreign Office had 'never lost its essential character as a nest of aristocratic singing birds mainly hatched out at Eton'4 had survived its author. To critics, British diplomatic activity savoured of conspicuous consumption and was an area for economies. The cost of diplomatic buildings overseas was a particular target for adverse comment. While overseas representation was a heavy user of foreign exchange, in 1975-76, as the Berrill Report observed, 'as a proportion of public expenditure on all programmes (0.5 per cent) or GNP (0.3 per cent)' the overall cost of overseas representation was 'very small'.5 Certainly, Britain no longer needed the diplomatic apparatus of a Great Power once she had ceased to be one. Moreover, Britain's continuing, indeed accelerating, economic decline relative to her main competitors, made it imperative that she should place much more emphasis than had been traditional on the export promotional side of overseas representation. Nonetheless, even allowing for the pace of change and of Britain's decline, the number of official inquiries into overseas representation risked debasing the activity. To judge from the reception given to the Berrill Report in 1977 this was what was widely felt to have occurred in the period after the Plowden Committee had first turned to the subject.

I   THE PLOWDEN REPORT ON REPRESENTATIONAL SERVICES OVERSEAS

'About once every twenty years, owing to wars or domestic failure to realise the magnitude of its task, the British Diplomatic Service almost grinds to a halt. Such a point had been reached by 1962; the Service was saved by the Plowden recommendations.' Sir Douglas Busk's verdict on the work of the Plowden Committee on Representational Services Overseas of 1962-63 was expressed in a more melodramatic manner than one would normally expect from a former diplomat. Nevertheless, his verdict reflected the generally favourable mood of the official reaction to the Plowden Report when it was published in 1964. The Committee had been appointed by Harold Macmillan 'to review the purpose, structure and operation of the services responsible for representing the interests of the United Kingdom Government overseas, both in Commonwealth and in foreign countries; and to make recommendations, having regard to changes in political, social and economic circumstances in this country and overseas'. It was a strong and experienced committee, a majority of whose members had worked in the areas of government concerned, including former Heads of the Foreign Service and the Commonwealth Relations Office. The Committee took evidence, which was not published. In addition, as one member, Sir Charles Mott-Radclyffe, later wrote, the Committee 'split into twos and threes like animals out of the Ark and virtually covered the world in order to see the problems on the spot. In the process, forty-two Foreign Office and Commonwealth Relations Office posts were visited. The members then returned to pool their findings'. The Conservative Government accepted the Plowden recommendations in toto.6

It had been about twenty years since the Foreign Service Order in Council of 1943 had brought together in one Service the Foreign Office and the Diplomatic Service, the Consular Service and the Commercial Diplomatic Service, and had thus fulfilled the main intention of the Eden White Paper of that year. However, the arrangements for representational services overseas had still remained complex. In 1946, when the Department of Overseas Trade had been absorbed into the Board of Trade, a Trade Commission Service had been established which operated in Commonwealth countries only. It was part of the Home Civil Service. This was also the case with the Commonwealth Service, which was established in 1947, when the Dominions Office and the India Office were merged to form the Commonwealth Relations Office. The Plowden Committee gently suggested that the world of 1943 had vanished. It indicated what the role of modern Overseas Services needed to be, emphasizing the paramount importance not of traditional diplomacy but of the promotion of trade. The Committee mildly criticized the policy planning arrangements in the existing departments and advocated their development. The bulk of the Plowden Committee's Report was concerned with the conditions of service of the various staffs involved in representational services overseas, and with the advocacy of the improvement of those conditions. The Committee recommended that a unified Service called HM Diplomatic Service should be created to take in the duties, personnel and posts of the existing Foreign Service, Commonwealth Service and Trade Commission Service. The Committee suggested that the new Service should be established at the beginning of 1965 - which it was - and that it should have a combined administration under a Chief of Administration. The Committee said that the Diplomatic Service needed flexibility in the control and deployment of manpower, arguing that without a larger margin of manpower, the requirements of training, travel, leave and sick leave could not be met. A reserve of 10 per cent was suggested.

The Committee devised a new Grades Structure for the Administrative, Executive and Clerical Classes. This maintained
separate pay scales (and ones which maintained existing links
with the Home Civil Service), promotion streams, and entry
points. On recruitment, the Committee noted the preponderance
of Administrative direct entrants whose educational background
was one of Public School followed by either Oxford or Cambridge. The Committee expressed concern at 'the present
meagre ration of successes' among candidates from other school
and university backgrounds. On the recruitment of women, the
Committee recommended that the existing Foreign Service
marriage bar regulation for women should be modified in the
Diplomatic Service. The Committee said that a greater degree
of specialization in languages, areas and functions was needed
in the new Service. In one of its few critical comments, the
Plowden Committee said that the 1943 reforms had carried with
them 'the implication that everyone would do everything and
become expert in everything. In practice, this could only
result in their not being expert in anything'.7
     The Plowden Report enjoyed a favourable reception in 1964.
The Report was nicely judged for the times. The Committee
recognized that 'the survival of Britain, let alone her
influence, depends on trade'. Yet, it also quoted, with an
approval that it believed the British people would share, a
Churchillian pronouncement that Britain should not be content
to be 'relegated to a tame and minor role in the world'.8
While it recommended a unified Diplomatic Service, Lord Plowden
said that the Committee came 'to the conclusion that public
opinion, more particularly in this country than in Commonwealth
countries, was not yet ready' for a merged Foreign and Commonwealth Office. Sir Charles Mott-Radclyffe later revealed that
this decision was a compromise partly to secure an agreed
Report. Arthur Henderson, who represented the Party on the
Committee, felt that a merger between the Offices would create
hostility in the Labour Party. The Committee was also
influenced by the question of whether one Secretary of State
could conceivably carry the burden which unification in
Whitehall would involve.9   What may well have commended the
Plowden Report in official circles was that it was mainly
about the favourite subject of civil servants - conditions of
service. Moreover, that subject was not approached in a spirit
of economy. 'The present cost of these Services is not un-
reasonable', the Plowden Committee declared. The Government
itself drew back from the target of 10 per cent excess
manpower, and opted for 7½ per cent, which subsequently
appears to have become the ceiling. The years between 1965 and
1968 were characterized by the consolidation of the merged
Service and then by the work which led to the merged FCO. The
Prime Minister at least seemed to deem the latter merger as
safe enough in relation to Labour Party sentiment in the wake
of the European initiative of 1966-67. The announcement of
the prospective creation of the FCO came as 'a complete

surprise' to the Head of the Diplomatic Service, Sir Paul
Gore-Booth, who also found that the merger was not the only
major administrative operation of 1968. A further review of
overseas representation was established.10

II   THE DUNCAN REPORT ON OVERSEAS REPRESENTATION

'In the somewhat panicky atmosphere of early 1968 it was
natural that the demand should be revived in the Government
for economy in the handling of our overseas representation',
Sir Paul Gore-Booth later recalled. 'My professional reaction
was that we had been spending the last three years methodically
working through the reforms proposed by the Plowden Committee
and that it would be pleasant if we could be allowed to get on
with a little uninterrupted diplomacy. However, I had to
agree that this further review was unavoidable. A tough
negotiation followed in resistance to terms of reference which
would have meant, like the trial in Alice in Wonderland,
"Sentence first, verdict afterwards". The result was a
compromise.' In August 1968, the Foreign Secretary, Michael
Stewart, appointed a committee comprising Sir Val Duncan of
Rio Tinto Zinc as chairman; Andrew Shonfield, the economist
and journalist; and Sir Frank Roberts, a former Ambassador to
Yugoslavia, the USSR and Western Germany. The Duncan
Committee was asked 'to review urgently the functions and
scale of the British representational effort overseas' in the
light of the announcement of the British withdrawal from East
of Suez, the balance of payments, and the changing international role which these implied. The Committee was invited
'to make recommendations particularly on the furtherance of
British commercial and economic interests overseas and, in
arriving at these recommendations, to consider the value to
HM Government of work done and information submitted by overseas posts in the political field; to have regard to the
functions and scale of representation by other major Western
European countries; to bear in mind, in the current need for
the strictest economy, the importance of obtaining the maximum
value for all British Government expenditure and the
consequent desirability of providing British overseas
representation at lesser cost'. The Duncan Committee had been
given 'a very free hand', as Gore-Booth observed. Despite,
among other things, visiting 34 Overseas Missions, as well as
taking a great deal of (unpublished) evidence, the Committee
was able to produce its Report as early as June 1969.11   It
was a very controversial Report.
    The Duncan Committee saw Britain as being 'a major power
of the second order', and described its own role as one of
'designing a system of representation for the mid-1970s'. The
Committee identified the central commitments in British
foreign policy as being to NATO and to a progressively
integrated Western Europe with the Common Market at its core.
It divided overseas countries into two broad, but sharply

131

distinguished categories. 'One is the category of advanced industrial countries with which we are likely to be increasingly involved to the point where none of us will be able to conduct our domestic policies efficiently without constant reference to each other. This group - to which we refer as the Area of Concentration of British diplomacy - will consist of about a dozen or so countries in Western Europe plus North America. There are also a few industrially advanced nations outside the European/North Atlantic area with whom British relations will be very close and important for different reasons. Examples are Australia and Japan. There is not the immediate prospect here of the mutual commitment in the day-to-day process of government that there is in Western Europe. But British representation in these countries will have far reaching responsibilities. The other category of countries comprises the rest of the world. There will be important differences in the kind of representation that will be appropriate, depending on whether the country concerned is in the Soviet bloc, commercially important, politically hostile, economically underdeveloped and so on. But none of them is likely to impinge on the day-to-day conduct of British Government business in quite the way that we expect the countries of the first group to do.'12

The Committee recommended that in future British Missions abroad should be divided into 'Comprehensive' Missions and 'Selective' Missions. Comprehensive Missions would be maintained in the Area of Concentration and in certain other important countries in the Outer Area. Selective Missions would constitute the majority in the Outer Area. Comprehensive Missions would retain a full apparatus for diplomatic representation including staff for political work. Whereas, political work and reporting would diminish to very small proportions in Selective Missions. The Committee saw economic work and the conduct of commercial policy as a large part of the substance of political work. It was this field which produced particularly striking examples of what the Committee chose to call the New Diplomacy, by which it meant 'the increasing regular contact at all levels between specialists from various countries in the complicated techniques of modern life and the switch to multilateral organizations of activities which would previously have been bilateral'. The Committee was clear that Britain's economic situation required commercial work to be the most urgent task of her overseas representatives. The Committee favoured cutting down on some traditional types of consular services in order to emphasize the work of export promotion. The Committee made recommendations about handling property overseas more efficiently, and about more travel and less correspondence on the part of officials. It did not see any urgent need to devote more Diplomatic Service resources to aid administration. It recommended cutting British Information Services overseas by half. By contrast, the Committee exempted the British Council

from economies, and advocated more expenditure on BBC External
Services in order to improve the audibility of broadcasts. In
addition, deeming that the existing accommodation was
'manifestly unbusinesslike for the conduct of a great Ministry
of State', the Committee recommended that the main FCO
building in Whitehall should be rebuilt.13

The Duncan Committee recorded that it had been impressed
by 'the quality of the Diplomatic Service and by its team
spirit. It is highly regarded in other countries'. Nevertheless, it was clear that quantitatively the Service faced a
period of contraction, primarily because of changed national
requirements resulting from Britain's altered role in the
world. While the Diplomatic Service should be allowed the
full 10 per cent manpower margin recommended in the Plowden
Report, the Duncan Committee said that the overall size of the
Service would have to be reduced, even though this meant the
premature retirement of a number of competent officials. The
Committee advocated a streamlined promotion system for the
ablest of those remaining. The Committee did think that the
Diplomatic Service was vulnerable to the charge of pursuing
'the cult of the amateur'. The Committee said, 'we do not
believe that the Diplomatic Service should be made up of
experts. Its members should remain generalists. But they
require professionalism as well. They should in fact be
professional generalists, not generalist amateurs. Their only
depth specializations will continue to be in hard languages ...
The professional skills of all members of the Service, however,
should include (a) a working knowledge of at least one and
preferably more European languages and (b) a certain familiar-
ity with the basic concepts of the social sciences (including
e.g. modern techniques of management and marketing).'14

When it was published, the Duncan Report had a generally
hostile reception from the Press, those connected with the
Diplomatic Service, and interested academics. 'According to
the Duncan Committee', one academic critic complained, 'a
diplomat is a man who goes abroad to sell washing machines for
his country'.15 Ennobled former diplomats were outspoken in
the relevant House of Lords debate. Lord Caccia, for instance,
challenged the belief expressed by the Duncan Committee that
Britain's role in the world had changed, and demanded evidence
that it had. Lord Gore-Booth preferred a tone of mild
dismissiveness. He wrote of the Duncan Report that 'the
passages on the shape and purpose of the Service were somewhat
overstated and the distinction made between what the Committee
called "areas of concentration" of our diplomatic effort and
the rest of the world was too stark. The chapters on
commercial work tended to give too much the impression that
nothing had been done hitherto. But I have always assumed that
these comments were underlined for the purpose of making
important points in a way which would catch the deaf ear and
the blind eye. There were some admirable "nuts and bolts"
recommendations ... There were weaknesses too, notably on

information work which the Committee did not seem to under-
stand'. The Government only endorsed the Committee's 'general
approach'. It did not give 'a specific endorsement to its
conclusions'. The Government eventually concluded that the
distinctions in the Duncan Report between the so-called 'area
of concentration' and the rest of the world, and between
'comprehensive' and 'selective' posts were too sharply drawn.
What the Duncan Committee thought it had done, according to
Andrew Shonfield, was 'to spell out, belatedly, the logic of
the end of Empire'.16   The Report's actual proposals were more
radical in tone than in content. Nevertheless, the FCO's taste
for change seemed to be exhausted, as was perhaps indicated in
1970 when it restored the traditional name of Chief Clerk for
the post of Deputy Under Secretary in charge of Administration.
However, a further external review had soon to be faced.

III   THE BERRILL REPORT ON OVERSEAS REPRESENTATION

Those who had shared George Brown's 'high hopes' of the Duncan
Committee had been disappointed. 'When I read their Report',
the former Foreign Secretary later recorded, 'I felt this was
possibly the most missed opportunity for quite several decades
to bring about a genuine reform of the Foreign Service. It is
a job somebody still has to carry out'. The appointment of
another review body in the near future seemed as unlikely as
the rebuilding of the FCO's 'magnificent slum' of a headquarters in Whitehall, a project duly abandoned in 1976. Yet,
in January of that year, a further external review was
established. The occasion was provided by revelations of, and
Press comments about, the costs incurred in housing the
British Ambassador to the OECD in Paris. These costs were
approximately equalled by those of the external review. This
was conducted by the Central Policy Review Staff which was
asked by James Callaghan, the Foreign and Commonwealth
Secretary, 'to review the nature and extent of our overseas
interests and requirements and in the light of that Review to
make recommendations on the most suitable, effective and
economic means of representing and promoting those interests
both at home and overseas. The Review will embrace all aspects
of the work of overseas representation, including political,
economic, commercial, consular and immigration activities,
whether these tasks are performed by members of HM Diplomatic
Service, by members of the Home Civil Service, by members of
the Armed Forces or by other agencies financially supported by
HM Government'. The review team consisted of Sir Kenneth
Berrill and six other members of the Think Tank. Besides
receiving and inviting a mass of (unpublished) evidence, the
Berrill team went on various journeys, in twos and threes like
the Plowden Committee, and, altogether, visited posts in 27
countries.17   Its Report was published in August 1977, and
proved to be very controversial.
      The Think Tank had been given wider terms of reference

than the Plowden and Duncan Committees so that it could undertake 'a comprehensive and radical review of the UK's overseas
representation'. The CPRS observed that 'this has not been a
review of the FCO and the Diplomatic Service. It has been a
review of all departments or parts of departments in London
responsible for the making and carrying out of overseas
policies and all those working overseas on behalf of HM Government (apart from formed units of the Armed Forces). Of the
35,000 people estimated to be working in 1976 in the areas
covered by our terms of reference, some 55 per cent were
working in the UK and only 45 per cent overseas. And of those
35,000, only one-seventh (5,000) were members of the Diplomatic
Service; ... the FCO accounts for less than half (16,000) of
the staff whose activities we have examined'. The Think Tank
said that its review had taken place 'after a period of
decline in the UK's power and influence ... In the last 20
years our share of the total GDP of the OECD countries had
fallen by a quarter and our share of world trade in manufactures has fallen by more than half. In today's world, a
country's power and influence are basically determined by its
economic performance. Inevitably, therefore, the UK's ability
to influence events in the world had declined and there is
very little that diplomatic activity and international public
relations can do to disguise the fact'. The Berrill team was
sceptical of a marked change in Britain's relative economic
performance over the 10-15 year 'time horizon' which it saw
itself as considering. What had changed since the Duncan
Report, the CPRS believed, was that, as a result of Common
Market membership, the EEC had added an overseas dimension to
many policies of home departments which before were almost
entirely domestic in character. Increasingly, the EEC provided
the channel through which the British voice was heard in international economic and political issues.18
    The Berrill team identified fourteen separate functions
which together made up the work of overseas representation.
These were economic, social and environmental work; export
services; foreign policy work (i.e. work connected with international political situations and activities in which the UK
was an active participant); defence work; consular services;
control of entry into the UK (i.e. immigration and visa work);
the administration of overseas aid; educational and cultural
work; external broadcasting; information work; political
work (i.e. the conduct of day-to-day bilateral political
relations and the political analysis of overseas countries);
communications; entertainment; accommodation and other
administration overseas. The Think Tank thought that, with
one exception, the distribution of resources between the
various functions reflected their relative importance and
effectiveness. Economic work and export services, which the
CPRS considered to be priority functions, accounted for about
31 per cent of total net expenditure, compared with only 10
per cent of foreign policy and defence work. The exception

was educational and cultural work, external broadcasting and information work which together accounted for 30 per cent of total net expenditure. With continuation of existing policies this proportion was likely to increase because of the heavy capital investment required to enable the BBC External Services to maintain their audibility in competition with other broadcasters. The Berrill team doubted whether it was right to give information and culture so large a share of resources. This is why it envisaged - but did not exclusively recommend - the abolition of the British Council; and why it recommended that universal world wide broadcasting by the BBC should be abandoned in favour of a greater concentration of resources on those parts of the world denied access to unbiased news and information.19

While the Think Tank believed that all the functions of overseas representation were valid objects of public expenditure, it did think that in most of them less work should be done or it should be done more selectively. The CPRS recommended major reductions in overseas information work and entertainment. It thought that in other cases, such as foreign policy work, defence work, and political work, insufficient account had been taken of the changes in the UK's position in the world. Resources were devoted to the collection of information which was not really necessary for policy makers in London, or to attempts to influence other governments which had little prospect of success. The Think Tank recommended a reduction of about one-third in the deployment of defence staff overseas and in the effort devoted to the political analysis of overseas countries. In many cases - such as foreign policy work, educational and cultural work, political work, communications and security - the CPRS found that the work was being done to an unjustifiably high standard. The Think Tank thought that this was particularly true of the Diplomatic Service which tended to err on the side of perfectionism in work whose importance was not always commensurate with the human and material resources devoted to it. The Berrill team recommended that the Service should recruit a smaller proportion of the ablest candidates, and that there should be a general downgrading of the jobs it did. In recruitment for the Diplomatic Service preference should be given to candidates who had studied relevant subjects at university. There should be more training. The Think Tank considered that more should be done to widen the social background of recruits to the Diplomatic Service. The CPRS concluded that current staffing arrangements failed to provide the specialization necessary to enable staff to acquire the expertise required for most functions. The lack of adequate specialization was especially noticeable in export promotion, and administration, economic work, immigration and the administration of posts overseas. The CPRS also thought that the existing arrangements did not provide enough interchange between staff working in the UK and staff working overseas in the same function. The Berrill team

came down marginally in favour of a merger of the Home Civil
Service and the Diplomatic Service, and the creation within the
combined Service of a Foreign Service Group, which would staff
most of the jobs in the UK and overseas.20
    The Think Tank believed that the UK maintained more
diplomatic and consular posts overseas than were required,
despite the cuts made since the Duncan Report. It recommended
substantial further cuts. The CPRS wanted the geographical
focus of the UK's overseas representation to be changed. In
non-Communist developed countries there would be reductions in
export promotion, consular services, educational and cultural
work, external broadcasting, information work and political
work. Much economic and foreign policy work would be done by
visitors from London. This should permit quite large reductions of resident staff in such countries. The Think Tank's
conclusions differed from those of the Duncan Committee. It
accepted that the bulk of the UK's overseas interests were
located in the developed countries which Duncan called the
Area of Concentration; but it thought that this was not a
sufficient guide to the distribution of overseas representation.
Account had to be taken of how far Government activity in each
country was necessary and effective for the protection and
advancement of UK interests. In closed societies and most of
the Third World, Government involvement was necessary; but
this was much less true of the developed world and the Think
Tank believed that the Government devoted an unjustifiably
high volume of resources to overseas representation there. The
Think Tank emphasized the need to develop Cabinet machinery in
relation to foreign policy and the changed role of home departments. The CPRS recommended the transfer to the Property
Services Agency of responsibility for all diplomatic and
consular accommodation overseas.21
    The Berrill Report had an even more unfavourable reception
than the Duncan Report. In its Report, the Think Tank
complained about 'the ill natured publicity' which had
accompanied its work. It recorded that it had 'encountered –
in this admittedly much reviewed field – a widespread
reluctance to accept that a further review was needed or that
present ways of doing things could be improved on'. The FCO
denied that it had set up a special anti-Tank unit to lie in
wait for the CPRS; but the Berrill Report proved to be an
easy target for critics anyway. One reason for this was the
political views associated with some members of the CPRS team.
These views surfaced in the Report where it said that 'a strong
and appealing ideology can give a country influence', and
offered the example of Nkrumah's Ghana. The Report complained
of 'a sort of "middle-classness" in the prevailing values' of
the Diplomatic Service. In this instance, Marxisant sentiments
were misleading. A more accurate description of the Diplomatic
Service was that it remained aristocratic in tone. The Report
also complained about diplomats having 'the sense of being in a
group apart and habitually moving in the highest circles of

local society'. This invited from the advocates of traditional diplomacy the response that the 'highest circles' have a disproportionate influence on policy in most systems of government, including those of socialist countries. So that, understandably, diplomatic activity tended to be concentrated on them. Some of the Think Tank's more definite recommendations read oddly. This was the case with its proposal to abolish the British Council at a time when the Americans, the French, the Germans, and the Japanese were stepping up their cultural diplomacy. The Callaghan Government rejected the relevant recommendation, just as it did the proposals to cut back on the BBC's external services. Indeed, that Government was generally dismissive of the recommendations of the Berrill Report.22

For all the shortcomings of its Report, the Think Tank team did leave behind a programme of economies which could be taken up later. It also left behind the impression that Britain's arrangements for overseas representation were characterized by Parkinson's Law. One earlier commentator sympathetic to this view pointed out that in 1914, as a Great Power, Britain had only a handful of embassies compared with the vast range of the present day.23 This ignored the realities of the different political situations. In 1914, other countries came to Britain, who had less need to go to them. It was a world of empires, in which the British Empire was sufficiently powerful to declare war on behalf of her Dominions. Fifty years later, by the time of the Plowden Report, the old empires had been displaced by a multiplicity of sovereign states, and with only a few of these could relationships be established other than on terms of some equity of representation. To the extent that a British presence is taken to mean effective British influence the scale of representation has been overdone. The importance of political reporting seems to be exaggerated. The main justification for the well developed structure of representation is the promotion of trade. As in most countries the State plays a leading part in conducting trade, the British representative has to be both diplomat and trader, doing the work of both permanent politician and export promoter. The cult of the generalist, which requires frequent movement of staff between posts, attracted the criticism of the Plowden and Duncan as well as Berrill Reports. One does not have to share the Berrill Report's sometimes grim Leveller instincts to wish for a more professional Service in terms of career patterns and recruitment and training policies. The Think Tank might have added a different dimension to its analysis if it had fully examined the equivalent arrangements for overseas representation in Japan, the most successful 'analogue' country; and especially the role of the Ministry of International Trade and Industry. 24

The separate existence of the Diplomatic Service and even of the FCO itself seems to be at least challenged by the changing context in which British overseas representation now takes place. Membership of the EEC has not restored the

position of the FCO. Indeed, the establishment of the
European Secretariat in 1972 and its retention emphasized its
decline. Why have a separate FCO at all ? The Think Tank
skirted the issue when it envisaged, but did not recommend, the
creation of a Department of Overseas Affairs from a combination
of the FCO, the Ministry of Overseas Development and the
external trade divisions of the Department of Trade.25 The
Think Tank envisaged the end of the separate existence of the
Diplomatic Service too. The FCO and the Diplomatic Service may
need the powers of obstructiveness commonly ascribed to them by
reformers to avoid these fates. They may be aided in opposition by the Home Civil Service, to whom the changes might well
be unwelcome. It is to the attempted reform of that Service
that we now turn.

References

1. As was remarked by Lord Hailsham (1975, p. 219) who
led the British negotiating team.
2. H.C. 260, (1960), pp. xxx-xxxiv; 'The End of the
Colonial Office', Public Administration, 44, (1966), pp. 480-
82; Cross (1969), pp. 113-19; Cmnd. 1308, (1961), p. 5;
Wilson (1971), pp. 10-11, 511, 521, 570-71; Cmnd. 4506,
(1970), p. 11.
3. In the 1960s, the American rate was estimated to be
an investigation into overseas representation every two years
since World War II (Walker, 1968-69, p. 309). The various
investigations were listed by Bacchus (1974), pp. 736-38.
4. Laski (1951), p. 161.
5. Berrill Report, para. 4.1.
6. Busk (1967), p. xii; Cmnd. 2276, (1964), p. vi;
Mott-Radclyffe (1975), p. 256.
7. Cmnd. 2276, (1964), paras. 2-23, 217-32, 44-5, 51,
54-5, 63-70, 72-5, 78-83, 86-104, 344-75, 117-23, 178-92.
8. Ibid., paras. 9-10.
9. 257 H.L. Deb. 5s. c. 65; Mott-Radclyffe (1975),
pp. 260-61 (confirmed in correspondence by Lord Plowden).
10. Cmnd. 2276, (1964), paras. 36, 605(b); 257 H.L. Deb.
5s. c. 119; Boardman and Groom (1973), p. 93; Gore-Booth
(1974), pp. 387-91.
11. Ibid., pp. 391-93; Cmnd. 4107, (1969), p. 5.
12. Ibid., pp. 23, 12-13.
13. Ibid., pp. 48-54, 59-62, 88, 124, 94, 113-14, 158.
14. Ibid., pp. 22-8, 31.
15. 'Editorial', Bulletin of the Institute of Development Studies, 2, (1969), p. 2; Donelan (1969), pp. 605-16;
The Economist, 19.7.1969, pp. 17-18.
16. 305 H.L. Deb. 5s. c. 997; Gore-Booth (1974), p. 393;
787 H.C. Deb. 5s. c. 611-17; 305 H.L. Deb. 5s. c. 941-54;
795 H.L. Deb. 5s. c. 15-16; Shonfield (1970), pp. 247-68.

17.   Brown (1971), p. 163; H.C. 473, (1975), pp. xvi-xvii; The Economist, 23.7.1977, p. 24; Berrill Report, pp. v-vi. As for how the Think Tank became involved, see Wallace (1978), p. 221.
18.   Berrill Report, pp. ix-x.
19.   Ibid., p. xi; paras. 13.14-15, 12.50-68.
20.   Ibid., pp. xi-xii, xv; paras. 14.39, 17.9-11, 21. 35-69, 21.86, 21.89-90, 21.93.
21.   Ibid., pp. xiii-xv; paras. 19.8, 19.11, 19.16-17, 20.7, 18.22.
22.   Ibid., paras. 21.82, 1.9, 2.8, 21.22-23; C. Larner, 'The Diplomat as Peacock', New Society, 4.8.1977, pp. 227-28; Beloff (1977), pp. 435-44; Cmnd. 7308, (1978), pp. 16-17. Regarding the well publicized political bias of the Berrill team, one of its members was reported to have told a diplomat: 'you don't seem to realize that we are building a new socialist Britain' (Sunday Telegraph, 7.8.1977). The Economist, 6.1.1977, p. 17 and The Times, 5.8.1977, reported that the FCO had established an 'anti-Tank unit', in the latter case suggesting that the unit fed black propaganda about the Think Tank team to the Press. The FCO did have a Review Unit - supervized by Sir Andrew Stark - but its work was officially described to me in terms of servicing the Think Tank team, acting as a liaison point for it.
23.   Watt (1969), pp. 485-86.
24.   The Japanese arrangements are described in Scalapino (1977), pp. 3-35, 227-29.
25.   Berrill Report, paras. 20.43-47.

Chapter 10

CHANGING THE GUARDIANS: THE REFORM OF THE HOME CIVIL SERVICE

'Whether or not new wine is being poured into the Civil
Service these days ... it is certain that the old bottles are
there to receive it.' Thus ran C H Sisson's verdict from
within the Service on what he called the 'pseudo-revolution'
wrought by the Fulton Report of 1968. Committees of inquiry
and Royal Commissions have the reputation, not always deserved,
of not making much of a mark on the Civil Service. The
Priestley Report of 1955, for example, was described by one
eminent observer as being likely to share the reputation of
the Playfair, Ridley, MacDonnell and Tomlin Reports before it:
namely of being unread and unreadable. Worse, in the eyes of
critics, little action seems to follow from a Commission's or
committee's deliberations. The exception to these rules is
commonly seen as being the Trevelyan-Northcote Report of 1853.
Written in the forthright prose of the then official head of
the Treasury, Sir Charles Trevelyan, and possessing the virtue
of brevity, the Trevelyan-Northcote Report has a radical
reputation. This is despite the fact that it was almost
seventy years before its reform programme could be sensibly
said to have been implemented. The Organization Report of 1853
was undeniably important, but perhaps its reputation owed something to its style of presentation.1
    'The first full dress inquiry into the British Home Civil
Service since the Northcote-Trevelyan reforms of the early
1850s.' That was how Harold Wilson later described the work of
the Committee which, in February 1966, he set up under the
chairmanship of the Vice Chancellor of the University of Sussex,
Lord Fulton, 'to examine the structure, recruitment and
management, including training, of the Home Civil Service, and
to make recommendations'. Actually, the MacDonnell Commission
of 1912-15 had a broader remit which included the Foreign
Office and the Diplomatic Service, and its Report was an
important one. Nevertheless, to judge from the first chapter
of the Fulton Report when it was published in June 1968, it was
the Trevelyan-Northcote inquiry that the more critical members
of the Committee seemed to wish to emulate. Sir James Dunnett,
one of the two Permanent Secretaries involved (with Sir Philip

Allen), identified Robert Neild, Norman Hunt, and Fulton himself as closely associated with views about reforming the Civil
Service present in the then (he thought, securely established)
Labour Government. It was Dunnett's belief that 'nothing ...
would have been worse than for the Committee to have split -
Lord Simey ... and two Permanent Secretaries on the one hand
against change, and the rest of the Committee endorsing a more
extreme Report on the other'. The result was a compromise.
The first chapter - substantially the work of Hunt - contained
the views of the critics. Among other things, the chapter
berated the Civil Service for amateurism when the need was for
(an undefined) professionalism. Thereafter, as Dunnett said,
while it was 'not without recommendations for change', the
Fulton Report was 'broadly conservative'.2

    This was always a more likely result of the machinations
of the Fulton Committee than the 'fundamental and wide ranging
inquiry' into the Civil Service that Harold Wilson promised in
1966. The then Prime Minister, in fact, effectively ruled out
such an inquiry at the time of the Committee's appointment.
For Wilson emphasized that 'the Government's willingness to
consider changes in the Civil Service does not imply any
intention on its part to alter the basic relationship between
Ministers and Civil Servants. Civil Servants, however eminent,
remain the confidential advisers of Ministers, who alone are
answerable to Parliament for policy; and we do not envisage
any change in this fundamental feature of our parliamentary
system of democracy'. When the Fulton Report was published,
it was evident that this 'rider' to the Committee's terms of
reference had inhibited its discussion of the current working
of the doctrine of Ministerial responsibility. It prevented
the elucidation of the precise relationships with Ministers of
the men constituting the core of the Civil Service. As the
Committee also saw its terms of reference as excluding what
Wilson later called 'one most important subject, the machinery
of government', the Fulton Report was a much less 'wide ranging
and fundamental review' of the Civil Service than it should
have been.3

    Take, for example, the machinery of government. According
to its Chairman, the Fulton Committee, in framing its
recommendations, felt obliged to look 'to a period ahead of not
less than a quarter of a century'. How could the Committee
manage this without anticipating changes in governmental
machinery ? The difficulties of the exercise were indicated
in the Committee's discussion of the structure of government
departments and the promotion of efficiency in them. The
Committee was 'much impressed' by the Swedish system, whereby
small central departments have the main responsibility for
policy making, while the task of managing and operating
policies is hived off to autonomous agencies. This system is
used not only for activities of a commercial kind, as is
largely so with public corporations in Britain, but also for
public services in social fields. The Committee thought that

the separation of policy making from execution worked well in
Sweden, and considered that there was a wide variety of
activities in Britain - including parts of the social services -
to which the principle of 'hiving off' might be applied.   The
Committee observed that 'we have not been able to make the
detailed study which would identify particular cases; but we
see no reason to believe that the dividing line between
activities for which Ministers are directly responsible, and
those for which they are not, is necessarily drawn in the right
place today. The creation of further autonomous bodies, and
the drawing of the line between them and central government,
would raise parliamentary and constitutional issues, especially
if they affected the answerability for sensitive matters such
as social and educational services. These issues and the
related questions of machinery of government are beyond our
terms of reference. We think, however, that the possibility of
a considerable extension of "hiving off" should be examined and
we therefore recommend an early and thorough review of the
whole question'.4 The large scale 'hiving off' of part of the
activities of government departments to bodies that would
resemble public corporations would naturally have implications
for the Civil Service. Freed from concern about day-to-day
parliamentary control, the Civil Servants charged with 'hived
off' activities would have the opportunity of more fully
concentrating on managing them, and could be more easily seen
as responsible for their management. Some would argue that
only under such conditions can 'accountable management' - as
favoured by the Committee - be achieved in the Civil Service.
One need not agree with the Committee in order to appreciate
the undesirability of the limitations placed upon it. The
Committee was forced to recommend the setting up of a further
committee to consider what it needed to consider itself.

Another example was the convention of Ministerial responsibility. Despite its preclusion from making recommendations affecting basically the constitutional relationship between Ministers
and Civil Servants, the Fulton Committee did examine some problems of the political control of government departments.   It
found no need for the creation of Ministerial cabinets on the
French model, as had been advocated by the Labour Party in
their evidence to it, and none for political appointments on
a large scale.   However, it did say that a Minister should
be free to change some of the Civil Servants immediately
surrounding him, notably his Private Secretary and, subject to
safeguards, his Permanent Secretary (although that would be
'more exceptional'). A Minister was already free to change his
Private Secretary and even his Permanent Secretary. A recommendation of this sort was more of a hint than a statement, and
it hinted at something which wants altering in the Minister-
Civil Servant relationship: but what was it? More definite
statements by the Committee drew attention to the recent
widening of access to the work of Civil Servants, and made
important recommendations for even wider access. The Committee

again veered into the choppy waters of Ministerial responsibility by recommending that the whole process of policy-making
should be made more open. Again, it had to suggest a further
inquiry to examine means of making it more open. The Committee
also expressed hopes for the further strengthening of the
accountability of Civil Servants to Parliament and to the
public. In this context it noted the appointment of the
Parliamentary Commissioner for Administration. It also drew
attention to the potential significance of the development of
the new specialized parliamentary committees. It welcomed such
developments as lessening the secrecy surrounding policy-
making in the Civil Service. The Committee went on to argue
that the new developments had important implications for the
traditional anonymity of Civil Servants. This anonymity was
'already being eroded by Parliament and to a more limited
extent by the pressure of the Press, radio and television; the
process will continue and we see no reason to reverse it.
Indeed we think that administration suffers from the convention
which is still alive in many fields, that only the Minister
should explain issues in public and what his department is or
is not doing about them. This convention has depended in the
past on the assumption that the doctrine of Ministerial
responsibility means that a Minister has full detailed knowledge and control of all the activities of his department.
This assumption is no longer tenable. The Minister and his
junior Ministers cannot know all that is going on in his
department, nor can they nowadays be present at every forum
where legitimate questions are asked about its activities. The
consequence is that some of these questions go unanswered. In
our view, therefore, the convention of anonymity should be
modified and Civil Servants, as professional administrators,
should be able to go further than now in explaining what their
departments are doing, at any rate so far as concerns managing
existing policies and implementing legislation'. The Committee
decided against offering 'any specific precepts for the
progressive relaxation of the convention of anonymity'. However,
it did suggest that the further inquiry which it recommended
that the Government should undertake to examine ways and means
of getting rid of unnecessary secrecy both in policy-making and
administration 'may well result in specific recommendations on
this closely related problem'.5 Now here was an issue central
to any reconstruction of the Civil Service: but the Fulton
Committee was again forced to leave it to a further committee.
The comments about developments impinging upon the relationship
between Ministers and Civil Servants were useful. Nevertheless,
the Committee's inability to discuss the basis of the Minister-
Civil Servant relationship prevented it from working out the
implications of what it was saying. If it had attempted an
adequate historical introduction to its Report, the Committee
could have discussed the development of the conventions and so
at least implicitly indicated some of the consequences of its
recommendations on anonymity.

The fact of the matter is that the doctrine of Ministerial responsibility is the basis of the work of the Home Civil Service. The whole role of the Administrative Class - the main target of the critical first chapter - was built around the convention. Any full examination of 'the structure, recruitment and management, including training' of that Service had to include a consideration of the working of that doctrine. Given the qualifications added to its terms of reference, the Fulton Committee could not really fulfil its task.

The Committee had the consolation of having what were interpreted as being its main recommendations accepted by the Labour Government of the day. These were to transfer the central management of the Home Civil Service from the Treasury to a new Civil Service Department; to establish a Civil Service College to promote post-entry training in the Service; and to replace the Service's class system with 'a single, unified grading structure'. As we shall see, the Fulton Committee made other recommendations on, for example, direct entry recruitment, and on the establishment of policy planning units and the appointment of Senior Policy Advisers, which were deemed less generally acceptable. The implementation of the Fulton Report passed into the hands of the Home Civil Service. Under the chairmanship of the Head of that Service, Sir William Armstrong, a National Whitley Council Joint Committee on the Fulton Report was established shortly after that document's publication. The Armstrong Committee was 'not limited in its terms of reference to issues arising specifically from the Fulton Report'. Its task was the more general one of 'the reform of the Civil Service, taking full account of, but not bound by, what the Fulton Report had to say'. The Armstrong Committee, and the machinery of consultation built around it, had the opportunity to make a contribution to the development of the Civil Service of the kind made by the National Whitley Council's Reorganization Committee of 1920-21, which was similarly composed of leading Civil Servants and staff association representatives.6 Until it was wound up in 1973, the Armstrong Committee was one source of change in the Civil Service. Its appointment was a reminder of the extent to which the Civil Service was self governing, unionized, and an interest in its own right. This was reflected in many of the changes made in the post-Fulton period, but particularly in those made in the Civil Service's central management.

I   THE CENTRAL MANAGEMENT OF THE HOME CIVIL SERVICE

The Fulton Committee's proposal that the central management of the Home Civil Service should be taken away from the Treasury and given to a new Civil Service Department was immediately accepted by the Labour Government. The Civil Service Department came into formal existence on November 1st 1968. It took over the staffs and the responsibilities of the Civil Service Commission and the Pay and Management Divisions of the Treasury.

The Ministerial arrangements followed the pattern outlined in the Fulton Report. The Prime Minister became Minister for the Civil Service, with the day-to-day work being done by another Minister, usually one without a departmental portfolio. As for the Civil Servants, the Fulton Committee's suggestion that the Permanent Secretary to the new Department should be Head of the Home Civil Service was followed. In the first instance, this meant that the post was retained by Sir William Armstrong, who also held it under the previous arrangements.7

The creation of the Civil Service Department was of doubtful practical value. The Fulton Committee need not have been as worried as it seemed to have been because the British Civil Service was 'almost alone' in assigning its central management to the central finance department. What was not demonstrated was that other countries' experience of alternative arrangements similar to those which the Committee came to favour worked either better or even as well as the traditional British ones. The Committee failed to rebut satisfactorily the argument advanced by Armstrong's predecessor, Sir Laurence Helsby. This was that under concentrated control the two functions of controlling expenditure and managing the Service could be more effectively discharged through being combined in one department; and that such a single department must be more effective on both sides of its work by reason of the knowledge of departmental organization and personalities that was derived from its wide range of interest. The Committee considered that there would be reason to fear too great a concentration of power in one department if the enlarged responsibility for career development, which it envisaged being given to those conducting the central management of the Service, was added to the Treasury's responsibilities for financial and economic policy and for the control of public expenditure. The general view among Permanent Secretaries was that a strong and effective combined Treasury improved machinery of government as a whole. They preferred to deal with one central controlling department. They feared that it would complicate their task of management to have to 'clear their lines' with two departments. In particular, the pre-Fulton system enabled departments to get central approval of proposals involving both staff and expenditure in the same operation. The Permanent Secretaries disliked the prospect of two independent, though overlapping, operations. A staff association, the Institution of Professional Civil Servants also believed that the established arrangements had advantages. It said that 'the divisions dealing with staffing matters could no doubt be separated from the rest of the Treasury. But this would achieve nothing if the new department thus created had then to go to the Treasury to obtain financial approval for the arrangements it wished to implement. There are enough difficulties at present without creating an extra step. It is fundamentally important that departments and staff associations and other bodies should be able to consult and negotiate with a central organization which has effective power'. In addition and in view of the importance which it itself placed upon such work, the Fulton Committee's recommendation that the responsibility for the development and dissemination of administrative and management techniques should be transferred from the Treasury to the CSD was a particularly unfortunate one. This was because, as Sir Laurence Helsby pointed out, 'the dissemination of knowledge of these techniques, and their application to particular projects or blocks of expenditure call for close collaboration with the divisions dealing with expenditure and the advantages of conducting such a joint operation in a single department are obvious'.8

Whether or not it appreciated these advantages, the Fulton Committee did not believe that its general proposals for reform would be implemented in the radical spirit it deemed to be necessary if the central management of the Service remained with the Treasury. The Committee asserted that 'there is today among Civil Servants a lack of confidence in the Treasury as the centre of Civil Service management'. As no supporting evidence was referred to, this assertion was difficult to examine. According to Fulton, the CSD was supposed to be 'in a position to fight, and to be seen fighting, the Treasury on behalf of the Service'. Presumably, Civil Service morale was supposed to benefit, and some staff associations may have hoped for 'better' pay deals. The expectations of Fulton and of the associations were always likely to be unfulfilled, not least because of the sheer scale of the Service and its massive cost. If there was a Golden Age of the Civil Service, from the standpoint of morale and pay, it was the late 1930s. Then, so the veterans tell us, ordinary members of the Executive Class bought four bedroomed houses and reflected upon the rising cost of domestic servants. However, in 1939, the number of non-industrial Civil Servants was only 163,000. Thirty years later, this total was 475,000. At the beginning of 1978, the figure was 567,000. The Chancellor of the Exchequer had to have a major voice in decisions relating to the sums of public expenditure concerned. There was also the point that, however golden the past, the pay and conditions of the Service were currently generous, at least from the taxpayers' standpoint. This was a standpoint which was unrepresented in the much praised Whitley system of joint consultation. Following the Priestley Commission of 1953-55, pay research arrangements were established under which Civil Service salaries were determined by the principle of 'fair comparison with the current remuneration of outside staffs employed on broadly comparable work'. Given differences in security of tenure between Civil Servants and their counterparts in the private sector, it could be doubted if 'fair comparisons' were all that 'fair' to the latter. To add to the demands on the taxpayers, index linked pensions for the Civil Service were introduced by legislation in 1971.9

Such 'revolutionary improvements in the conditions of

employment of Civil Servants', as one staff association representative described the superannuation changes, did not prevent poor industrial relations characterizing the early years of the CSD's existence. Indeed, the first Civil Service strike took place in 1973. Under often militant leadership, industrial action remained a real threat thereafter. The Staff Side of the National Whitley Council continued to be in favour of a CSD, arguing that it had 'a firm role to play'. It did not say what this role precisely was, and why it needed to be performed in an organization separate from the Treasury. Many of the developments in post-entry training and in management services, which the Staff Side approved of, began under the Treasury. As for 'the more creative personnel work' that the Staff Side saw as characterizing the post-Fulton order, the most 'creative' proposals for change made were those which related to the employment of women in the Civil Service. These owed a good deal to the original initiative of Sir William Armstrong. It is difficult to believe that this initiative would not have been forthcoming if Armstrong had remained Joint Permanent Secretary to the Treasury as well as Head of the Home Civil Service. Indeed, the establishment of the CSD was a victory for the principle of change for its own sake.10

II   THE STRUCTURE OF THE HOME CIVIL SERVICE

The Fulton Committee's recommendation that the existing structure of the Home Civil Service should be replaced by what it called a unified grading structure was immediately accepted by the Government. Harold Wilson described the proposals as meaning 'the abolition of classes within the Civil Service'. In a sense, they did. For the Committee seemed to have followed advice, such as that received from the Treasury, that it would 'probably be right to abolish the word "class" throughout the Service, and substitute some less emotive word such as "group"'. Accordingly, insofar as it discussed the details of its proposed structure, the Fulton Committee talked in terms of occupational groups or groupings. One of its more definite recommendations was that Civil Servants of Under Secretary level and above should constitute a Senior Policy and Management Group.11

The Armstrong Committee shared this ambition of making 'the senior levels of the Service an "open society" in which each post is filled by the individual best fitted for it, irrespective of his profession, discipline, and previous history within the Service'. This meant 'the abolition of classes and the absorption of all posts at and above the level of Under Secretary and equivalent grades into a single, rationalized pay and grading structure'. Below this Open Structure, which was swiftly established, the Armstrong Committee generally followed a strategy of dividing up the Service into broad categories and occupational groups. In the autumn of 1971 a Science Group within the Science Category was formed by an amalgamation of the Scientific Officer, Experimental Officer and Scientific Assistant Classes. From the beginning of 1972, the Works Group of Professional Classes together with some associated classes were merged to help to form the Professional and Technology Category. The most important change was the merger of the Administrative, Executive and Clerical Classes to form a single Administration Group within the General Category with effect from January 1st 1971. The merger involved about 40 per cent of the staff of the Home Civil Service. As a result of the changes, at some points where the Administrative and Executive Class ladders previously ran in parallel, they were amalgamated. Another important change (at least in nomenclature) was the abolition of the Assistant Principal grade, the traditional point of entry for the best graduate direct entrants. It was replaced by two training grades called Administration Trainee and Higher Executive Officer (A).12

As the Civil Service which Fulton reviewed comprised 47 general and 1,400 departmental classes, there was scope for some rationalization of its structure. What was not established was anything resembling a unified grading structure. The changes that did take place were always more likely to be ones of form rather than of substance. Take, for instance, the creation of the Science Group. The Fulton Committee did not argue a case for such a merger. It seemed to think it analogous with the widely advocated amalgamation of the Administrative Executive, and Clerical Classes. However, in recruiting to the generalist side of the Service - with the exception of late entry recruitment - what was looked for in candidates was crude clerical, managerial, and administrative potential to be refined or realized by work within the Service. In the case of the Scientific Civil Service, there might well be advantages in having all candidates with first degrees entering at the same point, and a single promotion ladder might well make for greater flexibility. Nevertheless, the jobs remained specific and demanded certain levels of scientific knowledge. Recruitment and other arrangements had to reflect this. Much the same considerations applied to the merger connected with the Works Group. Despite its relative lack of complexity, the reconstruction of the generalist side of the Service was incomplete. The reconstruction more or less followed the lines of the Treasury's evidence to Fulton. This had included a revised structure which was remarkably similar to that designed by the Plowden Committee for the Diplomatic Service. The accompanying recruitment, promotion and training arrangements ensured that the Administrative Class - the prime target of the critics - survived, except in name.13

III DIRECT ENTRY RECRUITMENT TO THE HOME CIVIL SERVICE

The Fulton Committee's treatment of the problems of direct entry recruitment to the Civil Service was inadequate. It neglected to do more than briefly mention either the problems of recruiting specialists in particular or of non-graduates in general. The Committee wanted the Service to recruit specialists not only 'in the right numbers', but also of the 'right type and quality'.14   The Service would no doubt oblige if it could. The problem was how to do it.

The Fulton Committee also displayed confusion in discussing the problems associated with direct entry recruitment of graduates into the generalist side of the Service.   The main problem worrying reformers was the persistent dominance of the outside entry to the Administrative Class by Oxford and Cambridge liberal arts graduates. A majority of the Committee wanted to continue attracting such graduates, while at the same time giving preference to graduates in the natural sciences, engineering and the social sciences. The Government rejected 'preference for relevance'. It considered that the market for able graduates was competitive. Hence, a bias in favour of certain academic disciplines would be more likely to reduce than to increase the number of acceptable candidates. However, the Fulton Committee's recommendation that there should be an inquiry into the selection process was accepted. Indeed, two inquiries took place. One conducted by Cooper Brothers, a firm of accountants and management consultants, was completed by February 1969. Its report led to the speeding up of Civil Service Commission procedures. The other inquiry, conducted by a Committee under the chairmanship of J G W Davies (a former Secretary of the Cambridge University Appointments Board) investigated the selection arrangements for administrators.   It reported in September 1969.   It had been required to examine the current working of the Method II means of recruitment. This combined a qualifying written examination, a series of tests and interviews over two days (at the Civil Service Selection Board), and a Final Selection Board.   Method II, which had been introduced after the War had become more effective in attracting successful candidates than Method I, the traditional 'literary' means of entry to the Administrative Class. The Fulton Committee was divided over the future of Method I.   However, when the Government consulted university opinion it was found to be overwhelmingly against the retention of Method I.   Accordingly, in May 1969, it was announced that Method I would be discontinued after the 1969 examination. One of the factors which influenced the Government's decision was that the Davies Committee had no doubts about the fairness of Method II. Indeed, that Committee found 'no evidence of bias in Method II itself either in the procedures or on the part of the assessors'. It talked of Method II as 'a selection system to which the Public Service can point with pride'.   Nevertheless, the Davies Committee managed to produce 23 recommendations for changes, which the Government implemented in whole or in part. However, these recommendations were framed on the assumption of Method II continuing to be used for selecting 'graduates with the

qualities of Assistant Principals'. The Committee recognized
that 'if and when the wider graduate entry discussed in the
Fulton Report is introduced or other changes occur, consequent-
ial change in the selection system may well be needed'.15
    The essential problem in direct entry recruitment to the
generalist side of the Service by the time of Fulton was to
ensure that it reflected the expansion of university education.
Previously, the Administrative Class took what it defined as
'high fliers', disproportionately from the upper middle class
products of Oxford and Cambridge. The next major entry point
was the Executive Class, which, ideally, recruited from among
those with university entrance qualifications. Below that,
again ideally, the Clerical Class recruited from the 16 plus
school leaver. In fact, promotion from below ensured that a
substantial minority of the Administrative Class had begun
their Service careers elsewhere, usually in the Executive
Class. The Executive Class was numerically dominated by former
members of the Clerical Class, in whose ranks, in practice,
well qualified school leavers were a small minority. The
Society of Civil and Public Servants and the Civil and Public
Services Association understandably portrayed their membership in terms of massed ranks of untried talent. This is partly
what the leaderships of staff associations are paid to do. It
may even have been true, say, of the Civil Service of 1938.
University expansion and better educational opportunities and
a wider range of available careers made this an unconvincing
portrayal of the Civil Service of 1968. Under the arrangements devised by the Armstrong Committee, provision for
promotion from the ranks persisted. What the creation of the
Administration Group provided was the opportunity to markedly
increase the number of university entrants, broadening the
entry to include what Method II would have previously defined
as graduates of middle order ability. The critical decision
was whether the wider graduate entry was to be differentiated
or not. In its evidence to Fulton, the Treasury was clear that
the Service's 'first need is for the brightest young graduates
who at present come in as Assistant Principals'. It proposed
that, within the larger entry, such graduates 'might be
"starred" or otherwise designated on the strength of their
academic records and their performance at the selection
stage'.16 The exemption from the qualifying examination of
those with the best academic records was actually stopped, at
the suggestion of the Davies Committee. What did continue was
that performance in the recruitment process was overwhelmingly
the determinant of the graduate entrants' future career. The
'starred' entry was the old Administrative Class in all but
title. It was assured from the outset that the familiar
career opportunities were there. The alternative of leaving
differentiation to depend upon performance in the Service,
notably in the training period, never seems to have been
seriously considered.

IV   POST-ENTRY TRAINING IN THE HOME CIVIL SERVICE

Despite a good deal of talk in its Report about the need for greater professionalism in the Service, the Fulton Report gave surprisingly little attention to post-entry training. The Fulton Committee's proposals were very similar to those put forward in January 1967 by a Treasury Working Party on Management Training in the Civil Service. The most novel recommendation on training in the Fulton Report - and one accepted by the Government - was that a Civil Service College should be established. The provision of post-entry training available in the Service increased markedly in the post-Fulton period. This was particularly so in comparison with the period before the establishment of the Treasury's Centre for Administrative Studies in 1963. Although the Fulton Report relatively neglected them, this increased provision applied to specialists as well as to non-graduates on the generalist side of the Service. Nonetheless, any advances made in post-entry training were overshadowed by what was widely seen as the failure of the Civil Service College.

From the outset, it was difficult to see how the Civil Service College could succeed. The appointment of an academic, Eugene Grebenik, as the first Principal of the College, did not help. It seems that the Service feared that the post would go to Norman Hunt if it did not act swiftly. Grebenik's appointment quickly followed. The first Principal, a negativist by temperament, made no secret of confusions about the College's role. As for his own role, Grebenik once followed the example of a colleague, and likened himself to 'the driver of a train of camels across a poorly chartered desert. The beasts have wills of their own, the passengers, some of whom have not wanted to make the journey, see mirages in the form of oases to left and right. The leader, his body kicked and his soul damned at every twist and turn of the route, has just to keep on smiling and crying "onward" !' In Grebenik's case, the direction - if there was one - was always more likely to be 'backwards'. The appointment of an experienced Civil Servant - like Grebenik's eventual successor - might have made some difference, but not decisively so. The staff associations were determined that the institution should not be a Higher Civil Service College, and that it should serve the needs of their members. As the critical Heaton-Williams Report observed in 1974, the Civil Service College ended up being expected 'to combine the roles of All Souls and an adult education centre, with some elements of technical education and teacher training thrown in for good measure'. To which Grebenik added 'Amen'.17

The Fulton Committee should have made its own mark on post-entry training, and escaped the grip of the Treasury Working Party and the staff associations. As even in the mid-1970s, with the College firmly established, 94 per cent of Civil Service training took place elsewhere, the Committee should have gone for excellence. What was - and remains -

needed was a British version of the <u>Ecole Nationale</u>
<u>d'Administration</u>. At that institution both graduate and non-
graduate entrants to the French Higher Civil Service undergo an
arduous two-and-a-half year course primarily in economics,
public administration and related subjects, combined with
practical work. For the graduates, moreover, this course
begins immediately upon entry. The Fulton Committee, like the
Treasury Working Party before it, and then the Service, not
only wanted British graduate entrants to undertake a less
substantial course, but it also wanted such graduates to
receive what formal instruction they were going to get after
successfully completing their probation. However, the numbers
failing to pass probation had been very small in the past.
There was no reason for supposing that they would be very
great in the future. One of the functions of a training
programme begun immediately upon entry could be to sort out
those unlikely to make the grade. Such evaluation could be
conducted over a longer period than that possible under the
recruitment machinery, no matter how fairly run. Moreover, the
placing of the training course at the very outset of a
graduate's career on the administrative side of the Service
would be an act of obvious professionalization which might make
the Service more attractive to more graduates of the desired
quality. As it was, it was unclear why the British administrative cadets should be required to make do with less instruction in subjects relevant to their future careers than their
French counterparts who, anyway, were much more likely to have
already undertaken university studies in such subjects. An
additional point was that more provision needed to be made for
non-graduates if they were to have a fair chance of competing
with graduates for promotions in the Service.18

Particularly after the establishment of the Centre for
Administrative Studies, much has been achieved in the sphere
of post-entry training in the Home Civil Service. Nevertheless, it was to be regretted that, despite its references to
the need for greater professionalism in the Civil Service, the
Fulton Committee managed no more than a cursory treatment of
post-entry training arrangements. Since, obviously, those
arrangements were one of the major determinants of the
Service's level of professionalism.

V   SENIOR POLICY ADVISERS AND PLANNING UNITS

The most interesting proposals in the Fulton Report were those
relating to policy planning units and Senior Policy Advisers.
This was because, however unconsciously, the Fulton Committee
was pointing to the policy 'gap' in British government, and
suggesting a means of at least partially closing it.

The Fulton Committee proposed that in most departments a
planning unit should be established. A Senior Policy Adviser
would be at its head 'whose prime job, like that of the unit,
would be to look to, and prepare for, the future and to ensure

that day-to-day decisions are taken with as full a recognition
as possible of likely future developments'. He was intended to
be able to by-pass the Permanent Secretary and be guaranteed
access to the Minister. As things stood, of course, the
Permanent Secretary was the Minister's chief policy adviser.
It was unclear how the Committee could, on the one hand, accord
the Permanent Secretary the day-to-day responsibility for
running the department and, on the other, preclude him from
responsibility for long term policy planning and the associated
research. Because of the nature of his duties as 'head of the
office under the Minister', the Permanent Secretary's advice on
long term policy might well have particular value. Permanent
Secretaries did carry 'a heavy burden': but they were well
placed to delegate lesser duties to their senior colleagues.
The Committee's words about access to the Minister read oddly.
It envisaged the Senior Policy Adviser being of at least
Deputy Secretary status. That would ensure access. What the
Committee seemed to want for him was privileged access, but it
did not argue a case for that. The Fulton Committee said that
'the main task of the planning unit should be to identify and
study the problems and needs of the future and the possible
means to meet them'. The Committee also envisaged that the
Senior Policy Adviser 'would be free to determine, after
consultation with the Permanent Secretary but subject only to
the approval of the Minister, what problems his planning unit
should tackle'.19 Nevertheless, at least in constitutional
theory, policy, long term or otherwise, was a sphere for
Ministerial initiative. To conceive of it in another manner
was to see policy formation as a continuing process. What
about political control of this process ? Could any Minister
bind his successors to any conclusions that the unit would
reach ? The Committee did not point up the constitutional
significance of what it was saying.

On the tenth anniversary of the publication of the Fulton
Report, there were fourteen policy planning units, officially
described as such, in central government departments. They
were to be found in the following departments: the Civil
Service Department, the Board of Customs and Excise, the
Ministry of Defence, the Department of Education and Science,
the Department of Employment, the Department of the Environ-
ment, the Foreign and Commonwealth Office, the Department of
Health and Social Security, the Home Office, the Board of
Inland Revenue, the Scottish Home and Health Department, the
Department of Transport, the Treasury, and the Welsh Office.
What did or did not officially qualify as a planning unit
varied considerably. While the rest of the units were
'relatively small' as Fulton suggested, the Ministry of
Defence's planning unit - which it dated from 1964 - seemed to
embrace much of its higher decision making structure. A
minority of the units pre-dated Fulton. For example, the
Intelligence Branch of the Board of Customs and Excise had been
originally established in 1922. Following Fulton, its name was

changed to the Departmental Planning Unit. The Board of Inland Revenue established a planning unit in 1965. In the previous year, the Foreign Office, as it then was, had created a Planning Staff in anticipation of the recommendation of the Plowden Report. The DES had a planning unit from 1966, when, on the insistence of Anthony Crosland, a Planning Branch was established. The other units which survived in 1978 were all post-Fulton creations: but none were Fulton type planning units.20

Certainly, there were no Fulton style Senior Policy Advisers to be found in government departments ten years after the publication of the Report. From time to time in the intervening years, there have been highly placed policy advisers in departments, who were not regular Civil Servants, and who often had privileged access to Ministers on a personal basis. None of these advisers has been supported by Fultonite planning units. This is not to say that they always lacked support. Indeed, the organization that first developed under Christopher Foster, when he was Director General of Economic Planning at the Ministry of Transport 1966-69 and then in the DOE 1974-77, became a substantial enterprise. The most controversial policy adviser was Nicholas Kaldor (Special Adviser to the Chancellor of the Exchequer 1964-68, 1974-76). The longest serving proved to be Brian Abel-Smith, Professor of Social Administration in the University of London since 1965. He was a part-time Senior Adviser to the Secretary of State for Social Services from 1968 to 1970, and then from 1974 to 1979. This meant that he served Richard Crossman, Barbara Castle, and David Ennals. Abel-Smith's role at the DHSS was to advise the Secretary of State on all his responsibilities. He had no supporting unit. Crossman wrote of Abel-Smith in 1970 that 'he has been my closest personal friend and without him I could have done very little in the past two years'. Abel-Smith was a member of what Crossman called his 'circus' which helped him to prepare his National Superannuation Bill. Abel-Smith was one of the architects of Crossman's National Health Service Green Paper. He was also associated with the decisions to give higher priority to expenditure on hospitals for the subnormal, and to set up the Hospital Advisory Service. Crossman called the White Paper on Mental Handicap 'Brian's White Paper'.21

The Fulton recommendations for policy planning units resulted from disquiet about existing provision in government departments. The appointment of policy advisers in recent years was indicative of an unwillingness on the part of Governments to rely solely on the resources of the conventional Civil Service machinery. While Kaldor, Foster and Abel-Smith were all Labour appointees, this unwillingness extended to Conservatives too. For example, the role accorded to Sir Arthur Cockfield, as Adviser on Taxation in the Treasury between 1970 and 1973, in assisting the implementation of the tax strategy that he had helped to devise in Opposition. Advisers of this type differed from the political or special

advisers who were widely introduced into government departments
when Labour returned to office in 1974. Although some of these
latter advisers had specialized expertise, their primary role
was to provide general political support to the Minister within
a department, acting as the Minister's eyes and ears. Political advisers of this kind seem to be a surrogate for good
junior Ministers. The policy advisers of the Foster, Kaldor,
Cockfield and Abel-Smith kind, while not lacking political
commitment, were more obviously brought into government for
their specialized abilities. The experience of, and contacts
with, the Civil Service which Sir Arthur Cockfield possessed
made his introduction into the Treasury in 1970 all the
easier.22

It was unfortunate that the Fulton Committee did not make
the attempt to more obviously place its proposed Senior Policy
Advisers and planning units within the conventional departmental framework. The examples which it had in mind were so placed
(the Economic Section of the Treasury, and the Economic
Adviser to HM Government, in the person of Sir Robert Hall,
1947-61).23 As it was, the particular manner in which the
Fulton Committee presented its recommendations helped to ensure
the muted response which they received.

VI   THE FULTON LEGACY

The desire of at least some members of the Fulton Committee to
produce a radical Report was not satisfied. Given the
constraints imposed on the Committee's terms of reference this
was a tall order from the outset. Moreover, the climate of
opinion which had in the end led to the Committee's appointment
had induced the Civil Service to make some changes. The actual
appointment of the Committee persuaded the Service to make, or
promise to make, some more. By the time that the Fulton
Committee reported, the process of Civil Service reform had
been going on for some time. Insofar as its terms of reference
permitted, the Committee's job was to take a synoptic view of
the Service's problems; and to give it a decisive prod in such
areas as post-entry training where it remained reluctant to go
the whole way. The Fulton Committee did nothing of the kind.
The Fulton legacy was a meagre one in terms of worthwhile
change. Its contribution on the critical matter of training
was cursory and inadequate. More generally, it lacked an
informed overview of its task. As we have seen, the Government
selected what it deemed to be the main recommendations. Of
these, the Armstrong Committee seemed to decide that a unified
grading structure might be alright for, say, British Petroleum,
but not for the Home Civil Service. In the eyes of their
critics, the Civil Servants remained a law unto themselves.
Some looked to a reform of the Official Secrets Act to open up
the Service.24 This change came to have the power of
intellectual fashion behind it, in much the same way as the
campaign for a British Ombudsman had once had.

References

1.   Sisson (1971), p. 250;   Mackenzie (1956), p. 129;
Fry (1969), pp. 35-6.
2.   Wilson (1971), p. 539;   Fulton Report, p. 2;   Dunnett
(1976), pp. 372-73;   information supplied by Lord Boyle.
3.   724 H.C. Deb. 5s. c. 209-10;   773 H.C. Deb. 5s. c.
1555;   767 H.C. Deb. 5s. c. 454.
4.   295 H.L. Deb. 5s. c. 1167;   Fulton Report, pp. 61-2.
5.   Ibid., pp. 91-4.
6.   767 H.C. Deb. 5s. c. 455-56;   Armstrong Report
(Feb., 1969), pp. iii, 28.
7.   Ibid., p. 3;   Fulton Report, pp. 83-4.
8.   Ibid., pp. 81, 86;   Fulton Evidence, 5(i), pp. 101-2,
292.
9.   Fulton Report, p. 82;   Civil Service Opinion,
October 1973, pp. 319-20;   Civil Service Statistics 1970, p.5;
Civil Service Statistics 1978, p. 31;   Priestley Report, p.25;
Fry (1974), pp. 319-33.
10.   'Annual Report of IPCS 1972', State Service, March
1973, p. 14 (William McCall);   Whitley Bulletin, January 1972,
p. 2;   326 H.L. Deb. 5s. c. 800.
11.   767 H.C. Deb. 5s. c. 456;   Fulton Evidence, 5(i),p.5;
Fulton Report, pp. 69-78.
12.   Armstrong Report (Feb., 1969), pp. 24-5;   Armstrong
Report (July, 1969), para. 4;   Armstrong Report (March, 1972),
pp. 2, 5-10, 27-30.   The Administration Trainee Scheme and the
related structure was clearly set out in H.C. 535-III, (1977),
pp. 882-86.
13.   Fulton Report, pp. 65, 70;   Fulton Evidence, 5(i),
pp. 1-7.
14.   Fulton Report, p. 17.
15.   773 H.C. Deb. 5s. c. 1553;   Armstrong Report (Feb.,
1969), pp. 8-9;   Fulton Report, pp. 26-33, 157-62, 196;   770
H.C. Deb. 5s. Written Answers c. 357-68;   784 H.C. Deb. 5s.
Written Answers c. 137-38;   Davies Report, pp. iv, 82-6.
16.   Fry (1969), pp. 179-82, 442;   Fulton Evidence, 5(i),
pp. 1, 4.
17.   Information supplied by Lord Boyle;   Civil Service
College 1972-73, p. 15;   Heaton-Williams Report, p. 14;   Civil
Service College 1974-75, p. 2.   Before going to the College,
Grebenik was a colleague of mine at Leeds.
18.   H.C. 535-I, (1977), p. xxii;   A. Stevens, 'The
Ecole Nationale d'Administration' in Rhodes (1977), pp. 64-78;
Fry (1969), pp. 311-25;   Fulton Report, pp. 37-38.   Fry (1969)
indicates how an Anglicized ENA might be organized.   The
training of ATs in 1976 was described in H.C. 535-III, (1977),
pp. 880-81.
19.   Fulton Report, pp. 57-61.
20.   Fry (1972), pp. 139-55;   with information up-dated
by the author in the summer of 1978.

21.   Crossman, III, (1977), pp. 53, 66-7, 428, 456, 466, 746, 752, 753, 759, 775, 868, 921, 943; information from Abel-Smith; Cmnd. 4683, (1971).

22.   Interview with Lord Cockfield, 2.6.1978; Wilson (1976), pp. 202-5; Klein and Lewis (1977), pp. 1-25; R. Darlington, 'Why There Should be More Special Advisers in Whitehall', The Times, 18.7.1978. The number of political advisers seemed to vary from a peak of 38 in May 1974 to between 25 and 27 in June 1978 (G.W. Jones, 'Advise and Resent', The Guardian, 22.6.1978).

23.   Interview with Lord Boyle, 16.6.1971.

24.   This agitation was intensified following the acquittal of the accused in The Sunday Telegraph secrets case in 1971. Summing up, Mr. Justice Caulfield suggested that Section 2 of the sixty year old Official Secrets Act should be 'pensioned off' (The Times, 3.2.1971). The Franks Committee soon followed, but not repeal.

Chapter 11

GUARDING THE GUARDIANS: THE PARLIAMENTARY COMMISSIONER FOR
ADMINISTRATION

'The Government has chosen the weakest and clumsiest way of
fulfilling its promise to give to the individual citizen a
means of redress against possible administrative abuses by
public servants.' Thus ran the verdict of The Economist on
the Labour Government's proposals for the appointment of a
Parliamentary Commissioner for Administration or Ombudsman,
when they were published in October 1965.   The Economist
reflected what seemed to be the opinion of a majority of the
interested. It added that 'the most startling thing about the
relevant White Paper was 'how much the Government wants to
leave out of the Parliamentary Commissioner's field of action.
There would be no recourse against abuses by the police; nor
(this is a huge gap) by local authorities; nor by nationalized
industries'. As for governmental departments, The Economist
said that 'Ministers would have the right to suppress the
publication of any information that seems inconvenient'.   It
concluded that 'this catalogue of omissions makes the whole
exercise almost pointless'. Its reaction was the dominant one.
In various journals the Parliamentary Commissioner was
described as being a 'muzzled watchdog', a 'crusader without a
sword', an 'Ombudsmanque' and an 'Ombudsmouse'. Because the
'Ombudsomissions' were so blatant it was even suggested that
the fact that the Parliamentary Commissioner first took office
on April Fool's Day (1967) was significant. The academic
verdict was scarcely more favourable. One distinguished
political scientist dismissed the establishment of the
Ombudsman as being ' relatively unimportant' for the development of the Civil Service. The lawyers tended to be even more
dismissive. The more radical of them wanted the introduction
of an institution comparable with the French Conseil d'Etat.1
     In relation to the range of modern British central
government activity, and the scale of the administrative
discretion that this involved, the Parliamentary Commissioner
for Administration faced a formidable task. Some thought that
the office was hindered rather than helped by complaints
having to be filtered first by MPs. The list of exclusions
from the PCA's field of review was a long one. Moreover,

confining the PCA to investigating maladministration also
seemed to some observers to be needlessly restrictive. Nevertheless, what the critics failed to recognize was the potential
of the actual role accorded to the Ombudsman. For example, the
third holder of the office, Sir Idwal Pugh was clear that
limiting his investigations to maladministration had made
little difference in practice. 'Bias, neglect, inattention,
delay, incompetence, ineptitude, perversity, turpitude and
arbitrariness' - the famous 'Crossman catalogue' - was a wide
definition of maladministration to work with. Despite the
constraints on the PCA, his powers were similar to those of
other Ombudsmen in other countries. He had the power to
investigate, recommend, and correct an action and issue
reports. These reports did not have mandatory force on the
departments. However, departments were bound to find it
difficult not to comply with them. Sir Idwal Pugh rightly
described the powers of investigation of the PCA's as 'very
great'. The PCA could require 'any Minister, officer or
member of the department or authority concerned or any other
person who ... is able to furnish information or produce
documents relevant to the investigation to furnish any such
information or produce any such document'. The Macmillan
Government's earlier concern for the effect of an Ombudsman on
the working of the convention of Ministerial responsibility was
clearly well founded.2
    The potential of the office of PCA was soon demonstrated
in the Sachsenhausen Concentration Camp Case. After that
Case - an analysis of which follows - the Ombudsman principle
was firmly established in British government, and was always
likely to be extended.

I   THE OMBUDSMAN AND THE SACHSENHAUSEN CONCENTRATION CAMP
     CASE

On June 9th 1964, the Foreign Secretary, R A Butler, informed
the House of Commons that the Government had concluded an
Agreement with the Federal German Republic whereby the latter
paid the sum of £1 million to British victims of Nazi
persecution. The sum was to be distributed at the discretion
of the British Government. After making this announcement,
Butler invited a number of Conservative backbenchers to a
meeting in his room at the House of Commons. At that meeting
he explained the Agreement and outlined the arrangements for
registering claims as well as the method of distribution. The
Foreign Secretary emphasized that detention in a concentration
camp or comparable institution would be the criterion on which
Nazi persecution was to be defined. Airey Neave, who was
present at the meeting, had raised in correspondence with
Butler the question of prisoners of war (especially RAF
officers who had escaped from Stalag Luft III) who were
detained in concentration camps. In a replying letter on
August 15th 1964, Butler told him that if the RAF officers

concerned had in fact been detained in concentration camps they would automatically be eligible.3

It was decided that the money secured through the Agreement should be distributed through administrative channels within the Foreign Office. Notes for Guidance were prepared for the use of officials administering the scheme and for the use of applicants. The scheme was widely publicised both at home and overseas. Applications were invited from those who considered they were eligible for compensation. In addition, application forms were distributed to, among others, certain potential ex-Service applicants (or their dependants) who were shown in Ministry of Defence records as possible victims of Nazi persecution. The Foreign Office tried to ensure that no potential applicant was denied the opportunity of submitting a claim. Moreover, applications that were clearly eligible were registered with the minimum delay. All other applications were acknowledged and inquiries were made to check the statements of applicants. Various sources of information were available to the Foreign Office. These included the records of the Service departments, the interrogation reports of released prisoners of war, and the records of the International Tracing Service of the Red Cross. The closing date was extended and final payments were made by the end of 1966.4

Among the claimants were Group Captain H M A Day, Lieutenant Colonel John Churchill, and Squadron Leader S H Dowse. They claimed because they believed that they had been interned in Sachsenhausen Concentration Camp, which had been situated some twenty miles north of Berlin. At various times, the three claimants had been held in a special camp (Sonderlager A) and in a cell block (the Zellenbau) at Sachsenhausen. Day's claim was initially considered a good case for the period of his detention in Zellenbau and was registered, only to be later struck out. This was because of the accounts of conditions in the Zellenbau and Sonderlager A contained in interrogation reports taken from officers in 1945; and because of the evidence contained in Captain Payne Best's book The Venlo Incident and in Captain Peter Churchill's book, The Spirit in the Cage about conditions there. The rejection of Day's claim formed part of a general Foreign Office decision that the group was disqualified because Sonderlager A was outside the perimeter of the Sachsenhausen Concentration Camp proper, and that the evidence of their treatment showed that it was in no way a comparable institution. The letters of rejection stated that the prisoners were never subjected to the well known inhuman and degrading treatment of a concentration camp proper. In later stages of the case the Foreign Office sought to prove that Sonderlager A and the Zellenbau were not part of the main camp because the severity of treatment and the Nazi persecution element in those places were not of concentration camp standard. The Foreign Office held that treatment for some in the Zellenbau, while harsh, was in line with the Germans' normal treatment for escaped prisoner of war. Although, it might well have been in contravention of the Geneva Convention. The Foreign Office insisted that the treatment was without the concentration camp hallmark, which was to overwork or to maltreat to destruction. The Foreign Office also contended that if they were to compensate these men in fairness they would have to call for a new registration of claims for all maltreated prisoners of war.5

In October 1965, Day, Churchill and Dowse went to see Airey Neave, with the letters that they had received from the Foreign Office refusing their claims for compensation. Since two of these (Day and Dowse) had been among those RAF officers who had escaped from Stalag Luft III, Neave went to see George Thomson, Minister of State at the Foreign Office. Neave argued that Day, Churchill and Dowse were at all times in parts of Sachsenhausen Concentration Camp, which was under the control of the Gestapo and the SS; that this applied both to the Sonderlager A and the Zellenbau; and that they were 'in a concentration camp or comparable institution' within the meaning of the Foreign Office's Notes of Guidance. Neave offered to supply Thomson with an aerial photograph of the Camp given to him by Day and also with sketch maps. Thomson promised to look at the matter again. However, Thomson proceeded to follow the advice of his officials, and so did his successor, Eirene White. Parliamentary questions secured no shift of opinion. Neither did a visit to the Foreign Secretary himself, George Brown. He followed his officials' advice too. In February 1967, he told Day and his friends 'to forget it and get it out of their systems'. He said that 'all the money was gone'. Neave, however, had been rallying parliamentary support for the claimants. Further rebuffs from another Foreign Office Minister, W T Rodgers, and from the Prime Minister did not deflect Neave. An all-party motion was placed on the Commons Order Paper asking for an independent inquiry with power to award compensation in appropriate cases. It was signed by over 350 MPs. Richard Crossman, the Leader of the House, agreed to find time for a debate. After further discussion, Neave agreed to submit the case to the PCA, which he did in May 1967.6

The PCA (Sir Edmund Compton) decided that it would be appropriate to review the cases of all twelve former Sachsenhausen prisoners who had had their claims for compensation rejected, and not limit himself to the grievances of Group Captain Day and his friends. Sir Edmund took advantage of his access to all Foreign Office files and papers dealing with each individual's claim and the case in general. He obtained written and oral evidence from the Foreign Office officials who drew up and administered the scheme, and from the complainants and other rejected claimants. He secured other materials available about Sachsenhausen Concentration Camp. Reviewing the evidence, the PCA came to the conclusion in December 1967 that there were 'defects in the administrative procedure by which the decisions on these claims were reached

in the first place and defended when subsequently challenged'.7
    Sir Edmund Compton found the Zellenbau at least to be part
of the Sachsenhausen Concentration Camp by means of three
sources of evidence, each available to the Foreign Office. The
first was the aerial photograph supplied by Day to Neave who
had passed it to the Foreign Office. Sir Edmund secured
confirmation from the Ministry of Defence that this was either
an RAF or USAAF photograph, and that it had been taken as late
as the summer of 1944 (Day and his friends having been moved
into the Zellenbau in the September and October of that year).
Another source was a plan in the Ministry of Defence Air
Historical Branch which had been drawn in August 1944 by an
officer who had been employed by the SS authorities as a
draughtsman, but who had subsequently escaped from Sachsenhausen. A third source was a book, published in Berlin in
1961, called Damals in Sachsenhausen. This included a
description of the Camp and of the Zellenbau as part of the
Camp.8
    From the evidence in Damals in Sachsenhausen, the PCA
found that Zellenbau prisoners faced a real threat of liquidation. The book indicated that towards the end of 1944 the
Head Warder was ordered to reduce by execution the number of
prisoners held there. At his trial by the Russians, he
admitted that of the 100 or more prisoners in the cells in
October 1944 only thirteen remained in April 1945 when the
Camp was evacuated. The PCA also found that there was
variation of treatment in the Zellenbau. Captain Payne Best's
book was the personal record of an officer held in isolation
from all contact with his fellow prisoners in the cell block
and knowing nothing of their circumstances. Peter Churchill's
book was no evidence for the Zellenbau, because he had only
been held in Sonderlager A. The PCA also found out that there
had been a wide range of living conditions and treatment in
the main compound, presence in which did not necessarily mean
concentration camp treatment as generally understood. In their
submissions to Ministers, the Foreign Office made much of the
brutal treatment handed out to one prisoner, while neglecting
the more lenient treatment of another.9
    Sir Edmund Compton's investigation led him to three
conclusions. First, he criticized the process by which the
Foreign Office decided against Sonderlager A and Zellenbau
being part of Sachsenhausen Concentration Camp. This was
because in his view the original decision was 'based on partial
and largely irrelevant information'; and also because the
'decision was maintained in disregard of additional information
and evidence, particularly as regards Zellenbau'. Secondly,
the PCA recognized that he could not question 'the merits of
the general ruling as applied throughout the compensation
scheme that claimants judged not to have been held in a
concentration camp had to establish detention in conditions
comparable with those in a concentration camp "as generally
understood", meaning severe forms of Nazi persecution

treatment'. Nevertheless, Sir Edmund recorded his opinion that this ruling could mean that a non-camp claimant had to pass a more severe test than a camp claimant, and that this happened in the Sachsenhausen case. Finally, the Parliamentary Commissioner criticized 'the treatment by the Foreign Office of the evidence submitted by the complainants in support of their claims as regards their own conditions under detention in Zellenbau and as regards conditions in the main compound of Sachsenhausen'.10

In the final part of his Report, the PCA drew attention to the complainants' feeling that the Foreign Office had dealt with their representations in terms which implied that in order to secure a share of the compensation they had magnified the severity of their treatment, and made fantastic claims of more lenient treatment received by other Sachsenhausen prisoners. Sir Edmund Compton believed that the result of his investigation had vindicated their veracity and sincerity in both respects. As for financial compensation, Sir Edmund could make no recommendation, but he successfully asked the Foreign Office to review the cases. On December 20th 1967, Airey Neave was informed of this in a letter from the Foreign Secretary.11

On February 5th 1968, in a debate in the House of Commons on a Motion to take note of the PCA's Report on Sachsenhausen, the Foreign Secretary, George Brown talked in terms of a victory for Neave. While he disagreed with Sir Edmund Compton's findings, Brown said that he had 'nevertheless decided that compensation will be paid on the appropriate basis to all these claimants or, in the case of those who have died, to their dependants'.12

II   THE OMBUDSMAN AND THE DOCTRINE OF MINISTERIAL RESPONSIBILITY

In his speech in the Sachsenhausen debate, George Brown talked 'personally and not for the Cabinet' about what he saw as the implications of the creation of 'the "Ombudsman" as we call him' for the convention of Ministerial responsibility. It was a subject on which he had 'strong feelings'. The then Foreign Secretary said that 'we will breach a very serious constitutional position if we start holding officials responsible for things that are done wrong. In this country, Ministers are Members of Parliament. That is not true of many countries. I think we have the best Parliamentary democratic system in the world and one of the reasons for this is that our Ministers are responsible to Parliament. If things are wrongly done, then they are wrongly done by Ministers and I think that it is tremendously important to hold to that principle. If things have gone wrong, then Ministers have gone wrong and I accept my full share of the responsibility in this case. It happens that I am the last of a series of Ministers who have looked at this matter and I am the one who got caught with the ball when the lights went up. But I accept, I repeat, my share of the

responsibility. I could not possibly do other. I read every
page of all the information. It is Ministers who must be
attacked, not officials'. Brown added that 'the office of
Parliamentary Commissioner was intended to strengthen our form
of democratic government, but let me say that if that office
were to lead to changing this constitutional position so that
officials got attacked and Ministers escaped, then I think that
the whole practice of Ministers being accountable to Parliament
would be undermined. I think that the morale of the Civil and
Diplomatic Services would be undermined and I am not sure that
many experienced right hon. and hon. Members want to think
twice about that situation'.13
          George Brown's comments about Ministerial responsibility
were, in fact, poorly received by such Members. For instance,
Airey Neave himself suggested that the Foreign Secretary had
proposed 'some rather unusual constitutional doctrines ... with
regard to the position of the Parliamentary Commissioner'.
Charles Pannell, a former Labour Minister, said, 'We really did
not want that long lecture upon him accepting responsibility'.
A Conservative Member, Sir Arthur Vere Harvey complained about
the Foreign Secretary choosing to 'prevaricate for twenty-five
minutes in defence of his officials, while agreeing that this
was wrong and that was wrong'. Sir Arthur and a fellow
Conservative, Sir David Renton, were among those Members who
objected to Brown's suggestion that the Ombudsman's judgment
could be wrong. Douglas Houghton, a former Cabinet colleague
of Brown's, found disturbing the Foreign Secretary's unwillingness to accept the Ombudsman's findings. Houghton said
that 'when the Foreign Secretary thinks that his judgment is as
good as that of the Parliamentary Commissioner, he is mistaking
the function of the Parliamentary Commissioner'. Charles
Pannell also objected to the Foreign Secretary's disagreeing
with the Ombudsman's Report. He said that 'there must be no
argument at the end of the day. This is almost like a
judicial procedure, when one calls in an arbitrator. One
cannot argue afterwards'. Sir Arthur Vere Harvey even asked,
'Who is the Foreign Secretary to question the Parliamentary
Commissioner's judgment ? We have his Report before us'.14
          A Liberal Member, Dr Michael Winstanley, complained that
George Brown seemed to 'cast doubt on the whole concept of maladministration. He said, very clearly, that "if things have
gone wrong, then Ministers have gone wrong". He returned
constantly to the point that the Minister was always
responsible. In other words, he appeared to reject utterly
the concept that the Commissioner must deal only with maladministration. The Foreign Secretary seemed constantly to
tell us that the only thing that could arise was a Ministerial
decision. In other words, he seemed to be rejecting the terms
of the Act'. Dr Winstanley said that this was clearly a
matter which had to be looked into carefully both by the House
as a whole and by the Select Committee for the Parliamentary
Commissioner for Administration which it had set up. It seemed

to Dr Winstanley that 'in his statement the Foreign Secretary was rejecting the basic idea underlying the whole work of the Parliamentary Commissioner'.15

As for an explanation of Mr Brown's behaviour, Charles Pannell felt qualified to advance a view because he knew the Foreign Secretary 'as well as anybody in the House does, and certainly far better than anybody in his Department does. He has a vein of quixotry in his nature. He is a gallant man and is very loyal, and I can honestly say that he would never have been as loyal to himself as he had been to his Civil Servants. He would have come cleaner on his own trouble, but he spoke as he did for his Civil Servants'. Mr Pannell said that as a result 'what the Foreign Secretary has put up is the curious false proposition that the buck does not stop at the Parliamentary Commissioner but "the buck stops with me" '. Pannell made it evident that he shared the view of Douglas Houghton that the position of the Ombudsman was analogous with that of the Comptroller and Auditor-General, and the Public Accounts Committee. Pannell went on, 'All of us, certainly those of us who have been Ministers, accept the idea of Ministerial responsibility. At no time did the Foreign Secretary say, "I dealt with my Civil Servants". It is his job to deal with maladministration in his own department. The anonymity of the Civil Service is always preserved, and it is the Minister at the end of the day who has to take it, as the unfortunate Sir Thomas Dugdale took it, on very insubstantial grounds. But, having done that, it is for the Minister to turn on the department. What are the Administrative Class for in the Civil Service if they are not to protect the Minister ?'. Sir Thomas Dugdale's resignation over the Crichel Down affair in 1954 was also mentioned in Sir Arthur Vere Harvey's speech. He said that 'the Foreign Secretary can say what he likes, but he must bear the responsibility. I do not want to blow this up into a great issue, but other Ministers in the past - in the case of Crichel Down and so on - have had to accept full responsibility. If the Foreign Secretary wants to excuse officials in the Foreign Office, then, he and he alone, is to blame'. David Ginsberg observed that 'none of us was seeking a ministerial scalp', but perhaps some had civil service scalps in mind.16

The Leader of the House, Richard Crossman, did not take up this point in replying to the debate, the quality of which he felt justified the decision to hold it before the Sachsen-hausen case had been considered by the appropriate Select Committee. Crossman also did not, on this occasion, see the positions of the Ombudsman and the Comptroller and Auditor-General as being analogous. For he described the creation of the Parliamentary Commissioner for Administration as 'a complete constitutional innovation'. Crossman said that the powers that the PCA had been given were unique because he had 'a power of investigation greater than any back bencher or Minister because he is empowered to look at the most secret

documents and all the files, to cross-examine every official
and Minister from the top to the bottom, and has in his one
personality, greater power of investigation than anyone has
ever had before. What we look at in the Report is the top of
the iceberg. What he has been able to print is but a fraction
of the amount he obtained, upon the basis of which he built
these conclusions'. Crossman added that 'one must remember,
therefore, that he has had an absolutely unique six months, to
which British administration has not been subjected previously.
We have invented here an instrument of investigation sharper,
more precise, going deeper, than ever before'. This did not
mean, however, that Crossman thought that the Foreign Secretary
could not differ from the Parliamentary Commissioner's findings
in the Sachsenhausen case. Crossman observed that 'if we were
to take the view that Ministers had automatically to stand on
their heads and say the opposite of what they thought directly
the Ombudsman came up with a view, we would have an impossible
position'. Moreover, as Dr Winstanley had earlier pointed out,
there was 'nothing in the Act to compel the Minister to follow
the directions of the Commissioner'. Yet, the onus was surely
on a Minister to accept the Ombudsman's version of a case. As
George Brown said in the Sachsenhausen debate, 'having
established the office of Parliamentary Commissioner, whether I
think his judgment is right or wrong, I am certain that it
would be wrong to reject his views. I think that public
opinion would be outraged if I rejected his views on an issue
which affects personally a few very gallant men'. Even in a
less controversial case than Sachsenhausen, a Minister would
find it difficult not to act as the Ombudsman recommended.
When the PCA reported on a case, his impartial position (which,
as we have seen, led some experienced Members to suggest that
his judgment was virtually infallible over Sachsenhausen)
placed the Minister concerned in much the same position as
used to be the case when he received a report from the Public
Accounts Committee. Criticisms of the department more or less
have to be accepted, and appropriate remedial action undertaken. Moreover, it was not just financial accounts that were
open to scrutiny, but potentially almost all the government
department's area of administration.17
   So George Brown's concern about the implications for the
convention of Ministerial responsibility of the establishment
of the PCA was not as misplaced as some MPs suggested in the
Sachsenhausen debate. Brown was far from, in his general
argument, propounding 'some unusual constitutional doctrines'
about Ministerial responsibility. He was taking the traditional view of the relevant convention. What Brown was complaining
about was that the Ombudsman (and so the House of Commons)
could criticize the actions of Civil Servants. Whereas, as he
interpreted the Constitution, such officials could only be
responsible to Ministers. As Sir Ivor Jennings put it, 'the
overriding constitutional convention which regulates the whole
(Civil) Service was that 'each Minister is responsible to

Parliament for the conduct of his department' and that 'the act
of every Civil Servant is by convention regarded as the act of
his Minister'. A similar 'traditional' view was recorded by
Herbert Morrison, who wrote that only the Minister and neither
Parliament nor the public has 'official control over his Civil
Servants. One of the fundamentals of our system of government
is that some Minister of the Crown is responsible to
Parliament and through Parliament to the public, for every act
of the Executive. This is a cornerstone of our system of
Parliamentary Government. There may, however, be an occasion
on which so serious a mistake has been made that the Minister
must explain the circumstances and processes which resulted in
the mistake, particularly if it involves an issue of civil
liberty or individual rights. Now and again the House demands
to know the name of the officer responsible for the occurrence.
The proper answer of the Minister is that if the House wants
anybody's head it must be his head as the responsible Minister,
and that it must leave him to deal with the officer concerned
in the department'.18

Herbert Morrison advanced similar views in the House of
Commons debate on the Crichel Down affair in 1954. Some of his
points were taken up by the then Conservative Home Secretary,
Sir David Maxwell Fyfe, who attempted to 'state fairly and
fully the doctrine of Ministerial responsibility'. Sir David
said that 'the position of the Civil Servant is that he is
wholly and directly responsible to his Minister. It is worth
stating again that he holds his office "at pleasure" and can
be dismissed at any time by the Minister; and that power is
nonetheless real because it is seldom used. The only exception relates to a small number of senior posts, like Permanent
Secretary, Deputy Secretary, and Principal Finance Officer,
where, since 1920, it has been necessary for the Minister to
consult the Prime Minister, as he does on appointment'. The
Home Secretary then put 'the different categories where
different categories apply'. He agreed with Morrison that 'in
the case where there is an explicit order by a Minister, the
Minister must protect the Civil Servant who has carried out
his order. Equally, where the Civil Servant acts properly in
accordance with the policy laid down by the Minister, the
Minister must protect and defend him'. Sir David also agreed
with Morrison about a third category which was 'different'.
This was 'where an official makes a mistake or causes some
delay, but not on an important issue of policy and not where
a claim to individual rights is seriously involved, the
Minister acknowledges the mistake and he accepts the
responsibility, although he is not personally involved. He
states that he will take corrective action in the department'.
Sir David agreed with Morrison that, in those circumstances,
the official should not be exposed to public criticism.
However, when one came to the fourth category, the Home
Secretary argued, 'where action has been taken by a Civil
Servant of which the Minister disapproves and has no prior

knowledge, and the conduct of the official is reprehensible, then there is no obligation on the part of the Minister to endorse what he believes to be wrong, or to defend what are clearly shown to be errors of his officers. The Minister is not bound to defend action of which he did not know, or of which he disapproves. But, of course, he remains constitutionally responsible to Parliament for the fact that something has gone wrong, and he alone can tell Parliament what has occurred and render an account of his stewardship. The fact that a Minister has to do that does not affect his power to control and discipline his staff. One could sum it up by saying that it is part of a Minister's responsibility to Parliament to take necessary action to ensure efficiency and the proper discharge of the duties of his department. On that, only the Minister can decide what is right and just to do, and he alone can hear all sides, including the defence'.19

Herbert Morrison expressed 'general agreement' with Sir David Maxwell Fyfe's views and said that the Crichel Down case caused 'a reconsideration, if not a redefinition of the relations of the Civil Servant with his Minister and with the public'. One leading political scientist felt that Morrison's writings and Maxwell Fyfe's statement meant that the doctrine of Ministerial responsibility was confirmed. However, neither Morrison's views nor the then Home Secretary's 'reconsideration' was of much help regarding George Brown's attitude over the Sachsenhausen case. Brown said that at the outset, as was recorded on the relevant file, he wondered whether the Foreign Office was not being 'over legalistic'. He came to share the Office's view but was satisfied that all the information he needed was supplied to him. Brown said: 'I read every piece of paper on the file and I came to my conclusions by my own processes of judgment. That these conclusions were the same as the department's does not, of course, invalidate them, and that they were the same as every previous Minister's does not invalidate them. I want to make it quite clear that every Minister who has looked at these things has come by his own processes of judgment to the same conclusion'. The then Foreign Secretary took issue with the Ombudsman's 'allegation that there were defects in the procedure by which the Foreign Office reached its decisions on these claims. I have examined this with all the thoroughness at my command and I say quite frankly that I do not believe that I was misled by officials. I regard it as a Minister's job to see that he has all the necessary information. If he does not have it, that is a very severe mark against him. If, having got it, he does not take it aboard, that is an even severer mark against him, and I reject completely the Parliamentary Commissioner's allegation that officials did not submit the evidence that Ministers right up to and including me should have had'. Brown stated, 'the House ... should deal with Ministers where we think that things have gone wrong. Ministers must, in my view, remain responsible to Parliament, and I am willing to do so.

Officials must remain responsible to their Ministers'.20

The then Foreign Secretary's comments, and some of the evidence submitted to it on the Sachsenhausen case, led the Select Committee on the Parliamentary Commissioner for Administration to ask for an opinion from the Attorney-General, Sir Elwyn Jones, about 'the general question of ministerial responsibility in relation to the office of the Parliamentary Commissioner'. In his statement, the Attorney-General said that 'the Minister in charge of the department is answerable to Parliament for the workings of the department. The action of the department is action for which the department is collectively responsible and for which the Minister in charge is alone answerable to Parliament. It is only in exceptional cases that blame should be attached to the individual Civil Servant and it follows from the principle that the Minister alone has responsibility for the actions of his department that the individual Civil Servant who has contributed to the collective decision of the department should remain anonymous'. In its report on Sachsenhausen, the Select Committee refrained from publishing passages in evidence submitted to it by Airey Neave which referred to an official by name. The Committee reserved the right to take evidence from Civil Servants of other than Permanent Secretary status. However, it also fully recognized advice given to it by the Attorney-General that it had to try to maintain a balance between its function and 'the protection of Ministerial responsibility upon which the efficiency of democratic Government depends'.21

The Committee on Ministers' Powers, which reported in 1932, was told by the Treasury Solicitor, Sir Maurice Gwyer, that any departure from the principle of Ministerial responsibility would imply the adoption of a new theory of government. Yet, whereas Ministerial responsibility was 'the crux of the English system of government in the nineteenth century', it has developed in such a way that one constitutional commentator has suggested that it is 'now little more than a formal principle used by Ministers to deter parliamentary interference in their affairs'. A member of the Select Committee on the Parliamentary Commissioner, Charles Fletcher-Cooke, in phrasing a question, stated that 'the purpose in the public mind' in setting up the office of Ombudsman was 'because, ever since the days of Crichel Down and probably before, the doctrine of Ministerial responsibility ... was really becoming either a fiction or unworkable'. Fletcher-Cooke went on, 'Behind the desire to set up a new system was, I think, a desire which can only be expressed in the vernacular: when something has gone wrong, the public feel that somebody ought to be summoned, in the words of the old song, and since it cannot always be the Minister ... the office of the Commissioner was set up to examine what has gone wrong. But then comes the next stage after he has reported, and it is, I should have thought, our duty particularly as a Committee and ultimately of the House to see that the blame lies fairly where it should lie and that the public's desire that maladministration should not go unvisited is really frustrated if, in fact, as soon as the Parliamentary Commissioner has reported the screen goes up again between the Civil Service and Parliament'.22

At the time of Crichel Down, another Conservative backbencher, Viscount Lambton, made similar complaints in talking about the Civil Servants concerned being placed 'beyond punishment' because of the convention of Ministerial responsibility. He thought there was a need to 'review the whole scheme of Ministerial responsibility'. Such sentiments were presumably a motive in Sir David Maxwell Fyfe's well-known 'reconsideration' of the convention. He replied to Lord Lambton saying that 'we all recognize that we must have that principle in existence and that Ministers must be responsible for the acts of Civil Servants. Without it, it would be impossible to have a Civil Service which would be able to serve Ministries and Governments of different political faiths and persuasions and with the same zeal and honesty which we have always found. I hope that answers the point made by my noble Friend'. Of course, it did nothing of the kind. When examined, Sir David Maxwell Fyfe's statement over Ministerial responsibility at the time of Crichel Down was much less than a definition, but more a collection of saving cases. Yet, it is doubtful if the convention can be 'saved' by the then Home Secretary's 'categories'. Either the Minister is responsible 'for every act done in his department', or he is not, and if he is not, then who is ? Not least because of the now recognized rarity of Ministerial resignations over such matters,23 the establishment of an Ombudsman to examine maladministration was an indication that the House, while not as yet expecting to know the name(s) of the erring official(s), no longer regards Herbert Morrison's 'proper answer' as sufficient.

The confusions over the current state of the doctrine of Ministerial responsibility were, indeed, evident in the Select Committee on the Parliamentary Commissioner's report on Sachsenhausen. For instance, although, as had been noted, it undertook to 'protect' the convention of Ministerial responsibility, the Committee recognized that in setting up the office of Ombudsman, Parliament had 'undermined the doctrine to some extent, in that the power of the Commissioner to carry out an independent investigation within the department, and publish what he finds is an encroachment upon the Minister's responsibility'. The Committee did not receive clear guidance from the Attorney-General. In making his statement to it, Sir Elwyn Jones said that Ministers were responsible for departments 'traditionally, and I submit for very good reason'. Nonetheless, he agreed that it was clear that, in appointing the Ombudsman, Parliament intended to undermine the convention of Ministerial responsibility 'up to a point'. Sir Elwyn said that 'to let this independent official go through the files behind the Minister's back and talk to Tom, Dick or Harry in his department is a tremendous encroachment upon his responsibility'.24

III   THE 'COMPLETE CONSTITUTIONAL INNOVATION' OF THE OMBUDSMAN

Ministerial responsibility was rightly described by Sir Ivor Jennings as 'the most essential characteristic of the Civil Service'.25   The doctrine was 'the overriding constitutional convention' which governed the Service's work. It followed that a development like the establishment of the PCA which undermined and encroached upon that convention could hardly be 'relatively unimportant' for the Civil Service. The Sachsen-hausen case was early evidence for taking this view.

The Sachsenhausen case soon showed too that the Ombuds-man's role was not so circumscribed as to make the establish-ment of his office an 'almost pointless' exercise. Airey Neave himself acknowledged that 'we would never have got the Government to change their (sic) mind without the assistance of Sir Edmund Compton ... I could not even with all the assistance that I had from so many hon. and right hon. Members on both sides of the House, have achieved the result of reversing a decision with regard to these claims without Sir Edmund'. Another of that 'very determined group of campaigners', David Ginsberg admitted that they might never have broken through 'without the Parliamentary Commissioner and his very special powers'. From the outset it was clear that what The Times had called 'half an Ombudsman'26 was better than none.

In the first decade of the office's existence, the PCA investigated about 3,500 cases. Unsurprisingly, the largest groups of cases involved the departments which had the most dealings with the public - the Inland Revenue and the DHSS. The percentage of investigated cases in which the PCA found elements of maladministration that had led to some measures of injustice ranged from 10 per cent at first to 43 per cent in 1976. There was sufficient work to justify the existence of the office.27   The critics of the 1965 White Paper and of the 1967 legislation looked too much at what the Ombudsman could not do, and not enough at what he could.

The Wilson Government's intention was to place the Ombudsman 'in a position comparable with that of the Comptroller and Auditor-General'. As we have noted, Richard Crossman described the PCA as 'a complete constitutional innovation'. The PCA has a wider role than the Comptroller and Auditor-General, whose function is to check expenditure as against the authority to spend. The PCA's task is to examine the competence and fairness with which administrative cases have been handled. The Sachsenhausen debate demonstrated early in the history of the office that a number of MPs considered the PCA's judgment in such matters to be definitive. Later cases such as Duccio (1969), Invalid Vehicles (1975) and

Court Line (1975) were important: but Sachsenhausen was the
critical breakthrough for the office of Ombudsman. It was the
victory that was necessary to emphasize the independence of the
PCA from the Civil Service, and showed that his judgment could
be brought home. If the Foreign Office could be forced to
concede, then so could the other powerful departments like the
Home Office - as, indeed, happened in the Television Licences
Case in 1975.28   The office of Ombudsman swiftly became an
established feature of British central government, and one
which was copied elsewhere in the system.

As for the present state of the convention of ministerial
responsibility, it is such that when Sir Arthur Vere Harvey
suggested in the Sachsenhausen debate that the then Foreign
Secretary could have avoided a political row by accepting 'full
responsibility' for the handling of the case, it was unclear
what the phrase actually meant. What remains of what Herbert
Morrison once called that 'vital doctrine' of ministerial
responsibility ?   The increased size of the civil service and
the volume, extent and complexity of its work has meant that
many have found it difficult to accept the notion of intimate
ministerial control over the affairs of a Government department. Nonetheless, the practice of leading civil servants is
based on an assumption of ministerial initiative, and it can
hardly be denied that Government departments are responsive to
ministerial policy initiatives. Some departments probably do
'run' their Ministers. But this may be a reflection on the low
calibre of some ministerial appointees in relation to the sometimes formidable departmental tasks facing them, and of the
practice of treating Ministers as all-rounders supposedly able
easily to change between not necessarily related posts. It
does not follow that opportunities no longer exist for
Ministers of the requisite talents to 'run' their departments
at least at policy level. Ministers also remain answerable in
the sense that they are liable to report upon the activities of
the Government department of which they are a political head to
the Crown, to the Prime Minister and Cabinet, and to Parliament.
Civil servants remain non-political in the sense that they
normally receive their appointments independently of Ministers,
that they are not allowed an overt political allegiance, and
that they are not required to politically perform on the floor
of either House. One notes that the Administrative Class's
representatives told the Fulton Committee that the anonymity of
civil servants was being cut away by the activities of the
specialized committees of the House of Commons,29 but it is
still the case that civil servants are not publicly responsible
either for the advice that they have given to Ministers, or for
the efficiency with which they carry out their work. The
notion of the collective responsibility of a Government
department for decisions does not block the possible identification of individual civil servants. After all, in the past
civil servants have been named in the reports of official
inquiries. The Attorney-General used the concept of the

collective responsibility of a Government department in the Sachsenhausen case as a way of indicating that decisions are not usually the responsibility of a single individual, and that, even when they are, the individual is acting within the framework of justified expectations. To go further than this would require a very extensive paraphernalia, including safeguards for the civil servants themselves. The office of Ombudsman, however, may be the breach through which such developments could take place.

References

1. _The Economist_, 16.10.1965, p. 249; Rowat (1968), p. ix; W.J.M. Mackenzie in Crick (1967), p. 183; Smith (1967), pp. 23-42; Mitchell (1962), pp. 24-33; Mitchell (1965), pp. 95-118; Mitchell (1967), pp. 360-74; Mitchell (1968), pp. 167-69; Mitchell (1972), pp. 203-6.
2. 734 H.C. Deb. 5s. c. 51; Fry (1969), pp. 265-67; Pugh (1978), pp. 132-33.
3. 696 H.C. Deb. 5s. c. 242; H.C. 258 (1968), pp. 53-4.
4. H.C. 54 (1967), pp. 3-4.
5. Ibid., pp. 4-5, 21, 29 (map).
6. H.C. 258 (1968), pp. 54-8; 725 H.C. Deb. 5s. c. 890-92; 736 H.C. Deb. 5s. Written Answers c. 18-19; 735 H.C. Deb. 5s. c. 977; Fry (1970), pp. 339-43.
7. H.C. 54 (1967), pp. 3, 5-15.
8. H.C. 258 (1968), pp. 3-4.
9. H.C. 54 (1967), pp. 13, 14, 16-17.
10. Ibid., p. 18.
11. Ibid., pp. 19-20; H.C. 258 (1968), p. 58.
12. 758 H.C. Deb. 5s. c. 115, 116, 123.
13. Ibid., c. 108, 112, 113.
14. Ibid., c. 115, 117, 130, 131, 148-49, 150, 152.
15. Ibid., c. 154.
16. Ibid., c. 134, 136, 142, 150, 151-52.
17. Ibid., c. 116, 153, 163-64, 169; Fry (1969), pp. 266-67.
18. I. Trethowan, 'Who carries the can for Bumbledom?', _The Times_, 8.2.1968; 758 H.C. Deb. 5s. c. 111-13; Jennings (1959), pp. 207-8; Morrison (1964), p. 332.
19. 530 H.C. Deb. 5s. c. 1275-77, 1285, 1286-87.
20. Morrison (1964), p. 333; Chester (1954), p. 401; 758 H.C. Deb. 5s. c. 108,111, 112.
21. H.C. 258 (1968), p. xiii; H.C. 350 (1968), pp. x-xiii.
22. Vile (1967), pp. 231, 235, 341; H.C. 350 (1968), p. 107.
23. 530 H.C. Deb. 5s. c. 1273; Ibid., c. 1285; Jennings, _Cabinet Government_, p. 499; Finer (1956), pp. 377-96.
24. H.C. 350 (1968), pp. xi, 73, 82.

25.   Jennings, <u>Cabinet Government</u>, p. 499.

26.   758 H.C. Deb. 5s. c. 118, 141; <u>The Times</u>, 15.2.1966.

27.   In his first ten Annual Reports, the PCA indicated
the percentage of investigated cases in which there had been
elements of maladministration that had led to some measure of
injustice. The percentages were 10 (1967), 10 (1968), 16
(1969), 23 (1970), 37 (1971), 30 (1972), 37 (1973), 37 (1974),
37 (1975), 43 (1976).

28.   758 H.C. Deb. 5s. c. 136; H.C. 385 (1969); H.C.
498 (1975); Gregory (1977), pp. 269-92; H.C. 529 (1975),
pp. 162-82; H.C. 680 (1975).

29.   758 H.C. Deb. 5s. c. 131; Morrison (1964), p. 171;
<u>Fulton Evidence</u>, 5(i), pp. 122-23.

Chapter 12

'THE PARTY IS OVER'

The apogée of administrative change in British central government was reached in the first part of the 1970s. 'We are in
sight of having nine (or perhaps ten) major departments in
Whitehall, apart from the Treasury (and the revenue departments) and the Civil Service Department in the centre', Sir
Richard Clarke wrote in 1971. The Central Policy Review Staff
had just been established. PESC, of which Clarke was the
effective architect, was at or near the height of its
reputation as a system of public expenditure control. PAR, the
recent introduction of which he applauded, had yet to reveal
its limitations. Clarke saw PESC and PAR as eventually
supplanting the traditional forms of public accounting. Could
there not be another 'giant', 'federal', Jumbo department, this
time at the centre ?   Or should there be two, but different
departments ?   Such questions were the very stuff of the
Administrative 'Revolution'.1
      Six years later, and out of office, these questions still
engaged the minds of Edward Heath and Harold Wilson, Prime
Ministerial builders of the 'Revolution'. In the meantime,
however, the political atmosphere had changed dramatically.
The supposedly rationalized structure envisaged by Sir Richard
Clarke, and, to some extent, indicated by the 1970 White Paper
had not existed for long even in form. The belief that
'national efficiency' could be obtained through administrative
change did not long survive the experience of the Heath
Government and the impact of the Oil Crisis, nor too did a
consensual belief in the Managed Economy Welfare State. It
became more widely recognized that the State could not at one
and the same time guarantee full employment, obtain price
stability, ensure perennially increasing real incomes, and
continually expand the social services. The Keynesian prop had
been knocked away from under the structure of the particular
form of the Positive State that Britain had adopted. The
assumption behind the Administrative 'Revolution' was that the
machinery of government was sufficiently malleable to fit the
role chosen for the State. Once this had been proved false, a
reaction against administrative change set in. Sir Samuel
Goldman, formerly of the Treasury, reflected this mood, in

176

evidence to a Select Committee in 1977, when he opposed the
return of the CSD to the Treasury, despite having compared the
original 1968 change to a division in a seamless garment.
Goldman, said: 'I have always felt that there has been too
much playing about with the machinery of government, too much
chopping and changing. There is no doubt that most (but not
all) of the experiments in this direction over the last decade
or more have turned out to be failures; they have been
acknowledged as failures and have been gone back on'.2
     This seems broadly to have been the case. Some of the
administrative changes had been worth making, but more had not
been. Many changes had been of form rather than of substance.
     The administrative changes which took place in the sphere
of defence and external affairs generally made more sense than
similar attempts to re-construct other parts of central government machinery. Some of the changes made in relation to
responsibility for overseas aid and development did seem
cosmetic.3 Admittedly, unlike the comforting Plowden
Committee, the Duncan and Berrill inquiries still found scope
for economies in overseas representation. Nevertheless, the
mergers which led to the establishment of the FCO and the
unified Ministry of Defence had an administrative logic to
support them. The demise of the Service Ministries and the
downgrading of the Service Ministers when the merged Ministry
of Defence was formed in 1964 did represent a major change in
defence administration. So did the centralization of the
defence programme and budgeting, and the increase in the
controlling apparatus at the disposal of the Chief Scientific
Adviser. Although the structure was incomplete until the
creation of the Procurement Executive in 1972 finally brought
in the old Ministry of Supply functions, the establishment of
the unified Ministry of Defence in 1964 probably did add up to
an administrative revolution in the defence sphere not matched
since Haldane was at the War Office. Compared with the
situation before 1964, Britain did in the end come to have a
defence organization more in keeping with her realistic role in
the world and her reduced economic circumstances. These
factors, together with the increasingly emphasized European
bias in her foreign policy, also encouraged changes in the
administrative organization of Britain's external relations.
De-colonization having gathered pace after Suez, the Colonial
Office no longer had sufficient work to justify its separate
existence by the mid-1960s. So it was logical to merge it with
the Commonwealth Relations Office to form the Commonwealth
Office. The further merger which created the Foreign and
Commonwealth Office in 1968 had been anticipated three years
before when a unified Diplomatic Service had been formed. The
timing of this merger was about right. It was not until about
1968 that the Commonwealth had come to almost universally mean
little to the British, and particularly to the Labour Party,
that the countries concerned could begin to be treated as
foreign.4

Britain's relative economic decline, which among other factors compelled changes in her administrative arrangements for defence and external relations, showed no sign of being either halted or reversed by the numerous changes made in the economic machinery of government. It was characteristic of the period of the Administrative 'Revolution' that Governments acted as if such changes could have these results. As the British economy lost ground, economic planning, incomes policy, industrial policy, and regional policy were among the panaceas tried, and sometimes tried together. Most were thought to need a new institution to administer them. Given that few of the established economic departments, from the Treasury downwards, escaped reconstruction, the general scale of institutional change was considerable, at least in terms of structure.

The Mintech and DEA experiments were perhaps the most ambitious essays in administrative change in the economic sphere. What necessity was there for a body like the DEA representing 'the interest of the economy as a whole' and with 'no executive responsibilities in the ordinary sense' ? This remit recalled that of the Economic Advisory Council of the 1930s, an institution which was composed of a massed array of talent, including Keynes. It produced no results, just advice. The EAC could propose, but the Treasury disposed. The same was always likely to be true of the DEA committed to the long-term, while the Treasury ran short-term policy. While it had other work, the DEA's fate was bound up with the National Plan. According to its Permanent Under Secretary, the Plan gave the work of the DEA its coherence. The July 1966 measures effectively marked the demise of the National Plan, which was a poor testament for the DEA. As the Plan had no revising mechanism, it was more a one-and-for-all exercise than a proper plan. Part of the DEA was eventually absorbed into Mintech in 1969. There was always overlap between the two Wilsonian institutional creations, not least as regards relations with the IRC. Mintech was organized in no less than three different forms during its six year history. While it was remarkable that anybody could believe that Mintech would swiftly work wonders in revivifying British industry, the scale of government commitment involved suggested something like the 1969 structure from the outset. That is provided one assumes that there ever was a need for more than an expanded Board of Trade equipped with something like the Industrial Development Executive of the later DTI.5

The DTI itself was soon broken up into what were deemed to be its constituent parts, and few of the institutional ventures in the economic sphere of the period had either a long or successful existence. The failure of successive prices and incomes policies condemned to eventual death almost all the various institutions established in that field.6 The regional economic planning machinery which the first Wilson Governments elaborated seemed to add little.7 As might be expected, activities like renaming the Ministry of Labour as the

Department of Employment and Productivity had little positive effect on either employment or productivity. Similarly, engaging in structural changes in the Treasury in 1956, 1962, 1964 (when the core of the DEA was taken out), 1968 (when the CSD was taken out), 1969 (when the core of the DEA was put back in again) and 1975 had no obviously beneficial effect on economic management. Indeed, by 1975 Britain was not just facing continuing relative economic decline. There was a real risk of her experiencing absolute economic decline.8

If the British economy perennially tended to lack the necessary momentum, this could not be said of institutional change in the period of the Administrative 'Revolution'. The 'old building' of British central government had needed reconstruction. The form that this took, however, was always more likely than not to be carried out in a manner which did not justify the scale of the activity. An important political dimension was neglected by the administrative reformers. The 'reform process' lacked a coherent overview until temporarily given one of a kind by the 1970 White Paper. Edward Heath later said of the 1970 changes: 'When I did this reorganization I had very much in mind that we had lived through 15 or 20 years in which most of the decisions taken in Whitehall about the allocation of responsibilities were done for political reasons and with very little consideration of the rationale behind it. I wanted to bring about a rational arrangement which ... would last'. Heath favoured large departments because he believed them to be more efficient, expecting from them an internally settled strategy in relation to the relevant policy areas. He favoured them too because they made possible a reduction in the number of senior Ministers, and hence in the size of the Cabinet. Heath found that, in the same way that the number of people who could run a company the size of Unilever or ICI or Shell or BP was small, this was also true of the number of politicians who could successfully run large Ministries. Health also found that, even though the policy responsibilities of the subordinate Ministers were made clear, the Secretary of State in charge of a large Ministry was always under real threat of being overloaded. This was because 'under our parliamentary system, somehow everybody still expects to be able to go to the man at the top'.9

The roles played by politicians and their parties in the machinery of central government received little attention during the Administrative 'Revolution'. The financial position of the parties forced a review towards the end of the period (by the Houghton Committee of 1975-76) but their role in relation to government was not a major concern. To a limited extent, the Fulton Committee recognized the problems of political direction with its proposals for policy planning units. However, precluded from examining the current working of the convention of Ministerial responsibility, Fulton was unable to coherently indicate how such units would operate in government departments, and no Fulton style units have been

established. Peter Shore, subsequently a Labour Cabinet
Minister, unwittingly underlined the fundamental problem of
political direction when he wrote in 1966 that 'the contribution made by the top men in the Civil Service to the success or
failure of Government policy can scarcely be exaggerated.
Ministers bring with them broad ideas of how future policy
should develop. But in the transformation of policy goals into
realistic plans, in the execution of those plans and, still
more, in policy responses to new and unexpected developments,
Ministers are largely, if not wholly, dependent on their
official advisers'.10

As a former member of the Labour Research Department,
Shore may well have accurately recognized his own political
party's limitations in the area of preparing for office. His
remarks were a reminder of Emanuel Shinwell's comments about
the absence of the 'necessary blueprints' for nationalization
measures in 1945. To suggest, as Sir Norman Chester does, that
Shinwell was only saying that there were a great number of
points to be thought about for the first time in the process of
translating a Party programme into legislation and practice is
not adequate. What Shinwell was more obviously complaining
about was the position of extreme dependence in which he was
placed in relation to his officials. Shinwell was honestly
acknowledging his own irresponsibility, and that of his Party,
for advocating nationalization without previously working out
essential practical details. On the Tory side, even in 1970
only the work done on taxation reform seems to have been
obviously of the desired standard. All else was improvized
without adequate preparation. British political parties are
only properly organized to compete for office. The parties are
organized for slogan making but not for policy preparation.
The difficulty is that if political parties do not do the work
of policy preparation then normally nobody does. For policy
purposes, the Civil Service is primarily organized around
Ministerial initiatives. These have not usually been forthcoming in a coherent form. There is thus a policy 'gap' in
British central government.11

Unsurprisingly, this also appears as a strategy 'gap' at
the centre of the system, which Edward Heath recognized when he
set up the Central Policy Review Staff. Heath said that 'what
I wanted to have was a piece of machinery which did not exist
in my knowledge of government which would keep a continuous
watch on the strategy of the Government and be able to tell the
Government when they were departing from that strategy in any
respect and analyse the reasons'.12 Strategy is supposed to
be the responsibility of the Cabinet. Heath was in effect
saying that the Cabinet either could not or would not do the
work. To fill the 'gap' and to monitor the Cabinet's performance, Heath, a Conservative Prime Minister, appointed the
CPRS, a formally non-political body, in fact headed by an
Opposition peer, to do a political job.

Even the more valuable reforms made in British central

government during the Administrative 'Revolution' were like
rare nuggets in a dross of usually worthless changes,
particularly outside the sphere of defence and external
affairs. Neddy survived its early association with economic
planning to act as an extra-parliamentary forum which Governments, like the other participants, found useful. The
establishment of the Ombudsman was worth doing. (Doubtless,
advocates of the alternative, a British Conseil d'Etat have
noted that since 1973 the French have had a type of Ombudsman,
the Mediateur.) Otherwise, the beneficial results of the
various reforms were very doubtful.13

The Administrative 'Revolution' was encapsulated in the
rise and fall of PESC. In 1957, the ratio of public sector
expenditure to GDP was 41 per cent. By 1973, this ratio was
51.4 per cent. The effective author of PESC on the Plowden
Committee, the ubiquitous Sir Richard Clarke conceded that
'over a comparatively short period of years the most favourable post-war public expenditure/resources situation had been
transformed to the worst'. The famous administrator did not
go on to say so, but it is difficult to believe that PESC did
not help to fuel inflation. PESC was essentially a system
geared up to economic growth. Built into it was the
assumption that resources would match prospective expenditures.
The 'forward look' distracted from the immediate look at
public expenditure in the round. The span of control was
extended to cover the whole public sector at a time when
control over spending in the central area was no more assured
than before. In fact, PESC had no system of financial control.
While any system of public expenditure control would have been
in difficulties in an era dominated by Keynesian assumptions
and Croslandism, PESC reinforced the prevailing tendency
instead of acting as a means of bringing resources and
spending into realistic balance. The failure of the Plowden
Revolution was recognized by the imposition of cash limits on
public spending in 1976.14

That year also witnessed the Funeral Oration for
Keynesian economic management spoken by James Callaghan at the
Labour Party Conference. 'We used to think that you could
spend your way out of a recession, and increase employment by
cutting taxes and boosting government spending. I tell you in
all candour that that option no longer exists, and that
insofar as it ever did exist, it only worked on each occasion
since the War by injecting a bigger dose of inflation into the
economy, followed by a higher level of unemployment as the
next step'. In the reaction that witnessed Keynesianism
toppled from its intellectual throne, and the halo removed
from around public expenditure, the fashion for administrative
change was a casualty. It did seem that as, appropriately,
Anthony Crosland observed, 'the party is over'.15

References

1. Clarke (1971), pp. 37-71.
2. H.C. 535-II, (1977), pp. 760-62, 766, 780-82, 802.
3. This was particularly true of the changes of 1974-75 when, in a matter of months, Overseas Development was moved out of the FCO and then, at least at Ministerial level, moved back again.
4. Howard (1970), pp. 18-19. Howard, a distinguished military historian, believes the changes to represent the biggest revolution in defence administration since Cardwell. As for external affairs, Sir Richard Clarke (in Thornhill, 1975, p. 76) advanced the view that it was unfortunate that the FCO merger did not take place ten years earlier because the CRO was 'always a brake upon our approach to Europe'. It may well have been; but as an obstacle at the time when it really mattered the CRO was overshadowed by the FO with whom, as later, it would have been merged.
5. Roll (1966), pp. 4-5; Lester (1973), pp. 91-93, 198, 200, 204.
6. For evidence of the failure of incomes policies, and from a sympathetic source, see Blackaby (NIESR, 1978), pp. 31-9.
7. For instance, the South West Economic Planning Council produced a quite detailed regional plan called Region With A Future in 1967, while the Northern Economic Planning Council's exercise, Challenge of the Changing North, published in 1966, with a less ambitious effort which, by and large, simply called for more Government money to be spent in the area. In neither case did the Council's Report make much difference.
8. To judge from the statistics on productivity presented in Cairncross et. al. (1977), pp. 9-13.
9. Heath and Barker (1978), pp. 361-90.
10. Shore (1966), p. 153.
11. Chester (1975), pp. 1008-9; Fry (1969), p. 296; Fry (1972), pp. 153-55.
12. H.C. 535-II, (1977), p. 763.
13. Neddy's survival was and is by no means assured, always given the possibility of trade union withdrawal in the face of an insufficiently 'cooperative' Government. Neddy's well developed supporting committee structure has been a factor in its survival thus far.
14. Clarke (1978), pp. xi, 147-49, 151, 158.
15. Report of the 75th Annual Conference of the Labour Party, p. 188 (cf. the advice given to Richard Crossman by the Keynesian economist Michael Stewart in 1966: Crossman, II, 1976, p. 41); DOE Press Notice 9.5.1975.

SELECT BIBLIOGRAPHY

I   GENERAL

Burke, E. Works, 6 Vols. (1883 edn.).
Crosland, C.A.R. The Future of Socialism, (1956).
Galbraith, J.K. The Affluent Society, (1958).
Galbraith, J.K. The New Industrial State, 2nd edn., (1972).
Hayek, F.A. The Road to Serfdom, (1944).
Hayek, F.A. The Constitution of Liberty, (1960).
Hayek, F.A. Law, Legislation and Liberty, 3 Vols., (1973-79).
Keynes, J.M. The General Theory of Employment, Interest and
    Money, (1936).
Marx, K. Capital, 3 Vols., (1906-33: trans. S. Moore and
    E. Aveling and E. Untermann).
Oakeshott, M.J. Rationalism and Other Essays, (1962).
Popper, Sir K. R. The Poverty of Historicism, 3rd edn., (1969).
Popper, Sir K. R. The Open Society and Its Enemies, 2 Vols.,
    5th edn., (1966-74).
Schumpeter, J.A. Capitalism, Socialism and Democracy, 5th edn.
    (1952).
Smith, A. An Inquiry into the Nature and Causes of the Wealth
    of Nations, 2 Vols., (ed. E. Cannan, 1904).

II   THE MACHINERY OF GOVERNMENT

(i) Official Material

Report of the (Haldane) Machinery of Government Committee,
    Cd. 9230, (1918).
Report of the (Redcliffe-Maud) Royal Commission on Local
    Government in England, Cmnd. 4040 (1969).
Report of the (Wheatley) Royal Commission on Local Government
    in Scotland, Cmnd. 4510, (1969).
The Reorganization of Central Government, Cmnd. 4506, (1970).
Clarke, Sir R. New Trends in Government, (1971).
Report of the (Crowther-Kilbrandon) Royal Commission on the
    Constitution, Cmnd. 5460, 5460-I.

Report of the (Houghton) Committee on Financial Aid to
    Political Parties, Cmnd. 6601, (1976).

(ii) Books and Articles

Attlee, C.R. 'Civil Servants, Ministers, Parliament and the
    Public', Political Quarterly, 25, (1954).
Avon, Lord, Full Circle, (1960).
Avon, Lord, Facing The Dictators, (1962).
Avon, Lord, The Reckoning, (1965).
Beer, S.H. Modern British Politics, (1965).
Beichman, A. 'The Conservative Research Department: The Care
    and Feeding of Future British Political Elites', Journal
    of British Studies, XIII, (1973-74).
Bevan, A. In Place of Fear, (1952).
Bevins, R. The Greasy Pole, (1965).
Birkenhead, Lord, The Prof in Two Worlds, (1961).
Birkenhead, Lord, Walter Monckton, (1969)
Bogdanor, V. & Skidelsky, R. (eds.), The Age of Affluence
    1951-1964, (1970).
Boyle, Sir E. & Playfair, Sir E. 'Who are the Policy Makers?',
    Public Administration, 43 (1965).
Bridges, Lord, The Treasury, 2nd edn., (1966).
Brown, G. In My Way, (1971).
Brown, R.G.S. & Steel, D.R. The Administrative Process in
    Britain 2nd edn., (1979).
Butler, Lord, The Art of the Possible, (1971).
Campion, Lord, et. al., British Government since 1918, (1950).
Campion, Lord, et. al., Parliament. A Survey, (1952).
Chandos, Lord, Memoirs, (1960).
Chapman, R.A. 'The Vehicle and General Affair: Some
    Reflections on Public Administration in Britain', Public
    Administration, 51, (1973).
Chester, D.N. & Willson, F.M.G. The Organization of British
    Central Government 1914-1964, (1968).
Churchill, R. The Rise and Fall of Sir Anthony Eden, (1959).
Clark, A. 'Ministerial Supervision and the Size of the
    Department of the Environment', Public Administration, 55,
    (1977).
Coombes, D. The Member of Parliament and the Administration,
    (1966).
Craig, F.W.S. British General Election Manifestos 1900-1974,
    (1975).
Crick, B.R. (ed.), Essays on Reform 1967, (1967).
Crick, B.R. The Reform of Parliament, (1964, 1970).
Crosland, C.A.R. The Future of Socialism, (1956).
Crosland, C.A.R. The Conservative Enemy, (1962).
Crosland, C.A.R. Socialism Now and Other Essays, (1975).
Crossman, R.H.S. (ed.), New Fabian Essays, (1953).
Crossman, R.H.S. Inside View. Three Lectures on Prime
    Ministerial Government, (1972).

Crossman, R.H.S. The Diaries of a Cabinet Minister, 3 Vols.,
    1975, 1976, 1977.
Daalder, H. Cabinet Reform in Britain 1914-1963, (1964).
Dalton, Lord, High Tide and After, (1962).
Davenport, N. Memoirs of a City Radical, (1974).
Donoughue, B. & Jones, G.W. Herbert Morrison. Portrait of a
    Politician, (1973).
Drucker, H.M. Doctrine and Ethos in the Labour Party, (1979).
Dunsire, A. Administration. The Word and the Science, (1973).
Feiling, K. The Life of Neville Chamberlain, (1946).
Finer, S.E. 'The Individual Responsibility of Ministers',
    Public Administration, 34, (1956).
Finer, S.E. (ed.), Adversary Politics and Electoral Reform,
    (1975).
Fisher, N. Iain Macleod, (1973).
Foot, M.M. Aneurin Bevan 1897-1945, (1962).
Foot, M.M. Aneurin Bevan 1945-1960, (1973).
Foot, P. The Politics of Harold Wilson, (1968).
Fry, G.K. 'Thoughts on the Present State of the Convention of
    Ministerial Responsibility', Parliamentary Affairs, 23,
    (1969-70).
Fry, G.K. The Growth of Government. The Development of Ideas
    about the Role of the State and the Machinery and
    Functions of Government in Britain since 1780, (1979).
Gilmour, Sir I. Inside Right. A Study of Conservatism, (1977).
Gunn, L.A. 'Politicians and Officials: Who is Answerable?',
    Political Quarterly, 43, (1972).
Hague, D.C., Mackenzie, W.J.M. & Barker, A. Public Policy and
    Private Interests, (1975).
Hailsham, Lord, The Door Wherein I Went, (1975).
Haines, J. The Politics of Power, (1977).
Headey, B. British Cabinet Ministers. The Roles of
    Politicians in Executive Office, (1974).
Heath, E. & Barker, A. 'Heath on Whitehall Reform',
    Parliamentary Affairs, 31, (1978).
Hill, Lord, Both Sides of the Hill, (1964).
Hood, C.C. The Limits of Administration, (1976).
Holland, P. & Fallon, M. The Quango Explosion. Public Bodies
    and Ministerial Patronage, (1978).
Hunter, L. The Road to Brighton Pier, (1959).
Hurd, D. An End to Promises. Sketch of a Government 1970-74,
    (1979).
Ince, Sir G. The Ministry of Labour and National Service,
    (1960).
Jenkins, Sir G. The Ministry of Transport and Civil Aviation,
    (1959).
Jenkins, R. The Pursuit of Progress, (1953).
Jenkins, R. The Labour Case, (1959)
Jennings, Sir W.I., Cabinet Government, 3rd edn., (1959).
Johnson, N. In Search of the Constitution, (1977).
Johnston, Sir A. The Inland Revenue, (1962).
Kilmuir, Lord, Political Adventure, (1964).

King, A. et. al., Why is Britain Becoming Harder to Govern ?, (1974).
King, C. The Cecil King Diary 1965-70, (1972).
King, Sir G.S. The Ministry of Pensions and National Insurance, (1958).
Laing, M. Edward Heath. Prime Minister, (1972).
Laski, H.J. Democracy in Crisis, (1933).
Laski, H.J. Parliamentary Government in England, (1938).
Laski, H.J. Reflections on the Constitution, (1951).
Lee, J. M. Reviewing the Machinery of Government 1942-1952, (1977).
Leemans, A.F. (ed.). The Management of Change in Government, (1976).
Lindblom, C.E. The Policy Making Process, (1968).
Low, Sir S.J.M. The Governance of England, (1904).
McKie, D. & Cook, C. (eds.). The Decade of Disillusion. British Politics in the Sixties, (1972).
Mackintosh, J.M. The British Cabinet, 3rd edn., (1977).
Macmillan, H. The Winds of Change 1914-1939, (1966).
Macmillan, H. The Blast of War 1939-1945, (1967).
Macmillan, H. Tides of Fortune 1945-1955, (1969).
Macmillan, H. Riding the Storm 1955-1959, (1971).
Macmillan, H. Pointing the Way 1959-1961, (1972).
Macmillan, H. At The End of The Day 1961-1963, (1974).
Martin, B.K. Harold Laski 1893-1950, (1953).
Maudling, R. Memoirs, (1978).
Milne, Sir D. The Scottish Office, (1957).
Minogue, M. Documents on Contemporary British Government, 2 Vols., (1977).
Moran, Lord, Winston Churchill. The Struggle for Survival 1940-1965, (1966).
Morrison, H. Government and Parliament, (1954, 1964).
Pelling, H. Winston Churchill, (1974).
Pollitt, C. 'The Central Policy Review Staff 1970-1974', Public Administration, 52, (1974).
Radice, L. Reforming the House of Commons, (1977).
Richards, P.G. Parliament and Conscience, (1970).
Richards, P.G. The Reformed Local Government System, 2nd edn.,
Robertson, J.H. Reform of British Central Government, (1971).
Rose, R. The Problem of Party Government, (1974).
Roseveare, H. The Treasury. The Evolution of a British Institution, (1969).
Roth, A. Enoch Powell. Tory Tribune, (1971).
Rothschild, Lord, Meditations of a Broomstick, (1977).
Sampson, A. Macmillan. A Study in Ambiguity, (1967).
Searle, G.R. The Quest for National Efficiency. A Study in British Politics and Political Thought 1899-1914, (1971).
Self, P.J.O. Bureaucracy or Management ?, (1965).
Self, P.J.O. Administrative Theories and Politics, (1972).
Self, P.J.O. Econocrats and the Policy Process, (1975).
Sharp, E. The Ministry of Housing and Local Government, (1969).
Shore, P. Entitled to Know, (1966).

Sissons, M. & French, P. (eds.). The Age of Austerity 1945-51, (1963).
Smith, B.C. & Stanyer, J. 'Administrative Developments in 1970: A Survey', Public Administration, 49, (1971).
Smith, B.C. & Stanyer, J. 'Administrative Developments in 1971 and 1972: A Survey', Public Administration, 51, (1973).
Smith, L. Harold Wilson. The Authentic Portrait, (1964).
Steel, D.R. & Stanyer, J. 'Administrative Developments in 1973 and 1974: A Survey', Public Administration, 53, (1975).
Steel, D.R. & Stanyer, J. 'Administrative Developments in 1975 and 1976: A Survey', Public Administration, 55, (1977).
Strachey, J. Contemporary Capitalism, (1956).
Strang, Lord, The Foreign Office, (1955).
Thornhill, W. (ed.). The Modernization of British Government, (1975).
Vile, M.J.C. Constitutionalism and the Separation of Powers, (1967).
Wheare, K.C. Government by Committee, (1955).
Wheeler- Bennett, Sir J. John Anderson, (1962).
Wigg, Lord, George Wigg, (1972).
Williams, M. Inside Number Ten, (1972).
Williams, P. Hugh Gaitskell, (1979).
Wilson, J.H. The Labour Government 1964-70. A Personal Record, (1971).
Wilson, J.H. The Governance of Britain, (1976).
Winnifrith, Sir A.J.D. The Ministry of Agriculture, Fisheries and Food, (1962).
Woolton, Lord, Memoirs, (1960).

III   THE MANAGEMENT OF THE ECONOMY

(i)   Official Material

Employment Policy, Cmd. 6527, (1944).
Economic Implications of Full Employment, Cmd. 9725, (1956).
Incomes Policy: The Next Step, Cmnd. 1626, (1962).
NEDC, Conditions Favourable to Faster Growth, (1963).
NEDC, Growth of the UK Economy to 1966, (1963).
Machinery of Prices and Incomes Policy, Cmnd. 2577, (1965).
Prices and Incomes Policy, Cmnd. 2639, (1965).
The National Plan, Cmnd. 2764, (1965).
Prices and Incomes Policy: An 'Early Warning System', Cmnd. 2808, (1965).
Prices and Incomes Standstill: Period of Severe Restraint, Cmnd. 3150, (1966).
Prices and Incomes Policy After June 30 1967, Cmnd. 3235, (1967).
NBPI, Report No. 36: Productivity Agreements, Cmnd. 3311, (1967).

Productivity, Prices and Incomes Policy in 1968 and 1969, Cmnd.
    3590, (1968).
Report of the (Donovan) Royal Commission on Trade Unions and
    Employers' Associations, Cmnd. 3623, (1968).
In Place of Strife. A Policy for Industrial Relations, Cmnd.
    3888, (1969).
DEA, The Task Ahead. Economic Assessment to 1972, (1969).
Productivity, Prices and Incomes Policy after 1969, Cmnd. 4237,
    (1969).
Treasury, Economic Prospects to 1972. A Revised Assessment,(1970).
Department of Employment, People and Jobs. A Modern Employment
    Service, (1971).
Report of the (Robens) Committee on Safety and Health at Work,
    Cmnd. 5034, (1972).
Price and Pay Code. Consultative Document, Cmnd. 5247, (1973).
Price and Pay Code for Stage 3. A Consultative Document, Cmnd.
    5444, (1973)
The Counter Inflation Policy: Stage 3, Cmnd. 5446, (1973)
Shepherd, J.R., Evans, H.P. & Riley, C.J. The Treasury Short
    Term Forecasting Model, (1974).
The Attack on Inflation, Cmnd. 6151, (1975).
Report of the (Ball) Committee on Policy Optimization, Cmnd.
    7148, (1978).
Cassels, J.S. 'The Manpower Services Commission', Management
    Services in Government, 34, (1979).

(ii) Books and Articles

Allen, Sir D. 'The Department of Economic Affairs',
    Political Quarterly, 38, (1967).
Bacon, R. & Eltis, W. Britain's Economic Problem. Too Few
    Producers, 2nd edn., (1978)
Balogh, T. Germany. An Experiment in 'Planning' by the 'Free'
    Price Mechanism, (1950).
Balogh, T. Planning For Progress. A Strategy for Labour,
    (1963).
Beckerman, W. (ed.). The Labour Government's Economic Record
    1964-1970, (1972).
Beveridge, W.H. Full Employment in a Free Society, (1944).
Blackaby, F. et. al. 'Three Aspects of Incomes Policy',
    National Institute Economic Review, No. 85,(August, 1978).
Blackaby, F. (ed.). British Economic Policy 1960-74, (1978).
Blank, S. Industry and Government in Britain. The Federation
    of British Industries in Politics 1945-65, (1973).
Brandon, H. In The Red. The Struggle for Sterling 1964-66,
    (1966).
Bray, J. Decision in Government, (1970).
Brittan, S. The Treasury under the Tories 1951-64, (1964).
Brittan, S. Steering the Economy. The Role of the Treasury,
    (1969, 1971).
Brittan, S. Is There An Economic Consensus ?, (1973).
Brittan, S. Second Thoughts on Full Employment Policy, (1975).
Brittan, S. The Economic Consequences of Democracy, (1977).

Brittan, S. & Lilley, P. The Delusion of Incomes Policy, (1977).

Brown, H. Phelps. 'The National Economic Development Organization', Public Administration, 41, (1963).

Brunner, J. The National Plan, (1965).

Cairncross, Sir A. (ed.). The Managed Economy, (1970).

Cairncross, Sir A. et. al. 'The Regeneration of Manufacturing Industry', Midland Bank Review, (Autumn, 1977).

Caves, R.E. et. al. Britain's Economic Prospects, (1968).

Chester, D.N. 'The Treasury 1956', Public Administration, 35, (1957).

Chester, D.N. 'The Treasury 1962', Public Administration, 40, (1962).

Clarke, R. 'The Plowden Report. II. The Formulation of Economic Policy', Public Administration, 41, (1963).

Clegg, H. How to Run an Incomes Policy and Why We Made Such a Mess of the Last One, (1971).

Cockfield, Sir A. 'The Price Commission and the Price Control', Three Banks Review, No. 117, (1978).

Cole, G.D.H. Principles of Economic Planning, (1935).

Cole, G.D.H. The Machinery of Socialist Planning, (1938).

Cole, G.D.H. Plan for Democratic Britain, (1939).

Congdon, T. Monetarism. An Essay in Definition, (1978).

Currie, R. Industrial Politics, (1979).

Davenport, N. The Split Society, (1964).

Deane, P. & Cole, W.A. British Economic Growth 1688-1959, (1962).

Denton, G., Forsyth, M. & MacLennan, M. Economic Planning and Policies in Britain, France and Germany, (1968).

Denison, E.F. & Chung, W.K. How Japan's Economy Grew So Fast, (1976).

Dow, J.C.R. The Management of the British Economy 1945-60, (1964).

Erhard, L. Prosperity Through Competition, 3rd edn., (1960).

Frank, I. (ed.). The Japanese Economy in International Perspective, (1975).

Friedman, M. The Counter-Revolution in Monetary Theory, (1970).

Friedman, M. Unemployment versus Inflation ? An Evaluation of the Phillips Curve, (1975).

Friedman, M. From Galbraith to Economic Freedom, (1977).

Friedman, M. Inflation and Unemployment. The New Dimension of Politics, (1977).

Gordon, R.J. (ed.). Milton Friedman's Monetary Framework: A Debate with his Critics, (1974).

Grant, W. & Marsh, D. The Confederation of British Industry, (1977).

Harris, R. & Sewill, B. British Economic Policy 1970-74. Two Views, (1975).

Harrod, R.F. The Life of John Maynard Keynes, (1951).

Hayek, F.A. Full Employment at Any Price ?, (1975).

Hayek, F.A. A Tiger by the Tail, 2nd edn., (1978).

189

Hayward, J.E.S. & Watson, M. (eds.). Planning, Politics and
    Public Policy. The British, French and Italian
    Experience, (1975).
Hennesy, J., Lutz, V. & Simone, G. Economic Miracles, (1964).
Hicks, Sir J.R. The Crisis in Keynesian Economics, (1974).
Hirsch, F. & Goldthorpe, J.H. The Political Economy of
    Inflation, (1978).
Howson, S. & Winch, D. The Economic Advisory Council 1930-1939,
    (1977).
Hutchison, T.W. Economics and Economic Policy in Britain
    1946-1966, (1968).
Hutchison, T.W. Keynes versus the 'Keynesians', (1977).
Hutchison, T.W. Knowledge and Ignorance in Economics, (1977).
Jay, P. Employment, Inflation and Politics, (1976).
Jenkins, P. The Battle of Downing Street, (1970).
Jewkes, J. The New Ordeal by Planning, (1968).
Johnson, H.G. Inflation and the Monetarist Controversy, (1972).
Johnson, H.G. & Nobay, A.R. (eds.). Issues in Monetary
    Economics, (1974).
Jones, A. The New Inflation. The Politics of Prices and
    Incomes, (1973).
Jones, A. (ed.). Economics and Equality, (1976).
Kahn-Freund, O. Labour and the Law, (1972).
Kaldor, N. Essays on Economic Policy, 2 Vols., (1964).
Kaldor, N. Causes of the Slow Rate of Economic Growth of the
    United Kingdom, (1966).
Keynes, J.M. Essays in Biography, (1933).
Keynes, Lord, 'The Balance of Payments of the United States',
    Economic Journal, 56, (1946).
Klein, L. & Ohkawa (eds.). Economic Growth. The Japanese
    Experience since the Meiji Era, (1968).
Lutz, V. Central Planning for the Market Economy. An
    Analysis of French Theory and Experience, (1969).
McFadzean, Sir F. The Economics of J.K. Galbraith. A Study
    in Fantasy, (1977).
Macrae, N. Sunshades in October, (1963).
Maddison, A. Economic Growth in the West, (1964).
Marris, R. The Machinery of Economic Policy, (1954).
Middlemas, R.K. Politics in Industrial Society. The
    Experience of the British System since 1911, (1979).
Mitchell, J. Groundwork for Economic Planning, (1966).
Mitchell, J. The National Board for Prices and Incomes,
    (1972).
Moran, M. The Politics of Industrial Relations. The Origins,
    Life and Death of the 1971 Industrial Relations Act,
    (1977).
Ohkawa, K. & Rosovsky, H. Japanese Economic Growth. Trend
    Acceleration in the Twentieth Century, (1973).
Paish, F.W. Studies in an Inflationary Economy. The United
    Kingdom 1948-1961, (1962).
Paish, F.W. Rise and Fall of Incomes Policy, 2nd edn., (1971).

Panitch, L. Social Democracy and Industrial Militancy. The Labour Party, the Trade Unions and Incomes Policy 1945-1974, (1976).

Parkin, M. & Summer, M.T. (eds.). Inflation in the United Kingdom, (1978).

Phillips, A.W. 'The Relation between Unemployment and the Rate of Change of Money Wage Rates in the UK 1861-1957', Economica, XXV, (1958).

Polanyi, G. Planning in Britain. The Experience of the 1960s, (1967).

Political and Economic Planning, Growth in the British Economy, (1960).

Pringle, R. The Growth Merchants. Economic Consequences of Wishful Thinking, (1977).

Reddaway, W.B. The Effects of UK Direct Investment Overseas, (1968).

Robinson, J. After Keynes, (1973).

Sir E. Roll et. al. 'The Machinery for Economic Planning', Public Administration, 44, (1966).

Shonfield, A. British Economic Policy since the War, (1958).

Shonfield, A. Modern Capitalism. The Changing Balance of Public and Private Power, (1965).

Showler, B. The Public Employment Service, (1976).

Skidelsky, R. (ed.). The End of the Keynesian Era, (1977).

Stewart, M. The Jekyll and Hyde Years. Politics and Economic Policy since 1964, (1977).

Surrey, M.J.C. 'The National Plan in Retrospect', Bulletin of the Oxford University Institute of Economics and Statistics, 34, (1972).

Thomson, A.W.J. & Engleman, S.R. The Industrial Relations Act. A Review and Analysis, (1975).

Weekes, B., Mellish, M., Dickens, L. & Lloyd, J. Industrial Relations and the Law, (1975).

Wigham, E. Strikes and the Government 1893-1974, (1976).

Winch, D. Economics and Policy. A Historical Study, (1969).

Woolton, B.F. Plan or No Plan, (1934).

Woolton, B.F. Freedom Under Planning, (1945).

Worswick, G.D.N. & Ady, P.H. (eds.). The British Economy 1945-50, (1952).

Worswick, G.D.N. & Ady, P.H. (eds.). The British Economy in the 1950s, (1962).

IV   THE CONTROL OF PUBLIC EXPENDITURE

(i) Official Material

Fourth Report from the Committee of Public Accounts, H.C. 241-I, (1950-51).

Sixth Report from the Select Committee on Estimates. Treasury Control of Expenditure, H.C. 254-I, (1957-58).

Seventh Special Report from the Select Committee on Estimates.
    Treasury Control of Expenditure. Observations of HM
    Treasury, H.C. 227, (1958-59).
Control of Public Expenditure, Cmnd. 1432, (1961).
Public Expenditure in 1963-64 and 1967-68, Cmnd. 2235, (1963).
Public Expenditure: Planning and Control, Cmnd. 2915, (1966).
Public Expenditure in 1968-69 and 1969-70, Cmnd. 3515, (1968).
First Report from the Select Committee on Procedure.
    Scrutiny of Public Expenditure and Administration, H.C.
    410, (1968-69).
Public Expenditure. A New Presentation, Cmnd. 4017, (1969).
Public Expenditure 1968-69 to 1973-74, Cmnd. 4234, (1969).
New Policies for Public Spending, Cmnd. 4515, (1970).
Public Expenditure 1969-70 to 1974-75, Cmnd. 4578, (1971).
Third Report from the Expenditure Committee. Command Papers on
    Public Expenditure, H.C. 549, (1970-71).
Public Expenditure 1969-70 to 1975-76, Cmnd. 4829, (1971).
Seventh Report from the Expenditure Committee. Public
    Expenditure and Economic Management, H.C. 450, (1971-72).
Public Expenditure to 1976-77, Cmnd. 5178, (1972).
H.M. Treasury, Public Expenditure White Papers: Handbook on
    Methodology, (1972).
Rees, P.M. & Thompson, F.P. 'The Relative Price Effect in
    Public Expenditure: its Nature and Method of
    Calculation', Statistical News, No. 18, (1972).
Sixth and Seventh Reports from the Committee of Public
    Accounts. Development and Production of the Concorde
    Aircraft, H.C. 335, 353, (1972-73).
Public Expenditure to 1977-78, Cmnd. 5519, (1973).
Goldman, Sir S. The Developing System of Public Expenditure
    and Control, (1973).
Ninth Report from the Expenditure Committee. Public
    Expenditure, Inflation and the Balance of Payments, H.C.
    328, (1974).
Fifth Special Report from the Expenditure Committee. Public
    Expenditure, Inflation and the Balance of Payments.
    Memorandum by the Treasury, H.C. 408, (1974-75).
Fourth Report from the Committee of Public Accounts, H.C. 502,
    (1974-75).
Twelfth Report from the Expenditure Committee. Cash Limits
    Control of Public Expenditure, H.C. 535, (1974-75).
Public Expenditure to 1978-79, Cmnd. 5879, (1975).
First Report from the Expenditure Committee. The Financing of
    Public Expenditure, H.C. 69-I, II, (1975-76).
Cash Limits on Public Expenditure, Cmnd. 6440, (1976).
The Government's Expenditure Plans, Cmnd. 6721-I, II, (1977).
Cash Limits 1978-79, Cmnd. 7161, (1978).

(ii) Books and Articles

Abramovitz, M. & Eliasberg, V.F. The Growth of Public Employ-
    ment in Britain, (1957).

Arrow, K. Social Choice and Individual Values, 2nd edn.,
    (1970).
Bacon, R. et. al. The Dilemmas of Government Expenditure,
    (1976).
Beer, S.H. Treasury Control, (1956).
Breton, A. The Economic Theory of Representative Government,
    (1974).
Bridges, Sir E.E. Treasury Control, (1950).
Brown, C.V. & Jackson, P.M. Public Sector Economics, (1978).
Buchanan, J.M. & Tollison, R. (eds.). Theory of Public Choice,
    (1972).
Buchanan, J.M. The Limits of Liberty. Between Anarchy and
    Leviathan, (1975).
Buchanan, J.M. & Wagner, R.E. Democracy in Deficit. The
    Political Legacy of Lord Keynes, (1977).
Buchanan, J.M. et. al. The Economics of Politics, (1978).
Chapman, L. Your Disobedient Servant, (1978).
Chester, D.N. 'The Plowden Report: I Nature and Significance',
    Public Administration, 41, (1963).
Chubb, B. The Control of Public Expenditure. Financial
    Committees of the House of Commons, (1952).
Clark, C. Taxmanship, 2nd edn., (1970).
Clarke, Sir R. The Management of the Public Sector of the
    National Economy, (1964).
Clarke, Sir R. Public Expenditure, Management and Control.
    The Development of the Public Expenditure Survey
    Committee (PESC), (1978).
Diamond, Lord, Public Expenditure in Practice, (1975).
Downs, A. An Economic Theory of Democracy, (1957).
Galloway, D. The Public Prodigals, (1976).
Godley, W. 'The Measurement and Control of Public Expenditure',
    Economic Policy Review, No. 2, (March, 1976).
Heclo, H. & Wildavsky, A. The Private Government of Public
    Money, (1974).
Johnson, N. Parliament and Administration. The Estimates
    Committee 1945-65, (1966).
Lyden, F.J. & Miller, E.G. (eds.). Planning Programming
    Budgeting. A Systems Approach to Management, (1971).
Meade, J.E. et. al. The Structure and Reform of Direct
    Taxation, (1978).
Niskanen, W.A. Bureaucracy and Representative Government,
    (1971).
Niskanen, W.A. Bureaucracy. Servant or Master ?, (1973).
Normanton, E.L. The Accountability and Audit of Governments.
    A Comparative Study, (1966).
Nutter, G.W. Growth of Government in the West, (1978).
Peacock, A.T. & Robertson, D.J. (eds.). Public Expenditure.
    Appraisal and Control, (1957).
Peacock, A.T. & Wiseman, J. (eds.). The Growth of Public
    Expenditure in the United Kingdom, 2nd edn., (1967).
Pollitt, C. 'The Public Expenditure Survey', Public
    Administration, 55, (1977).

Posner, M. (ed.). Public Expenditure. Allocation Between Competing Ends, (1977).

Prest, A.R. Public Finance in Theory and Practice, 5th edn., (1975).

Pryor, F.L. Public Expenditure in Communist and Capitalist Nations, (1968).

Robinson, A. Parliament and Public Spending. The Expenditure Committee of the House of Commons 1970-76, (1978).

Sandford, C. & Robinson, A. 'Public Spending. A Decade of Unprecedented Peacetime Growth', The Banker, 125, (1975).

Smith, B.L.R. & Hague, D.C. (eds.). The Dilemma of Accountability in Modern Government, (1971).

Tullock, G. The Politics of Bureaucracy, (1965).

Tullock, G. Private Wants Public Means, (1970).

Wright, M. 'Public Expenditure in Britain: The Crisis of Control', Public Administration, 55, (1977).

V   THE STATE AND THE PRIVATE SECTOR

(i) Official Material

Report of the (Barlow) Royal Commission on the Distribution of Industrial Population, Cmd. 6153, (1939).

Central Scotland. A Programme for Development and Growth, Cmnd. 2188, (1963).

The North East. A Programme for Development and Growth, Cmnd. 2206, (1963).

Monopolies, Mergers and Restrictive Practices, Cmnd. 2299, (1964).

Report of the (Plowden) Committee of Inquiry into the Aircraft Industry, Cmnd. 2853, (1965).

Investment Incentives, Cmnd. 2874, (1966).

The Industrial Reorganization Corporation, Cmnd. 2889, (1966).

Report of the (Geddes) Shipbuilding Inquiry Committee, Cmnd. 2937, (1966).

The Development Areas. Regional Employment Premiums, Cmnd. 3310, (1967).

Industrial Expansion, Cmnd. 3509, (1968).

Industrial Investment: The Computers Merger Project 1968, Cmnd. 3660, (1968).

Industrial Investment: The Production of Primary Aluminium, Cmnd. 3819, (1968).

The Intermediate Areas, Cmnd. 3998, (1969).

Investment Incentives, Cmnd. 4516, (1970).

Fourth Report from the Select Committee on Science and Technology. The Prospects for the UK Computer Industry in the 1970s, H.C. 621-I, II, III, (1970-71).

Sixth Report from the Expenditure Committee. Public Money in the Private Sector, H.C. 347, 347-I, II, (1971-72).

Rolls-Royce Ltd and the RB211 Aero Engine, Cmnd. 4860, (1972).

Shipbuilding on the Upper Clyde, Cmnd. 4918, (1972).

Industrial and Regional Development, Cmnd. 4942, (1972).

Public Money in the Private Sector, Cmnd. 5186, (1972).
Second Report from the Expenditure Committee. Regional
    Development Incentives, H.C. 85, 85-I, (1973-74).
The Regeneration of British Industry, Cmnd. 5710, (1974).
Central Policy Review Staff, The Future of the British Car
    Industry, (1975).
An Approach to Industrial Strategy, Cmnd. 6315, (1975).
Eighth Report from the Expenditure Committee. Public
    Expenditure on Chrysler UK Ltd, H.C. 596-I, II, III,
    (1975-76).

(ii) Books and Articles

Abraham, N. Big Business and the Government. The New
    Disorder, (1974).
Beesley, M.E. & White, G.M. 'The Industrial Reorganization
    Corporation: A Study in Choice of Public Management',
    Public Administration, 51, (1973).
Brown, A.J. The Framework of Regional Economics in the United
    Kingdom, (1972).
Bruce-Gardyne, J. Whatever Happened to the Quiet Revolution ?,
    (1974).
Bruce-Gardyne, J. Meriden. Odyssey of a Lame Duck, (1978).
Buchan, A. The Right to Work. The Story of the Upper Clyde
    Confrontation, (1972).
Burton, J. The Job Support Machine. A Critique of the
    Subsidy Morass, (1979).
Chataway, C. New Deal for Industry, (1972).
Chester, Sir D.N. The Nationalization of British Industry
    1945-51, (1975).
Clarke, Sir R. 'Mintech in Retrospect - I, II', Omega, 1,
    (1973).
Dean, Sir M. 'The Machinery for Economic Planning. IV The
    Ministry of Technology', Public Administration, 44,
    (1966).
Dell, E. Political Responsibility and Industry, (1973).
Ganz, G. Government and Industry, (1977).
Grove, J.W. Government and Industry in Britain, (1962).
Hallett, G., Randell, P. & West, E.G. Regional Policy for
    Ever ?, (1973).
Harris, N. Competition and the Corporate Society. British
    Conservatives, the State and Industry, (1972).
Hodges, M. The Multi-National Corporations and National
    Government, (1974).
Holland, S. (ed.). The State as Entrepreneur, (1972).
Jewkes, J. Delusions of Dominance, (1977).
Knight, A. Private Enterprise and Public Intervention, (1974).
Lester, T. 'The Unmaking of Mintech', Management Today,
    (November, 1973).
Lethbridge, D.G. (ed.). Government and Industry Relationships,
    (1976).

McClelland, W.G. 'The Industrial Reorganization Corporation 1966-71: An Experimental Prod', <u>Three Banks Review</u>, No. 94, (1972).
McCrone, G. <u>Regional Policy in Britain</u>, (1969).
Moonman, E. <u>Reluctant Partnership</u>, (1971).
Parr, M. 'The National Enterprise Board', <u>National Westminster Bank Quarterly Bulletin</u>, (February, 1979).
Prais, S.J. <u>The Evolution of Giant Firms in Britain</u>, (1976).
Reid, J. <u>Reflections of a Clyde Built Man</u>, (1976).
Rogow, A.A. & Shore, P. <u>The Labour Government and British Industry 1945-51</u>, (1955).
Skuse, A. <u>Government Intervention and Industrial Policy</u>, 2nd edn., (1972).
Smith, B.L.R. (ed.). <u>The New Political Economy. The Public Use of the Public Sector</u>, (1975).
Turner, G. <u>The Leyland Papers</u>, (1971).
Utton, M.A. <u>Industrial Concentration</u>, (1970).
Vernon, R. (ed.). <u>Big Business and the State. Changing Relations in Western Europe</u>, (1974).
Vig, N.J. <u>Science and Technology in British Politics</u>, (1968).
Young, S. & Lowe, A. <u>Intervention in the Mixed Economy</u>, (1974).

VI   THE STATE AND SOCIAL PROVISION

(i)   <u>Official Material</u>

<u>Social Insurance and Allied Services. Report by Sir William Beveridge</u>, Cmd. 6404, (1942).
<u>Educational Reconstruction</u>, Cmd. 6458, (1943).
<u>A National Health Service</u>, Cmd. 6502, (1944).
<u>Social Insurance. Part I</u>, Cmd. 6550, (1944).
<u>Social Insurance. Part II</u>. Cmd. 6551, (1944).
<u>Report of the</u> (Guillebaud) <u>Committee of Enquiry into the Cost of the National Health Service</u>, Cmd. 9663, (1956).
<u>15 to 18. A Report of the</u> (Crowther) <u>Central Advisory Council for Education</u> (England), (1959).
<u>Half Our Future. A Report of the</u> (Newsom) <u>Central Advisory Council for Education</u> (England), (1963).
<u>Report of the</u> (Robbins) <u>Committee on Higher Education</u>, Cmnd. 2154, (1963).
<u>Report of the</u> (Trend) <u>Committee of Enquiry into the Organization of Civil Science</u>, Cmnd. 2171, (1963).
<u>Report of the</u> (Seebohm) <u>Committee on Local Authority and Allied Personal Social Services</u>, Cmnd. 3703, (1968).
(Newsom-Donnison) <u>Public Schools Commission. First Report</u> (1968). <u>Second Report</u> (1970).
<u>Better Services for the Mentally Handicapped</u>, Cmnd. 4683, (1971).
<u>Select Committee on Race Relations and Immigration. Housing</u>, H.C. 508-I, II, III, (1970-71).
<u>Proposal for a Tax Credit Scheme</u>, Cmnd. 5116, (1972).

Equality for Women, Cmnd. 5724, (1974).
Select Committee on Race Relations and Immigration. The Organization of Race Relations Administration, H.C. 448-I, II, III, (1974-75).
Racial Discrimination, Cmnd. 6234, (1975).
Supplementary Benefits Commission Annual Report 1975, Cmnd. 6615, (1976).
Supplementary Benefits Commission Annual Report 1976, Cmnd. 6910, (1977).
Draper, P. Creation of the DOE. A Study of the Merger of Three Departments to form the Department of the Environment, (1977).
Supplementary Benefits Commission Annual Report 1977, Cmnd. 7392, (1978).
Supplementary Benefits Commission, Take-Up of Supplementary Benefits, Supplementary Benefits Administration Papers No. 7, (1978).
Department of Health and Social Security, Social Assistance. A Review of the Supplementary Benefits Scheme in Great Britain, (1978).
Supplementary Benefits Commission, The Response of the Supplementary Benefits Commission to 'Social Assistance', Supplementary Benefits Administration Papers No. 9, (1979).

(ii) Books and Articles

Abbott, S. (ed.). The Prevention of Racial Discrimination in Britain, (1971).
Abel-Smith, B. & Titmuss, R.M. The Cost of the National Health Service, (1956).
Abel-Smith, B. & Townsend, P. The Poor and the Poorest, (1965).
Atkinson, A.B. Poverty in Britain and the Reform of Social Security, (1969).
Barnett, M.J. The Politics of Legislation. The Rent Act of 1957, (1969).
Briggs, A. 'The Welfare State in Historical Perspective', Archives Europeenes de Sociologie, 2, (1961).
Brown, R.G.S. The Changing National Health Service, (1973).
Brown, R.G.S. The Management of Welfare. A Study of British Social Service Administration, (1975).
Davies, J.C.H. Permissive Britain. Social Change in the Sixties and Seventies, (1975).
Donnison, D.V. The Government of Housing, (1967).
Donnison, D.V. 'Social Policy since Titmuss', Journal of Social Policy, 8, (1979)
Eckstein, H. The English Health Service, (1958).
Eckstein, H. Pressure Group Politics. The Case of the British Medical Association, (1960).
Economist Intelligence Unit, Whose Benefit ?, (1978).
Gough, I. The Political Economy of the Welfare State, (1979).

Hall, P., Land, H., Parker, R. & Webb, A. Change, Choice and Conflict in Social Policy, (1975).

Heclo, H. Social Politics in Britain and Sweden. From Relief to Income Maintenance, (1974).

Hill, M.J. & Issacharoff, R.M. Community Action and Race Relations, (1971).

Jones, K. A History of the Mental Health Services, (1972).

Klein, R., Buxton, M. & Outram, Q. Social Policy and Public Expenditure 1976. Constraints and Choices, (1976).

Kegan, M. The Politics of Education. Edward Boyle and Anthony Crosland, (1971).

Lindsey, A. Socialized Medicine in England and Wales. The National Health Service 1948-1961, (1962).

Lowndes, G.A.N. The Silent Social Revolution, (1969).

Macdonald, I.A. Race Relations. The New Law, (1977).

Marshall, T.H. Social Policy, 4th edn., (1975).

Mullard, C. Black Britain, (1973).

Patterson, S. Immigration and Race Relations in Britain 1960-67, (1969).

Rathbone, E. The Disinherited Family, (1924).

Rimlinger, G.V. Welfare Policy and Industrialization in Europe, America and Russia, (1971).

Rodgers, B.N., Greve, J. & Martin, J.S. Comparative Social Administration, (1968).

Rose, E.J.B. et. al. Colour and Citizenship. A Report on British Race Relations, (1969).

Rowntree, B.S. & Lavers, G.R. Poverty in the Welfare State. A Third Social Survey of York, (1951).

Titmuss, R.M. Problems of Social Policy, (1950).

Titmuss, R.M. Income Distribution and Social Change, (1962).

Titmuss, R.M. 'The Welfare State - Images and Realities', Social Science Review, XXXVII, (1963).

Titmuss, R.M. Essays on 'The Welfare State', (1963).

Titmuss, R.M. Commitment to Welfare, (1968).

Titmuss, R.M. The Gift Relationship, (1970).

Townsend, P. Sociology and Social Policy, (1975).

Townsend, P. & Bosanquet, N. (eds.). Labour and Inequality, (1972).

VII DEFENCE

(i) Official Material

Central Organization for Defence, Cmd. 6923, (1946).

Defence. Outline of Future Policy, Cmnd. 124, (1957).

Central Organization for Defence, Cmnd. 476, (1958).

Office of the Minister for Science, The Management and Control of Research and Development, (1961).

Central Organization for Defence, Cmnd. 2097, (1963).

Second Report from the Committee of Public Accounts. Guided Weapons Contracts placed by the Ministry of Aviation with Ferranti Ltd, H.C. 183, (1963-64).

First Report of the (Lang) Inquiry into the Pricing of Ministry
    of Aviation Contracts, Cmnd. 2428, (1964)
Second Report of the (Lang) Inquiry into the Pricing of
    Ministry of Aviation Contracts, Cmnd. 2581, (1965).
Statement on The Defence Estimates 1965, Cmnd. 2592, (1965).
Statement on The Defence Estimates 1966. Part I. The Defence
    Review, Cmnd. 2901, (1966).
Statement on The Defence Estimates 1967, Cmnd. 3203, (1967).
Second Special Report from the Committee of Public Accounts.
    Bristol Siddeley Engines Ltd., H.C. 571, (1966-67).
Supplementary Statement on Defence Policy 1967, Cmnd.3357,(1967).
Report of the (Wilson) Committee of Inquiry into Certain
    Contracts made with Bristol Siddeley Engines Ltd., H.C.129,
    (1967-68).
Statement on The Defence Estimates 1968, Cmnd. 3540, (1968).
Third Special Report from the Committee on Public Accounts.
    Bristol Siddeley Engines Ltd., H.C. 192, (1967-68).
Supplementary Statement on Defence Policy 1968, Cmnd. 3701,
    (1968).
Statement on The Defence Estimates 1969, Cmnd. 3927, (1969).
Statement on The Defence Estimates 1970, Cmnd. 4290, (1970).
Supplementary Statement on Defence Policy 1970, Cmnd. 4521,
    (1970).
Statement on The Defence Estimates 1971, Cmnd. 4592, (1971).
Government Organization for Defence Procurement and Civil
    Aerospace, Cmnd. 4641, (1971).
Statement on The Defence Estimates 1972, Cmnd. 4891, (1972).
Statement on The Defence Estimates 1973, Cmnd. 5231, (1973).
First Report from the Expenditure Committee. Central
    Management of the Services, H.C. 220, (1974-75).
Second Report from the Expenditure Committee. The Defence
    Review Proposals, H.C. 259, (1974-75).
Statement on The Defence Estimates 1975, Cmnd. 5976, (1975).

(ii) Books and Articles

Aron, R. et. al. Problems of Modern Strategy, Parts I & II,
    (1969).
Bartlett, C.J. The Long Retreat. A Short History of British
    Defence Policy 1945-70, (1972).
Baylis, J. (ed.). British Defence Policy in a Changing World,
    (1977).
Bellini, J. & Pattie, G. A New World Role for the Medium
    Power: The British Opportunity, (1977).
Burt, R. New Weapons Technologies. Debates and Directions,
    (1976).
Cary, Sir M. 'Military Procurement', Journal of the Royal
    United Services Institute for Defence Studies, 119, (March,
    1974).
Cliffe, T. Military Technology and the European Balance,
    (1972).
Darby, P. British Defence Policy East of Suez 1947-1968,
    (1973).

Fuller, J.F.C. The Conduct of War, (1961).
Groom, A.J.R. British Thinking about Nuclear Weapons, (1974).
Howard, M. The Central Organization of Defence, (1970).
Howard, M. The Continental Commitment, (1971).
Howard, M. The British Way in Warfare. A Reappraisal,(1974).
Howard, M. War in European History, (1976).
Howard, M. War and the Nation State, (1978).
Howard, M. et. al. Does the Present Central Organization of
     Defence meet the Requirements of the 1970s ?, (1971).
Institute for Strategic Studies, The Military Balance 1964-65,
     (1964).
Institute for Strategic Studies, The Military Balance 1965-66,
     (1965).
Institute for Strategic Studies, The Military Balance 1966-67,
     (1966)
Institute for Strategic Studies, The Military Balance 1967-68,
     (1967)
Institute for Strategic Studies, The Military Balance 1968-69,
     (1968).
Institute for Strategic Studies, The Military Balance 1969-70,
     (1969)
Institute for Strategic Studies, The Military Balance 1970-71,
     (1970).
International Institute for Strategic Studies, The Military
     Balance 1971-72, (1971).
International Institute for Strategic Studies, The Military
     Balance 1972-73, (1972).
International Institute for Strategic Studies, The Military
     Balance 1973-74, (1973).
International Institute for Strategic Studies, The Military
     Balance 1974-75, (1974).
International Institute for Strategic Studies, The Military
     Balance 1975-76, (1975).
International Institute for Strategic Studies, Prospects of
     Soviet Power in the 1980s, (1979).
Klepsch, E.A. Two Way Street. USA-Europe Arms Procurement,
     (1979).
Martin, L.W. 'The Market for Strategic Ideas in Britain:
     The "Sandys Era"', American Political Science Review,
     LVI, (1962).
Martin, L.W. British Defence Policy. The Long Recessional,
     (1969).
Martin, L.W. Arms and Strategy. An International Survey of
     Modern Defence, (1973).
Martin, L.W. (ed.). The Management of Defence, (1976).
Mayhew, C.P. Britain's Role Tomorrow, (1967).
Orchard, L.C.J. et.al. Weapons Procurement, Defence Manage-
     ment and International Collaboration, (1972).
Reed, B. & Williams, G. Denis Healey and the Policies of
     Power, (1971).
Rosecrance, R.N. Defence of the Realm. British Strategy in
     the Nuclear Epoch, (1968).

Rosecrance, R.N. Strategic Deterrence Reconsidered, (1975).
Snyder, W.P. The Politics of British Defence Policy 1945-
    1962, (1964).
Williams, G., Gregory, F. & Simpson, J. Crisis in Procurement.
    A Case Study of the TSR-2, (1969).

VIII OVERSEAS REPRESENTATION

(i) Official Material

Proposals for the Reform of the Foreign Service, Cmd. 6420,
    (1943).
Fourth Report from the Estimates Committee. Colonial Office,
    H.C. 260, (1959-60).
Technical Assistance from the UK for Overseas Development,
    Cmnd. 1308, (1961).
Report of the (Plowden) Committee on Representational
    Services Overseas, Cmnd. 2276, (1964).
Report of the (Duncan) Review Committee on Overseas
    Representation, Cmnd. 4107, (1969).
Eighth Report from the Expenditure Committee. Diplomatic
    Manpower and Property Overseas, H.C. 473, (1974-75).
Ninth Report from the Expenditure Committee. Diplomatic
    Manpower and Property Overseas, H.C. 604, (1975-76).
Central Policy Review Staff, Review of Overseas Representation
    (1977).
Fourth Report from the Expenditure Committee. The Central
    Policy Review Staff Review of Overseas Representation,
    H.C. 286, (1977-78).
The United Kingdom's Overseas Representation, Cmnd. 7308,(1978)

(ii) Books and Articles

Ashton-Gwatkin, F. The British Foreign Service, (1950).
Bacchus, W.J. 'Diplomacy for the 70s: An Afterview and
    Appraisal', American Political Science Review, LXVIII,
    (1974).
Barnett, C. The Collapse of British Power, (1972).
Beloff, M. New Dimensions in Foreign Policy. A Study in
    British Administrative Experience 1947-59, (1961).
Beloff, M. 'The Think Tank and Foreign Affairs', Public
    Administration, 55, (1977).
Boardman, R. & Groom, A.J.R. (eds.). The Management of
    Britain's External Relations, (1973).
Briggs, E. Farewell to Foggy Bottom, (1964).
Busk, Sir D. The Craft of Diplomacy, (1967).
Clark, E. Corps Diplomatique, (1973).
Cross, J.A. 'The Beginning and End of the Commonwealth
    Office', Public Administration, 47, (1969).
Dilks, D.N. (ed.). The Diaries of Sir Alexander Cadogan
    1938-1945, (1971).

Donelan, M. 'The Trade of Diplomacy', International Affairs, 45, (1969).

Drummond, R. & Coblentz, G. Duel at the Brink. John Foster Dulles' Command of American Power, (1960).

Fieldhouse, D.K. Economics and Empire 1830-1914, (1973).

Furse, Sir R. Aucuparius. Recollections of a Recruiting Officer, (1962).

Garner, J. The Commonwealth Office 1925-1968, (1978).

Gerson, L.L. John Foster Dulles, (1967).

Gladwyn, Lord, Memoirs, (1972).

Gore-Booth, Lord, 'Historic Skills and New Tasks. The Diplomatic Service in the Seventies', International Affairs, 46, (1970).

Gore-Booth, Lord, With Great Truth and Respect, (1974).

Halberstam, D. The Best and the Brightest, (1972).

Heren, L. No Hail No Farewell, (1970).

Hinton, H.C. Communist China in World Politics, (1966).

Johnston, Sir J. 'The Relevance of Latter Day Diplomacy', Public Administration, 54, (1976).

Kelly, Sir D. The Ruling Few, (1952).

Kirkman, W.P. Unscrambling an Empire. A Critique of British Colonial Policy 1956-66, (1966).

Kirkpatrick, Sir I. The Inner Circle, (1959).

Kitzinger, U. Diplomacy and Persuasion, (1973).

McDermott, G. The New Diplomacy, (1973).

Moncrieff, A. (ed.). Suez. Ten Years After, (1967).

Moorhouse, G. The Diplomats. The Foreign Office Today, (1977).

Mott-Radclyffe, Sir C. Foreign Body in the Eye. A Memoir of the Foreign Service Old and New, (1975).

Northedge, F.S. Descent from Power. British Foreign Policy 1945-1973, (1974).

Nutting, A. No End of A Lesson, (1967).

Platt, D.C.M. The Cinderella Service. British Consuls since 1825, (1971).

Robertson, T. Suez. The Inside Story of the Suez Conspiracy, (1965).

Scalapino, R.A. (ed.). The Foreign Policy of Modern Japan, (1977).

Schlesinger, A.M. Jnr. A Thousand Days, (1965).

Shonfield, A. 'The Duncan Report and its Critics', International Affairs, 46, (1970).

Sorensen, T. Kennedy, (1965).

Strachey, J. End of Empire, (1959).

Strang, Lord, Home and Abroad, (1956).

Strang, Lord, The Diplomatic Career, (1962).

Thomas, H.S. The Suez Affair, (1967).

Trevelyan, Lord, Diplomatic Channels, (1973).

Walker, L. 'Our Foreign Affairs Machinery: Time for an Overhaul', Foreign Affairs, 47, (1968-69).

Wallace, W. The Foreign Policy Process in Britain, (1975).

Wallace, W. 'After Berrill: Whitehall and the Management of
British Diplomacy', _International Affairs_, 54, (1978).
Waterfield, G. _Professional Diplomat. Sir Percy Loraine_,
(1973).
Watt, D.C. 'Overseas Representation', _Political Quarterly_,
40, (1969).
White, A.J.S. _The British Council. The First 25 Years_, (1965).

IX   THE HOME CIVIL SERVICE

(i) Official Material

Report of the (Priestley) _Royal Commission on the Civil_
Service, Cmd. 9613, (1955).
Fifth Report from the Estimates Committee. Treasury Control
of Establishments, H.C. 228, (1963-64).
Sixth Report from the Estimates Committee. Recruitment to the
Civil Service, H.C. 308, (1964-65).
Report of the (Fulton) _Committee on the Civil Service_, Cmnd.
3638, (1968), being Vol. 1. Vol. 2: _Report of a_
Management Consultancy Group. Vol. 3 (1): _Surveys and_
Investigations Social Survey of the Civil Service.
Vol. 3 (2): _Surveys and Investigations_. Vol. 4:
Factual Statistical and Explanatory Papers. Vol. 5 (1):
Proposals and Opinions. Government Departments and Staff
Associations. Vol. 5 (2): _Proposals and Opinions._
Organizations and Individuals.
(Armstrong) _Report of the National Whitley Council Joint_
Committee on the Fulton Report. Developments on Fulton,
(February, 1969).
Civil Service Department, _The Civil Services of North_
America, (1969).
(Armstrong) _Report of the National Whitley Council Joint_
Committee on the Fulton Report. The Timing of Interim
Changes in the Grading Structure of the Civil Service,
(July, 1969).
Report of the (Davies) _Committee of Inquiry. The Method II_
System of Selection for the Administrative Class of the
Home Civil Service, Cmnd. 4156, (1969).
Civil Service Department, _Report of the Working Party on_
Material for Training in Government, (1970).
(Armstrong) _Report of the National Whitley Council Joint_
Committee on the Fulton Report. Fulton: A Framework for
the Future, (March, 1970).
(Armstrong) _Report of the National Whitley Council Joint_
Committee on the Fulton Report. Fulton - The Reshaping
of the Civil Service: Developments during 1970, (March,
1971).
Civil Service Department, _The Employment of Women in the Civil_
Service. The Report of a Departmental Committee, (1971).

(Armstrong) <u>Report of the National Whitley Council Joint Committee on the Fulton Report. The Shape of the Post-Fulton Civil Service</u>, (1972).

<u>Report of the Civil Service Joint Superannuation Review Committee. Civil Service Superannuation</u>, (1972).

<u>Report of the</u> (Franks) <u>Committee on Section 2 of the Official Secrets Act 1911</u>, Cmnd. 5104, (1972).

National Whitley Council Joint Committee on Training, <u>Four Reports on Civil Service Training</u>, (1974).

<u>Civil Service Training. Report by R.N. Heaton and Sir L. Williams</u>, (1974).

<u>Civil Servants and Change. Joint Statement by the National Whitley Council and Final Report by the Wider Issues Review Team</u>, (1975).

Sheriff, P. <u>Career Patterns in the Higher Civil Service, Civil Service Studies No. 2</u>, (1976)

<u>Eleventh Report from the Expenditure Committee. The Civil Service</u>, H.C. 535-I, II, III, (1976-77).

<u>Report of the</u> (Armitage) <u>Committee on Political Activities of Civil Servants</u>, Cmnd. 7057, (1978).

<u>The Civil Service. Government Observations on the Eleventh Report from the Expenditure Committee 1976-77</u>, Cmnd. 7117, (1978).

<u>Reform of Section 2 of the Official Secrets Act 1911</u>, Cmnd. 7285, (1978).

Civil Service Department. <u>Report of the Administration Trainee Review Committee</u>, (1978).

Civil Service Department, <u>Civil Service Statistics 1979</u>, (1979).

<u>Annual Reports of the Civil Service Commissioners, The Civil Service College, The Civil Service Department and the Civil Service Pay Research Unit</u>.

(ii) <u>Books and Articles</u>

Anon, 'Letters from Across the Channel: I Ministerial Cabinets', <u>Public Administration</u>, 50, (1972).

Anon, 'Letters from Across the Channel: III The Ecole Nationale d'Administration', <u>Public Administration</u>, 53, (1975).

Armstrong, Sir W. <u>Professionals and Professionalism in the Civil Service</u>, (1970).

Armstrong, Sir W. <u>Personnel Management in the Civil Service</u>, (1971).

Chapman, B. <u>British Government Observed</u>, (1963).

Chapman, R. <u>The Higher Civil Service</u>, (1970).

Dale, H.E. <u>The Higher Civil Service of Great Britain</u>, (1941).

Dunnett, Sir J. 'The Civil Service: Seven Years After Fulton', <u>Public Administration</u>, 54, (1976).

Fabian Group, <u>The Administrators. The Reform of the Civil Service</u>, (1964).

Fry, G.K. 'Some Weaknesses in the Fulton Report on the British Home Civil Service', <u>Political Studies</u>, XVII, (1969).

Fry, G.K. Statesmen in Disguise. The Changing Role of the
    Administrative Class of the British Home Civil Service
    1853-1966, (1969).
Fry, G.K. 'Policy Planning Units in British Central Government
    Departments', Public Administration, 50, (1972).
Fry, G.K. 'Civil Service Salaries in the Post-Priestley Era
    1956-1972', Public Administration, 52, (1974).
Keeling, C.D.E. 'Treasury Centre for Administrative Studies',
    Public Administration, 43, (1965).
Keeling, C.D.E. Management in Government, (1972).
Klein, R. & Lewis, J. 'Advice and Dissent in British Govern-
    ment: the Case of the Special Advisers', Policy and
    Politics, 6, (1977).
Mackenzie, W.J.M. 'The Royal Commission on the Civil Service',
    Political Quarterly, 27, (1956).
Parris, H. Staff Relations in the Civil Service, (1973).
Rhodes, R.A.W. (ed.). Training in the Civil Service, (1977).
Ridley, F.F. (ed.). Specialists and Generalists, (1968).
Ridley, F.F. & Blondel, J. Public Administration in France,
    2nd edn., (1969).
Robson, W.A. 'Editorial' and 'Recent Trends in Public
    Administration', Political Quarterly, 25, (1954).
Sisson, C.H. The Spirit of British Administration, (1959).
Sisson, C.H. 'The Civil Service - I, II, III', The Spectator,
    20.2.1971, 27.2.1971, 6.3.1971.
Stevens, A. 'The Role of the Ecole Nationale d'Administration',
    Public Administration, 56, (1978).
Stevens, A. 'Politicization and Cohesion in French
    Administration', West European Politics, 1, (1978).
Suleiman, E.N. Politics, Power and Bureaucracy in France. The
    Administrative Elite, (1974).
Suleiman, E.N. Elites in French Society, (1978).
Thomas, H.S. (ed.). The Establishment, (1959).
Walker, N. Morale in the Civil Service, (1961).
Wilding, R.W.L. 'The Post-Fulton Programme: Strategy and
    Tactics', Public Administration, 48, (1970).
Williams, L. 'The Role of the Staff Side in Civil Service
    Reform', Public Administration, 47, (1969).
Wraith, R. Open Government. The British Interpretation,
    (1977).

X   THE PARLIAMENTARY COMMISSIONER FOR ADMINISTRATION

(i) Official Material

Report of the (Donoughmore-Scott) Committee on Ministers'
    Powers, Cmd. 4060, (1932).
Report of the Public Inquiry Ordered by the Minister of
    Agriculture into the Disposal of Land at Crichel Down,
    Cmd. 9176, (1954).
Report of the (Franks) Committee on Administrative Tribunals
    and Enquiries, Cmnd. 218, (1957).

<u>Parliamentary Commissioner for Administration</u>, Cmnd. 2767,
    (1965).
<u>Annual Reports of the Parliamentary Commissioner for Adminis-</u>
<u>tration</u>:
    1967: 4th Report, H.C. 134, (1967-68)
    1968: 2nd Report, H.C. 129, (1968-69)
    1969: 2nd Report, H.C. 138, (1969-70)
    1970: 1st Report, H.C. 261, (1970-71)
    1971: 2nd Report, H.C. 116, (1971-72)
    1972: 2nd Report, H.C. 72, (1972-73)
    1973: 2nd Report, H.C. 106, (1973-74)
    1974: 2nd Report, H.C. 126, (1974-75)
    1975: 2nd Report, H.C. 141, (1975-76)
    1976: 2nd Report, H.C. 116, (1976-77)
    1977: J.C. 157, (1977-78)
<u>Special Reports of the Parliamentary Commissioner for Adminis-</u>
<u>tration</u>:
    1967: 3rd Report, H.C. 54, (1967-68) Sachsenhausen
    1969: 3rd Report, H.C. 316, (1968-69) Duccio
    1975: 5th Report, H.C. 498, (1974-75) Court Line
    1975: 6th Report, H.C. 529, (1974-75) Supplement on
           Three Wheeled Vehicles used by Disabled Persons
    1975: 7th Report, H.C. 680, (1974-75) Television Licences
<u>Reports from the Slect Committee on the Parliamentary</u>
<u>Commissioner for Administration</u>:
    1968: 1st Report, H.C. 258, (1967-68)
    1968: 2nd Report, H.C. 350, (1967-68)
    1969: H.C. 385, (1968-69)
    1969: 1st Report, H.C. 49, (1969-70)
    1970: 2nd Report, H.C. 127, (1969-70)
    1972: 1st Report, H.C. 215, (1971-72)

(ii) <u>Books and Articles</u>

Allen, Sir C.K. <u>Law and Orders</u>, 3rd edn., (1965).
Brown, L.N. & Lavirotte, P. 'Mediator: a French Ombudsman?',
    <u>Law Quarterly Review</u>, 90, (1974).
Chester, D.N. 'The Crichel Down Case', <u>Public Administration</u>,
    32, (1954).
Chinkin, C.M. & Bailey, R.J. 'The Local Ombudsman', <u>Public</u>
    <u>Administration</u>, 54, (1976).
Cohen, L. 'The Parliamentary Commissioner and the "MP
    Filter"', <u>Public Law</u>, (1972).
Crossman, R.H.S. <u>Socialism and the New Despotism</u>, (1956).
Ehrmann, H.W. <u>Comparative Legal Cultures</u>, (1976).
Elcock, H.J. 'Opportunity for Ombudsman: The Northern Ireland
    Commissioner for Complaints', <u>Public Administration</u>, 50,
    (1972).
Fry, G.K. 'The Sachsenhausen Concentration Camp Case and the
    Convention of Ministerial Responsibility', <u>Public Law</u>,
    (1970).
Gregory, R. & Hutchesson, P. <u>The Parliamentary Ombudsman</u>,(1975).

Gregory, R. 'Court Line, Mr. Benn and the Ombudsman', Parliamentary Affairs, 30, (1977).

Hamson, C.J. 'The Real Lesson of Crichel Down', Public Administration, 32, (1954).

Hewart, Lord, The New Despotism, (1929).

Jennings, Sir W.I. The Law and the Constitution, 5th edn., (1959).

Justice, The Citizen and the Administration, (1961).

Justice, Administration under the Law, (1971).

Justice, The Citizen and the Public Agencies, (1976).

Justice, Our Fettered Ombudsman, (1977).

Klein, R. 'The Health Service Commissioner: No Cause for Complaint', British Medical Journal, (1977).

Marshall, G. 'Maladministration', Public Law, (1973).

Marshall, G. 'Reforming the Parliamentary Commissioner', Public Administration, 55, (1977).

Mitchell, J.D.B. 'The Ombudsman Fallacy', Public Law, (1962).

Mitchell, J.D.B. 'The Causes and Effects of the Absence of a System of Public Law in the United Kingdom', Public Law, (1965).

Mitchell, J.D.B. 'Administrative Law and Parliamentary Control', Political Quarterly, 38, (1967).

Mitchell, J.D.B. 'Three Blind Mice', Public Administration, 50, (1972).

Pugh, Sir I. 'The Ombudsman - Jurisdiction, Powers and Practice', Public Administration, 56, (1978).

Robson, W.A. Justice and Administrative Law, 3rd edn., (1951).

Robson, W.A. 'Administrative Justice and Injustice: a Commentary on the Franks Report', Public Law, (1958).

Rowat, D.C. (ed.). The Ombudsman. Citizen's Defender, (1968).

Smith, M.H. 'Thought on a British Conseil d'Etat', Public Administration, 45, (1967).

Stacey, F. The British Ombudsman, (1971).

Stacey, F. Ombudsmen Compared, (1978).

Wade, E.C.S. & Phillips, G.C. Constitutional and Administrative Law, 9th edn., (1977).

Wade, H.W.R. Administrative Law, 4th edn., (1977).

Williams, D.W. Maladministration. Remedies for Injustice, (1976).

INDEX

International Monetary Fund
(I.M.F.) 57, 73, 92
Institute of Economic
Affairs 33
Institute of Professional
Civil Servants 146
Ismay Lord 122
Italy 5, 12
Invalid Vehicles Case 172

Jacob, Sir I. 122
Japan 4, 6, 12, 138
Jenkins, R. 39, 68, 71, 73,
85, 124
Jennings, Sir I. 167, 172
Job Creation 105
Joint Secretaryship of
State for Commonwealth
Relations and for the
Colonies 127
Jones, A. 66
Jones, Sir E. 170-1
Jones, J. 67
Joseph, Sir K. 115

Kaldor, N. 64, 155-6
Keynes, J.M. and
Keynesianism 14-5, 18,
21, 25, 32-3, 36, 57-9,
61-2, 67-8, 71, 73, 76,
78, 91-2, 94, 178, 181

Labour Party and Labour
Movement 15, 18, 21,
24-6, 28, 30, 36, 51-2, 63,
69, 70, 104, 108, 116, 130,
143, 177
Labour Party Conference 181
Labour Research Department
180
Lambton, Viscount 171
Land Commission 111
Laski, H. 15-6, 24, 128
Leathers Lord 31
Liberal Party 15, 33
Lloyd, S. 8, 59-60
Local Authorities 83
Local Employment Act (1970)
65, 96
Local Government Reform 36
Lord President of the
Council 96, 98

Low, S. 49, 50
Lyttleton, O. 31

Macleod, I. 11, 38, 51, 68
Macmillan, H. 5, 9-12, 19,
21-2, 31, 33-4, 110, 120-2,
127, 128-9
Makins, Sir R. 34
Managed Economy Welfare State
14, 17, 19, 21, 28, 34, 36,
43, 107-8, 176
Mandeville, B. 94
Manpower Services Commission
69
Marshall Aid 7, 17
Marx, K. 25
Maudling, R. 51, 59-60, 62,
120
Maxwell-Fyfe, Sir D. 30, 37-8,
168, 171
Mayhew, C. 123
Minister for the Civil Service
146
Minister for Industrial
Development 103
Minister for Science 96, 109
Minister for Social Security
115
Ministerial Responsibility
143-5, 164-72, 179
Ministers and Civil Servants -
Relationship of. 142-4, 168,
170
Ministry of Agriculture 30
Ministry of Agriculture,
Fisheries and Food 95
Ministry of Aviation 95,
98-9, 120-1, 124
Ministry of Aviation Supply
125
Ministry of Defence 9, 44,
119-25, 154, 161, 163, 177
Ministry of Economic Affairs
see Department of Economic
Affairs
Ministry of Education 108-9
Ministry of Fuel and Power
16, 51, 95
Ministry of Health 29, 94,
108, 113-5
Ministry of Housing and Local
Government 29, 108, 110-2